Rush

D0118986

DESERTS
OF AMERICA

DESERTS
OF AMERICA

by PEGGY LARSON

Illustrations by STANLEY WYATT

PRENTICE-HALL, INC.   Englewood Cliffs, N.J.

DESERTS OF AMERICA
by Peggy Larson

Library of Congress Catalog Card Number: 71–79948

Printed in the United States of America • *T*

13–199851–X

Prentice-Hall International, Inc., London
Prentice-Hall of Australia, Pty. Ltd., Sydney
Prentice-Hall of Canada, Ltd., Toronto
Prentice-Hall of India Private Ltd., New Delhi
Prentice-Hall of Japan, Inc., Tokyo

to
Merv . . .
the desert shared

Contents

Also by Peggy Larson:
Life in the Desert

with Mervin Larson:
All About Ants
Lives of Social Insects

Introduction

GEOGRAPHERS say that most of the great deserts of the world are "recent geomorphic features," and that those of the North American continent are probably not more than a few million years old. On the very different time scale of human history, interest in the desert for its own sake might also be called recent.

It was only after human life became relatively safe and comfortable that untamed nature was admired in any of her forms. To men of the Renaissance, only green fields and trim gardens were beautiful; and not until the eighteenth century did mountains become "sublime" rather than "gloomy" or "terrifying." A little later, the ocean began to be celebrated in prose and verse. But hardly more than a generation ago did our own Southwest cease to be what one of the first American explorers called "this profitless region" and of which Daniel Webster asked "To what use could we ever hope to put these great deserts and those endless mountain ranges?"

During the course of the decade just past, a number of books has been published which testify in one way or another to the awakened interest in the American deserts—in their scenic beauty and their natural history, or in their exploitation by agriculture, industry, vacation resorts, and real estate developments—and also in the threats to their unique character and beauty.

Many of these books have been excellent, each in its own way. But to the best of my knowledge there has been none which—to put it as simply as possible—covers the whole subject so thoroughly and so interestingly in one volume as the present one does. Mrs. Larson begins with the quotation from Daniel Webster from which a sentence was quoted above. She ends with a chapter called "How Shall the Desert Blossom?" whose title suggests very pointedly a question to which we do not yet know the answer. Is the future of the Southwestern desert to be one in which its unique characteristics have survived, or will exploitation of one sort or another result in that process of homogenization which has made the agreeable (as well as the disagreeable) features of one section of our country nearly indistinguishable from those of the others?

This more or less polemic aspect of Mrs. Larson's book is, however, merely incidental. Primarily it is an introduction to all the aspects of the desert, both as a "geomorphic feature" and as one of the distinctive haunts of life; to its origin, its distinguishing characteristics and their determinates, to its geology, geography, and natural history. In fact, there is hardly a question one is likely to ask which is not answered; and I believe that its accuracy everywhere can be taken for granted. Anyone who reads it will have learned a great deal about the desert. This is a popularization only in the sense that one needs no special previous knowledge to find it completely understandable. And it will, I believe, meet the tests of the specialist's knowledge.

—Joseph Wood Krutch

If one is inclined to wonder at first how so many dwellers came to be in the loneliest land that ever came out of God's hands, what they do there and why stay, one does not wonder so much after having lived there. None other than this long brown land lays such a hold on the affections.

Mary Austin, *The Land of Little Rain* *

* Reprinted by permission of The Houghton-Mifflin Co.

chapter one

A Desolate and Forbidding Prospect

"WHAT do we want with this vast worthless area—this region of savages and wild beasts, of shifting sands and whirlwinds of dust, of cactus and prairie dogs? To what use could we ever hope to put these great deserts and those endless mountain ranges?" Such was Daniel Webster's opinion of the large segment of land now known as the North American Desert.

Barren, worthless, menacing, a blight to agrarian-minded man, inhabited by Indians and dangerous animals, and representing obstacles to civilization's advance—this has been the traditional view of desert lands. Another Webster, this one of dictionary fame, also presents a traditional viewpoint by referring to *desert* as "a desolating and forbidding prospect."

Man must be the most fickle of animals, for in the little over one hundred years since the time of Daniel Webster, we have largely reversed our stand. Today, portions of the North American Desert support some of the most rapidly growing populations in the nation. Our particular desert area has gone from blight to blossom in 150 years, but its potential resources have not even yet been fully realized. Ores to be mined, land to be made fertile by the eventual addition of water, and—even more important—space for the burgeoning masses of mankind are only a few

3

Pinacate landscape with calderas in the distance (*M. W. Larson*)

of the riches the desert still holds. Perhaps the North American Desert's greatest value is simply its being a wilderness reserve where unusual, highly adapted plants and animals live in complex relationships with one another. Their ecology is fascinating, and still not completely understood.

Where is the North American Desert, and how did it get the way it is? What plants and animals live there and how do they survive? How is man altering its landscape, and what of its future? These and other questions we will try to answer as we survey the area.

One vast portion of the North American Desert stretches irregularly southward from eastern Oregon across most of Utah and Nevada and into portions of western Colorado and southwestern Wyoming, southeastern California, and much of western and southern Arizona. It continues over the lower portions of the Mexican state of Sonora and covers most of the Peninsula of Baja California. A second, very large area includes parts of southern New Mexico and southwest Texas and expands into the Mexican states of Chihuahua, Coahuila, eastern Durango, northern Zacatecas, western Nuevo Leon, and northern San Luis Potosí. Small areas detached from these two main blocks—including an area in western Washington state, and several small sections in the states of Hidalgo and Puebla in southern Mexico—are also recognized as desert country.

This large tract actually consists of four major deserts, each distinctive and interesting in its own right. The northern desert—including parts of Oregon, Idaho, Utah, Nevada, and small areas in Colorado, Wyoming, northern Arizona and eastern California—makes up the *Great Basin* desert. The *Mohave,* of southeastern California and southern Nevada, is a transition zone between the Great Basin and the *Sonoran* desert; the latter located in extreme southeastern California, parts of Arizona and the Baja Peninsula, and the Mexican state of Sonora. The second large area of desert, discontinuous from the first block which is composed of three contiguous deserts, is the *Chihuahuan,* located in New Mexico, Texas, and the several Mexican states to the south of these.

There is no certainty as to precisely where a desert begins and ends. Desert country merges gradually into semi-arid regions along its borders; and the distinction between arid and semi-arid land is seldom completely clear. Therefore, the total size of the North American Desert varies according to the authority quoted and the criteria he follows. But even granting the North American Desert its generally accepted area of some 500,000 square miles, it is actually puny, ranking only fifth in size when compared with the other deserts of the world.

Approximately one-seventh of our planet's land surface is classified as arid, but the various deserts making up this percentage are not scattered haphazardly over the globe. Due to complex meteorological conditions, they occur discontinuously along one belt of latitude in the Northern Hemisphere and along a second in the Southern Hemisphere. These belts lie between latitudes 15 and 40 degrees north and south, in the general areas of the Tropic of Cancer and the Tropic of Capricorn. Since the Northern Hemisphere has more land area within these latitudes, there is more desert country north of the equator.

The largest of the world's deserts is the Sahara. (Even *Roget's Thesaurus* lists "Sahara" as a synonym for desert.) This giant stretches from the Atlantic Ocean eastward across Africa for three thousand miles to the

Red Sea, and from areas bordering the Mediterranean south a third to a half the length of the great African continent. Its 3,300,000 square-mile area makes it nearly as large as the entire United States (3,700,000 square miles). But in defiance of romantic preconceptions, the Sahara has in fact a lower percentage of sand surface than the Arabian Desert, and is only one of the several deserts hosting camels and colorful nomads. (A little over a hundred years ago the North American Desert had its own imported camels.)

The Sahara holds the world's record for the highest temperature ever recorded. Its average rainfall in parts is probably about one inch per year, but in some regions, years can pass without a drop of rain. Some areas seldom or never support vegetation. It is no wonder then, that the Sahara, with its gigantic size, the harsh challenges it presents to life, and the remoteness of its interior, is popularly considered the epitome of deserts, just as Timbuktu, fabled settlement of the Sahara interior, has come to be a synonym for any remote region.

The Arabian Desert occupies the Arabian Peninsula and is separated from the Sahara by the Red Sea and the Gulf of Suez. This is the sandiest desert in the world, with one-third of its close to a million square miles covered by sand and dunes. The Sahara is traversed by the Nile, and the North American Desert by the Colorado River, but the Arabian lacks any permanent river within its borders.

Continuing eastward from the Arabian, one encounters the Thar or Indian Desert. It lies along the Indus River in northern India and covers slightly more than 200,000 square miles. North of the Thar and east of the upper portions of the Arabian Desert lies the Iranian Desert. This is a small desert, only 150,000 square miles in extent, but is distinguished by its sand dunes, some of which are probably the highest in the world.

Directly north of the Iranian lies the Turkestan Desert. Further to the east but at approximately the same latitude stretches a long arid area whose western portion is known as the Takla Makan. Its eastern portion is the more familiar Gobi. These are cool deserts, dry areas with warm summers but cold winters. They grade into steppes or semi-arid areas, and in fact, the Gobi is often considered a steppe. The Gobi is popularly known in the United States as the site of the explorations of Dr. Roy Chapman Andrews, whose expedition there discovered the first fossil dinosaur eggs.

The Sahara, Arabian, Indian, Iranian, Turkestan, Takla Makan, and

Gobi, in addition to the North American, comprise the deserts of the Northern Hemisphere.

Moving into the Southern Hemisphere, we find two rather long, narrow deserts in South America: the Atacama and the Patagonian. The latter lies in Argentina, directly east of the Andes Mountains which cut off its moisture supply and create the desert conditions over this area of approximately 260,000 square miles. The Atacama Desert stretches along South America's western coastline. Its approximately 140,000 square miles hold the record of being the driest area on earth. Over a period of 43 years, the rainfall in Africa, Chile, located in the Atacama Desert, averaged only 0.02 inches per year! In amazing contrast to such dryness, the coastal portions of this desert are extremely foggy—a phenomenon that is not uncommon in certain other west-coast deserts such as a portion of the desert in Baja California and the Namib.

The Namib is a long, narrow coastal desert of southwestern Africa. Like the Atacama, it is exceedingly dry, yet tends to be foggy at least in parts. The average rainfall is probably less than two inches per year. To the east of the Namib lies the Kalahari Desert, famous as the home of the South African Bushmen. Far less arid than the neighboring Namib, the Kalahari is sometimes considered a steppe rather than a desert proper. It is still arid, however, with an average rainfall varying from twenty inches per year in the northern sections to five inches in the southern. It supports a good seasonal cover of grass and a variety of shrubs and small trees, enough to support some game. These animals and the local fruits, roots, and seeds allow the Bushmen to support themselves through a gathering and hunting economy.

The final desert in our survey is the Australian, second largest in the world. Its 1,310,000 square miles of dry land stretch from the west coast out across the center of the continent, leaving an arable fringe of non-desert area between it and the southern, eastern, and northern coastlines. Even though its driest portions average five inches of rain per year, it is a far from hospitable land. Over 40 percent of Australia is classified as desert, making it the continent with the highest percentage of arid land. One UNESCO publication reports that approximately two-fifths of the continent is uninhabited and unstocked; in some areas, thirty to forty acres of land are needed to support a single sheep.

If we define a desert as a relatively dry, barren area, supporting only limited plant life, then we can think of the Arctic tundras as desert also.

Here most of the water is permanently frozen, but mainly, it is the frigid climate over most of the year that precludes plant growth. Therefore, while these areas may at times be referred to as "desert," they are not considered so for our purposes. We will be discussing warm deserts and cool deserts, but "cool" is not to be confused with the "cold deserts" of certain authors who use that term to cover the Arctic tundra.

Deserts are generally defined as areas receiving fewer than ten inches of rainfall per year. This figure, however, is misleading: although some parts of the world average only ten inches of precipitation per year, they may receive it at favorable seasons and at well-spaced intervals. Even scanty moisture, if properly regulated, is able to support definite grass-lands. Some authorities prefer to use a five-inch average rainfall to pin-point the desert limits; but many unquestionably desert areas average well above five inches of precipitation per year.

An inch of rain, if received from several brief showers, has a better chance to soak into the soil than does the same amount falling during a single storm, when most of it will be lost as runoff. Desert rainfall is often irregular; in many places it cannot be depended upon to fall at a particular season. Moisture received during the hot season may help the plants badly in need of it at that time; however, the water will be quickly evaporated due to the heat. In contrast, moisture received during the cool season when evaporation is not so rapid, is most beneficial to the living things in the desert, providing there is enough warmth for them to make use of it. Or, having an opportunity to soak into the soil, the moisture will act as a bank deposit which the plants can draw from at a later date when their need is greater.

The amount of moisture received in any one desert from year to year is also extremely variable. Although one region can *average* an annual rainfall of four inches over a twenty-year period, some of those years may be entirely rainless. Areas in the Sahara are reported to have been without rain for periods exceeding ten years; and Bagdad, California holds the United States record for the longest period with no measurable rainfall—767 days. Obviously, average precipitation figures do not give a complete picture of desert aridity, especially since average precipitation is not as important to desert life as the extremes of dampness or dryness to which they must adapt. Floods, as well as droughts, can take a deadly toll.

A second desert characteristic is the high temperatures that are reached during at least a part of the year. The highest official reading ever recorded was 136.4°F. at Azizia, Libya, in the Sahara. Second highest was the record of 134°F. in Death Valley, California.

Heat compounds the effects of aridity. Insolation—the solar radiation received by the earth—boosts the air's ability to absorb water from the surface of the earth. When air contains the maximum amount of water vapor it is capable of holding, it is said to be saturated, but this amount varies depending upon the temperature and pressure of the air. Warm air can absorb much more moisture than cool air before it reaches the saturation point. The amount of water vapor actually contained in air at any one time—compared to the amount it *can* hold under those conditions—is known as the relative humidity, and is expressed by a percentage (100 percent represents saturation). Air containing water vapor cools during the night, and since cool air has a lower saturation point, it releases any excess moisture in the form of dew. For this reason, dew often forms in deserts during the night.

Moisture in the air represents water evaporated from the surface of the land and sea and also that released by the transpiration of plants. (Roots absorb water from the soil, move it through their stems, and eventually lose it as vapor through pores on their leaves.) A negligible amount of vapor also enters the atmosphere from animal perspiration and respiration.

The constant flow of water into the atmosphere is called *evapotranspiration*. In the desert, the moisture available for evapotranspiration is usually meager, and consequently, the relative humidity is very low. Cloud cover is infrequent. With limited diffused water vapor in the air, limited cloud cover, and only infrequent plants to deflect the sun's radiation, 80–90 percent of it reaches the desert's surface to heat the soil, the air directly above it, and the living things that occur there. In turn, much of this daytime heat is re-radiated—unimpeded by cloud cover or humidity—back into the atmosphere after dark. This causes seesaws in daily temperature that can result in incongruously cold desert nights.

By contrast, humid or forested areas can deflect up to 50 percent of the sun's radiation through the cloud cover, moisture and dust in the air, and heavy vegetation. Only about one-half of the accumulated heat is re-radiated back toward the sky after dark. Such regions are literally covered by an insulating blanket that modifies and stabilizes climatic conditions. But with little beyond a thin dust blanket and a very small amount of moisture in the air to regulate the absorption and loss of radiation, desert temperatures swing, pendulum-like, from one extreme to another. These wide daily—and often annual—fluctuations provide temperature extremes which the desert's plants and animals must tolerate. Such climatic variations, however, often benefit animals who are able to adjust their activity to a wide choice of temperatures. Many, if not most, are active at the hottest time of year (i.e., summer), although only during the night, which is of course not the warmest part of the 24-hour day.

The rapid excessive heating and cooling of the desert's surface gives rise to winds—either local ones, such as whirlwinds, or more widespread cyclonic patterns. And while the winds themselves are usually not particularly violent, their effects are often far more dramatic in arid country than anywhere else. Much of the desert surface is bare, only lightly protected by vegetation; the soil is not damp and compact, but dry, more akin to sand than loam, and hence easily movable. Dust or sand storms are frequent. In addition, moving air masses tend to increase the evaporation of available moisture.

Since so many factors play a role in a region's climate, mathematical systems have been devised to define deserts, steppes, and other climatic classifications. One such is the Köppen system, devised by Dr. Wladimir Köppen early in this century. According to his calculations, approximately one-seventh of the earth's land surface consists of desert. Steppes—semi-arid lands—comprise another seventh. Other geographic classification systems have been developed by O. W. Thornthwaite and by Peveril Meigs.

The causes of aridity are not precisely the same for all deserts. The major factors are the highly complex circulation patterns of the atmosphere—which are in turn influenced by the rotation of the earth, the angle of its axis, the locations of land masses and large bodies of water, and other complex factors. In a very simplified manner, however, warm air at the equator tends to flow upward in the directions of the two poles. As the air rises, it cools and loses much of its moisture in precipitation. At approximately 30 degrees N. and S. latitude, this air descends and becomes heated by compression of the masses of air above it. As its heat increases, so does its capacity to absorb and retain moisture again. Therefore, in the general area of the "desert belts" circling the globe, the descending air displays increased evaporative power and decreased tendency to attain saturation—and therefore, is less likely to produce precipitation.

These particular belts of descending air occur in regions characterized by only light winds and nearly cloudless skies; known traditionally as the "horse latitudes." The origin of this nickname is now obscure. One theory has it that sailing ships headed for the New World were often becalmed in these latitudes and were forced to throw their cargoes of horses overboard when water supplies became scarce. Beyond the horse latitudes, the air ascends (thus producing more humid areas) and again begins descending over the cold, dry poles.

Deserts may also be created when the land is covered by a "rain shadow." If moisture-laden clouds encounter a mountain range while moving across a continent, they are forced up and over this natural barrier. Gaining altitude, the temperature drops, condensation takes place, and much or all of their moisture is dropped on the windward sides and summits of the range. The dry air then flows down the lee side of the mountain, bringing little or no moisture but plenty of evaporative power to the land beyond.

Other deserts, such as the Gobi, are arid simply because they lie in the centers of large continents, where the winds that do reach them have lost most or all of their moisture after travelling long distances over land. Certain strange coastal deserts owe their dryness to ocean currents which, flowing toward the equator from the poles, bring masses of cold sea water near the shore. Sea winds blowing over these currents are cooled before they reach the warm land, and bring little moisture—except in the form of fog or mist, which is not released as effective precipitation. Some of these coastal deserts, as the Namib and Atacama, are exceedingly arid.

Certainly not all the deserts of the world are alike. One may resemble another in many ways, yet each is distinctive. But regardless of the various factors that have produced various desert lands, their outstanding point shared in common is aridity.

chapter two

The North American Deserts

M APS drawn about two hundred years ago often referred to the Great American Desert, and one portion bore the melodious name of Pimeria Alta. Unfortunately, this romantic Spanish name was dropped by the Norteamericanos who came to live in this land of the Pima Indians. Also unfortunately, simple scientific conservatism has somehow managed to substitute the prosaic "North" for the colorful "Great" American Desert, though "great" is still an appropriate adjective to describe the majestic expanse of our desert land. The North American Desert covers so large an area that it encompasses a wide variety of physical conditions.

Its 500,000 square miles span 27 degrees of latitude stretching from a point fairly close to the Canadian border down to central Mexico. The desert floor ranges from 280 feet below sea level to approximately 5000 feet above. It is partly bordered by high mountain ranges, and other mountains often rise within the desert itself like green islands above an arid sea. The desert reaches from mid continent down to the tidelines. Depending on latitude, temperature and length of seasons vary; depending on locale, annual rainfall averages from less than two to fifteen or more inches per year, falling in the winter, in the summer, or both.

No single factor was responsible for the creation of the entire region. Separately or in combination, the circulation patterns of the atmosphere, rain shadow effects, locations far removed from oceanic moisture sources, and cold ocean currents influence the various sections of our North American Desert.

The northern region of the American Desert is primarily caused by a rain shadow. The Sierra Nevada and Cascade mountain ranges drain most of the moisture from clouds moving from the Pacific, thus creating the Great Basin Desert. Further to the south, the Mohave and Sonoran Deserts also lie in the rain shadows of western mountains. But in addition, these two deserts—including the more southern Chihuahuan—are located beneath more or less permanent anti-cyclones of descending dry air. All three deserts are in the horse latitudes, too far from the equator to benefit from tropical precipitation, and likewise too far south to catch moisture from ascending, cooling air. Moreover, the cold ocean currents flowing southward along the Pacific coast have a particularly apparent influence on the climate of the Sonoran Desert along the west coast of Baja California.

Of course, some precipitation does reach all of the North American Desert; enough to produce a generally predictable pattern of rainfall. Winter storms from the north and west, although well-wrung by the mountain barriers in their path, still manage to bring some moisture to the Great Basin and to desert areas as far down as southeastern Arizona. With summer, storm patterns shift away from the northern deserts. The more southerly Chihuahuan Desert receives most of its precipitation in the summer when storms from the Gulf of Mexico reach as far west as central Arizona.

As a general rule, winter rain falls in the northern and western portions of the desert, and summer rain in the southeast. These two primary storm patterns blend at their borders, producing an intermediate zone blessed with two "rainy" seasons, winter and summer. Tucson, Arizona lies in this area and receives approximately eleven inches of rain a year, rather evenly divided between the two seasons. In late summer, tropical hurricanes characterized by strong winds and heavy rainfall and known by their Spanish name of "chubascos" originate in the Pacific off Mexico and occasionally travel as far north as southern Arizona.

The driest portions of the North American Desert are those around the head of the Gulf of California, including the area in Baja California to the west of the gulf and the area stretching north from the gulf up into Death Valley. Two cities in this region, Mexicali and Yuma, boast mean

Baja California (*M. W. Larson*)

annual precipitations of 2.79 inches and 3.39 inches respectively. Moving northward and eastward from this area, average precipitation gradually increases.

Thus a great variety of physical conditions exists in different parts of the North American Desert. Plants and animals have evolved and adapted their ways of living to fit the climate and various soil conditions. Basically, however, four distinctive deserts have developed.

The Great Basin is the largest, most northern, coldest, and highest of the four. It covers almost all of the state of Utah and all but the southern tip of Nevada; it extends into southeastern Oregon, the southwestern portions of Idaho and Wyoming, the northwestern corner of Colorado, and small portions of northern and northeastern Arizona. A small, separate desert area in western Washington state is also included as part of the Great Basin.

The entire area lies at relatively high elevations, most of it over 4000 feet. The Great Basin is actually a good many basins, each separated from the others by low, roughly parallel north-south mountain ranges. We say this is a cool desert, for it has lower temperatures and a shorter summer season due to its more northern location, and extended periods of freezing temperatures are common in the winter. Precipitation averages four to eleven inches per year; and slightly more than half is received during late winter and early spring, often in the form of snow.

History is often shaped by lost causes. Early explorers were sure that a Northwest Passage traversed the continent to the Pacific, and they spent a great deal of effort searching for it. When this hope dimmed, they decided there must be at least a river or series of rivers traversing the continent from the Rockies to the Pacific. Lewis and Clark to the north, and the Spanish explorers to the south, determined that no such waterway lay in these areas. By process of elimination, hope focused on the last largely unknown section of middle North America, and so, exploration gained momentum in the area we now call the Great Basin. Great Salt Lake was already well known, and many of the trappers who worked nearby viewed its salty waters as indisputable proof of an undiscovered connection with the sea. Not until 1844, when Lieutenant Charles C. Frémont carried out his exploration of the area, was it definitely determined that this whole area was one of interior drainage. Frémont named the region the Great Basin and extinguished the hope of finding a waterway once and for all. Until that time the Great Basin Desert was one of the last main deterrents to westward expansion. Uncharted, forbidding, and dry, it stood across the path of pioneers seeking the Pacific. Frémont and others helped to clarify and map its features, but a mighty motivation was needed to spur the development of trails across it. A few more years provided the promise of fertile land in Oregon and the even stronger thrill of gold in California, and the desert was breached at last.

Great Salt Lake, one of the outstanding features of the Great Basin Desert, is seven times as salty as the ocean, and precisely because it is *not* connected to the sea. The water of the lake does not drain out, but is lost only by evaporation, leaving behind the minerals it originally leached from the soil of the surrounding mountains and desert over which it has passed. Over much of the Great Basin Desert, rainwater drains into the centers of the basins to form low-lying lakes. Unlike Great Salt Lake, most of these are temporary and do not attain any great volume. But again, evaporation leaves behind a residue of minerals, creating definite soil types which are often incapable of supporting plant life, or which support only very specialized plants.

Where the explorers searched, only to find water and waterways exceedingly scarce, water was once exceedingly plentiful—but that was some 30,000 years before they arrived! At the end of the last ice age, the Great Basin was a vast system of inland streams that drained the water of melting glaciers into gigantic lakes. Most outstanding of these was Lake Bonneville, which then covered much of southern Idaho, eastern Nevada, and western Utah. With the glaciers gone, Lake Bonneville gradually shrank, leaving behind a series of small lakes—including today's Great Salt Lake—in the deeper basins. Lake Bonneville's waters once rose at least a *thousand feet* above the level of today's Great Salt Lake; and its ancient shoreline is still apparent in many places today. Nor is its "remnant" any insignificant body of water, for the Great Salt Lake itself covers approximately 2000 square miles. Where Lake Bonneville dried up completely, vast residues of minerals were left behind to form such areas as today's Bonneville Salt Flats—hard, smooth, bereft of vegetation, and better known for fast automobiles than for hundreds of fathoms of water.

The vegetation of the Great Basin is the least diversified of any North American desert and is dominated by usually deciduous shrubs. The shrub popularly known as sagebrush, *Artemisia tridentata,* is the "trademark" of the region and is often present in nearly pure stands in areas of many square miles. Another shrub that blankets wide areas is the shadscale, *Atriplex confertifolia,* which replaces *A. tridentata* as the dominant plant at lower elevations and in the more alkaline soils. Cacti here are small and few; trees are rare, represented by only a few species such as willows and cottonwoods, and then occurring only along streambeds. Grasses and wildflowers grow whenever favorable moisture and temperature conditions coincide. At upper elevations, as on the higher mountain ranges, the desert vegetation gives way to xerophytic woodland, often composed of juniper and pinyon trees.

The Great Basin Desert's dominant shrubs are for the most part a gray-green in color. According to Dr. Forrest Shreve, in areas of many square miles, a single species such as sagebrush may make up as much as 95 percent of the total vegetative covering. Provided conditions are uniform, individuals of the same species all tend to attain the same approximate size and height. Much of the Great Basin is thus carpeted with large tracts of one or a very few species of plant shrub, generally of a monotonously uniform appearance. But though not diversified, the scenery is hardly dull. The Great Basin boasts the beauty and power of unobstructed views of distant rugged mountains, a gigantic unsmogged sky, and vast, relatively untouched stretches of open country as far as the eye can see—all of which are hardly dull.

Approximately 90 percent of the Chihuahuan Desert, second largest in size, lies south of the Mexican border. In fact portions of it lie farther south than any other North American desert. Its remaining 10 percent is divided between southeastern Arizona, the southern corners of New Mexico, and the southwestern wedge of Texas between the Pecos and the Río Grande. In Mexico, the bulk of the Chihuahuan lies on an intermountain plateau, bounded on the west by the Sierra Madre Occidental. To the east it is bordered by the Sierra Madre Oriental and by lowland plains. Much of the Chihuahuan Desert therefore lies in the rain shadow of these two ranges and is broken up by other, usually low ranges within its borders. Drainage is toward the Atlantic Ocean rather than the Pacific, although parts of the Chihuahuan drain into enclosed basins.

The Chihuahuan's average elevation is rather high, ranging between 3000 and 6000 feet. In winter, freezing temperatures may persist for as long as seventy hours. As we noted earlier, up to 80 percent of the year's precipitation falls in the summer and the annual average runs from approximately three to twenty inches depending on the section of the desert. Since the Chihuahuan is somewhat elevated and since the rainfall arrives during the period of heat stress when it is most needed, the desert conditions are ameliorated to some extent. Therefore this is not so extreme a desert as might conceivably be created in these lower latitudes.

Chihuahuan vegetation is characterized by a number of shrubs including the creosote bush, tarbush, all-thorn, and mesquite. Various types of yuccas, agaves, and sotol lend a distinctive appearance to the landscape, for their long, pointed, succulent or semi-succulent leaves form rosettes at the base of the plant, or on the outer parts of the branches if these are present. Yuccas, agaves, and sotols all produce a long stalk, the tip of which bear flowers. The well known "century plant," often used as an ornamental is one example of an agave; another is the lechuguilla, common in parts of the Chihuahuan. Trees are scarce, mainly located along watercourses. Cacti are present, but for the most part are small species and not particularly conspicuous. Flowering annuals follow the summer rains. Grasses spring up in many areas during favorable periods, and indeed, much of this desert merges with the grasslands along its borders.

Sweeping majestically out of Canada, the Rocky Mountains form a mighty ridge—the Continental Divide—down the North American continent. The Divide dwindles in size until it becomes simply an elevated grassland in New Mexico. But further south, the Divide rises again in the form of the Sierra Madre, which forms the western boundary of the Chihuahuan Desert. And though not terribly impressive in the southern United States, the Continental Divide is still sufficient to prevent the desert from running continuously across the southwestern United States. (Across the southwestern United States, grassland prevents the Sonoran Desert from meeting the Chihuahuan.) It is interesting, therefore, that west of the Continental Divide in the southeastern corner of Arizona, there occur small discontinuous desert areas whose vegetation is more characteristic of the Chihuahuan Desert than of the nearby Sonoran. There are indications that these isolated pockets are of somewhat recent development—or at least have become more pronounced within the last century.

Smallest of our North American Deserts is the Mohave, located primarily in southeastern California and in the southern wedge-shaped portion of Nevada. It also extends some very small bulges into western Arizona and extreme southwestern Utah. Though most of its territory lies between elevations of 2000 and 4000 feet, one part of the Mohave boasts the lowest elevation in the Western Hemisphere—282 feet below sea level—in Death Valley. The western sector of the Mohave lies at the higher altitudes, and the land slopes eastward toward the Colorado River that forms the desert's approximate eastern boundary.

Extremely arid, the Mohave's average rainfall varies from approximately two inches on its eastern borders to five inches in the west. The rain shadow of the mountains forming its western and southern boundaries cuts off much of the precipitation from the Pacific, and the little that does fall is received during the winter and spring months. The

The Pinacate Region of the Sonoran Desert (*M. W. Larson*)

Mohave itself is broken by numerous low mountain ranges which serve to divide it into basins, many of them undrained (like the Great Basin, the Mohave was covered with many lakes and rivers at the end of the last Ice Age). Along the desert's eastern border some drainage does occur into the Colorado River.

To the north of the Mohave lies the Great Basin Desert; to the south and along much of the Mohave's eastern borders lies the Sonoran. Many plants of both the Great Basin and Sonoran Deserts also thrive in the Mohave, which thus serves as a blending area between the two larger deserts. In general, the Mohave is a shrubby desert with the creosote bush and the bur sage the primary, ever-repeating species. Due to the aridity, however, these shrubs are often widely spaced and much of the soil lies bare. These two plants are shared by the Sonoran and Chihuahuan Deserts, but not by the Great Basin. (The creosote bush's northern limit of distribution is, for the most part, the northern boundary of the Mohave and Sonoran Deserts.) Some areas, particularly where the earth is saturated with saline deposits, are completely without vegetation. Trees are relatively scarce, found only along drainageways. Cacti are present, but are not as numerous or varied as those of the Sonoran.

About a quarter of the plant species that occur in the Mohave are endemic—that is, not to be found anywhere else. The most spectacular of these is the Joshua tree, often considered the Mohave's trademark. This strange plant is actually a giant yucca, a member of the lily family, which has achieved a tree-like form. Reaching up to thirty feet or exceptionally to fifty feet in height, its branches put forth sharply-pointed clusters of long leaves at their tips. Whole "forests" of these strange trees provide strikingly unusual scenery, and serve as a base for an interrelated community of living things.

It is in the Sonoran, fourth and last of the North American Deserts, that desert conditions and the development of desert plants to fit them reach a magnificent conclusion. Here the large size attained by many plants, the fine representation of cacti, and the many varieties of desert communities certainly make the Sonoran the most interesting and varied of the North American Deserts.

This desert lies like a giant horseshoe encircling the Gulf of California. From this point it spreads west and south to cover most of the peninsula of Baja California. To the east, it overlaps much of western and southern Arizona, continuing southward into the northwestern Mexican state of Sonora, from which it derives its name.

Due to its location and topography the Sonoran is subject to a variety of climatic conditions. We noted earlier that the area around the head of the gulf is extremely arid. The western parts of the Sonoran generally receive their precipitation only during the winter or early spring. Its eastern sections, however, lie far enough east to receive precipitation from the summer storms which bring the Chihuahuan Desert the greater percentage of its moisture. In addition, the eastern Sonoran Desert also receives moisture from the western winter storms. Therefore, the eastern reaches of the Sonoran average approximately ten to twelve inches of rainfall a year about evenly divided between the winter and summer

Transition Zone between the Mohave and Sonoran Deserts; note the Joshua tree (typical of the Mohave) and the saguaro (typical of the Sonoran) (*M. W. Larson*)

months; while parts of the western section may average only two inches per year, all falling in the winter. The left leg of the Sonoran horseshoe, formed by the Baja Peninsula, is enclosed by both the Gulf and the Pacific Ocean, whose cold offshore currents produce a special climate typified by great aridity and fog. The Sonoran's elevation ranges from below sea level to about 3000 feet. This desert's low elevation and the warm lower latitudes in which it lies are instrumental in producing its characteristically high temperatures.

The Sonoran Desert's climatic conditions determine what plants can survive there. Its central location among the North American Deserts contributes the variety of species represented there. This desert can draw upon those particular species able to survive its conditions which are derived from the desert areas to the north and west and which reach the Sonoran Desert by way of the Mohave. To some extent, its vegetation pattern also blends with types of vegetation which border the desert. Thus the boundaries of the Sonoran (where they do not meet the Pacific or the gulf) touch areas of higher elevations supporting grasslands, or more mountainous vegetation, or give way to more tropical plants, as to the south of the desert.

Dr. Forrest Shreve, who for many years was on the staff of Carnegie Institution's Desert Laboratory at Tucson, showed that the Sonoran Desert can be divided into seven subdivisions, based solely on the vegetation present in each. According to his schematic classification, these subdivisions are the *Lower Colorado Valley*, the *Arizona Upland*, the *Plains of Sonora*, the *Foothills of Sonora*, the *Central Gulf Coast*, the *Vizcaíno Region*, and the *Magdalena Region*.

The *Lower Colorado Valley* subdivision is the lowest in elevation, hottest, and driest of the seven. It comprises the low-lying areas at the head of the Gulf of California and along the eastern gulf coast of Baja California as far south as Bahía de los Angeles, the lower drainage area of the Colorado River, the Salton Sea of southeastern California, the southwestern corner of Arizona, and the low gulf coast areas of Sonora as far south as the Río Magdalena. Due to the extreme desert conditions, vegetation here is sparse and restricted to a limited number of species; the dominant ones being the familiar creosote bush and bur sage. This region is noted for its extensive dunes and areas of relatively recent volcanic activity.

The *Arizona Upland* subdivision, the northeastern portion of the Sonoran Desert, is primarily located in Arizona, but stretches across the border to the northern part of the Mexican state of Sonora. It is bordered by non-desert country to the north and east, and adjoins the Lower Colorado Valley to the south and west. Studded with numerous mountain ranges, this subdivision provides a variety of habitats for plants. The rainfall is generous, ranging as high as twelve to fourteen inches per year, and its biseasonal occurrence provides an extra bonus. It is in the Arizona Upland therefore, that some of the most interesting and outstanding desert plants occur, including the impressive saguaro cactus, a variety of smaller cacti, and a number of desert trees including the paloverdes, ironwoods,

Another view of a boojum forest, in which the carrot shape is particularly striking (*M. W. Larson*)

and mesquites. Creosote bush and bur sage are still dominant, especially in the valleys, but on hillsides the more varied and picturesque plants become common and lend a distinctive character to the terrain. Desert trees find improved moisture conditions along the usually dry streambeds and grow in relative abundance. Due to the occurrence of two rainy periods a year, one crop of annuals blooms following the winter rains and another following the summer rainy season. This ameliorated aridity in combination with varied topographical features has created what might be called a "lush" desert.

The *Plains of Sonora* and *Foothills of Sonora* subdivisions lie south of the Arizona Upland. When viewed as a unit, these two are bordered to the west by the gulf and by the Central Gulf Coast and Lower Colorado Valley subdivisions. Their eastern portions merge into areas of higher elevation approaching the Continental Divide. To the south this desert country is displaced by thorn forest vegetation. The plant growth of these subdivisions is characterized as "arborescent" or tree-like, the dominant plants being trees and shrubs.

The *Central Gulf Coast* subdivision consists of two narrow strips of land on either shore of the gulf. The one in Sonora stretches from the Río Magdalena south to the Río Yaquí. Across the gulf in Baja, the second extends along the coast almost to the southern tip of the peninsula. In the waters of the gulf, two large islands and a host of small ones lie like stepping stones between the opposing sections. They are literally "desert islands," and their flora and fauna are faithfully characteristic of the Central Gulf Coast subdivision.

The Central Gulf Coast is a hot, dry desert. Here live large, distinctive cacti such as the cardon, and bizarre plants such as the elephant tree. But the most outstanding plant by far is the boojum tree. Its appearance is as strange as its name, for it resembles a sixty-foot inverted grayish-green carrot.

The remaining two subdivisions known as the *Magdalena Region* and the *Vizcaíno Region* are both located in Baja California. North-south mountains and elevated areas divide the Baja peninsula lengthwise into two parts—the narrow eastern section with drainage to the gulf, and the much wider section draining into the Pacific. The *Vizcaíno* lies in approximately the central third of the peninsula to the west of this escarpment, bearing leaf-succulent plants such as agaves and yuccas in addition to the elephant tree, cardon cactus, and boojum. This strip is

The Vizcaíno Region of the Sonoran Desert, Baja California (*M. W. Larson*)

subject to high winds, which contributes to its barrenness; and fogs which foster the growth of lichens on plants and rocks. Most of the southern third of the peninsula (also to the west of the escarpment) composes the Magdalena Region characterized by desert trees including mesquites; a tree known as *Lysiloma* (called "palo blanco" by the Mexicans); peninsular ocotillo; and a variety of cacti including cardon, pitahaya, and the strange caterpillar cactus, whose trunks lie upon the ground. The trunks root themselves throughout their length, and the older parts gradually die off as the growing tip moves forward.

Each of our North American Deserts has a definite personality on the basis of its vegetation alone. The sagebrush of the Great Basin, the saguaros and boojums of the Sonoran, the lechuguilla of the Chihuahuan, and the Joshua trees of the Mohave attest that certain plants have met the challenge of desert conditions in a great variety of ways, and in so doing have produced some of the most interesting, if not *the* most interesting, plants and desert landscapes in the entire world.

chapter three

Water, Rock, Sand, and Soil

T HE North American Desert is geologically young, one of the most recent of the earth's developments on this continent. Dr. Daniel I. Axelrod proposes that our present deserts may be only one to five million years old. Our deserts, for the most part, demonstrate a basin and range topography; that is, they consist largely of roughly parallel mountain ranges separated by plains or basins. Rugged, jagged, and imposing, these mountains rise from the desert floor, cutting the smoothness of the far distant horizon. Little vegetation softens the outlines of their rocky nakedness. Timeless and permanent as they may seem when viewed from the standpoint of a human lifespan, they are constantly being worn down from assault by water, wind, freezing, and heating. If nothing vitally changes the process, they will be ground away until the surrounding desert assumes a near flatness similar to much of the Sahara.

"The land of little rain" Mary Austin called our desert country in her beautifully written book of the same name. And it is. Strange then that water is the great molding force of the desert landscape. When rain does come to the desert, some of it falls on the mountains. Often it arrives violently, accompanied by thunder and lightning, falling briefly but heavily. The usually rocky mantle of the mountain simply sheds it, much of it falling so quickly that it runs off before it can soak into cracks or

Flat Sonoran Desert country and mountains near Guaymas, Mexico (*M. W. Larson*)

shallow beds of soil. Racing down the mountainsides and gradually collecting into normally dry streambeds, this runoff flushes rocks, boulders, gravel, and dirt along in its path. Its momentum is slowed as it reaches the bottom of the slope and the material it is carrying is gradually dropped. At the foot of the mountain, a fan-shaped deposit of alluvial material gradually forms—a common feature of the desert wherever hills or low mountains appear. In time, the fans at the base of a single mountain may broaden sufficiently to coalesce with one another. When this happens, the resulting skirt about the base of the mountain sloping down toward the center of the intermountain plain or basin, is called a *bajada*. Any water which makes its way to the low center of the plain itself frequently drains away through usually dry waterways known as dry washes, or by their Spanish name, *arroyos*.

A usually dry streambed playing host to a flash flood (*M. W. Larson*)

One of the paradoxes of the desert is that each year a few people drown in these usually dry arroyos during a phenomenon known as a flash flood. Desert storms, particularly summer ones, are often restricted to small areas. One may see many groups of clouds in the distance whose rain is falling only in places. (This occurs particularly over the mountains.) A brief but violent storm on a mountainside can produce a heavy run-off which is soon channeled into waterways gouged out by countless previous storms. The flood, ever seeking lower levels, roars down upon the plain at the base of the mountain. Here it rushes onward in the arroyo until its momentum is at last spent or until most of it has soaked into the bed of the wash. But this great stream may form a wall of water several feet high at its forefront which travels down the wash at terrific speed. Once seen, such an occurrence is not easily forgotten. One may observe a com-

Two views of the same desert wash before and after a heavy storm (*M. W. Larson*)

pletely dry wash, then suddenly see a wall of water thundering down it, sweeping over the dry surface and filling the wash from bank to bank. People may thus be overtaken by a flash flood on a day with only a few clouds in the sky overhead, its water produced by a storm occurring so far away as to go unnoticed.

Accordingly, travelers are cautioned against camping or parking their vehicles in the beds of washes. Roads in the desert are often posted with signs that say "Dip," to warn the motorist that the road crosses a low area or wash at that point. The wise driver realizes that their apparent shallowness is deceptive. In Tucson, where some of the deeper washes are crossed by city streets, the roads have metal poles along the curb, marked to show the depth of the water that may be flowing there after a storm. Often two or three people lose their lives each summer by attempting to cross these arroyos during flooding and having themselves or their cars washed downstream. Such floods usually last only a few hours at most, and the next day the wash will very likely have only a muddy or damp surface as a reminder of the previous day's flood.

A playa or dry lake, here partly flooded following a storm (*M. W. Larson*)

In many cases, however, the water does not drain away so dramatically, but flows to the low-lying center of an undrained basin; this area is termed a *bolson*. When present in sufficient quantities, the water forms an ephemeral lake that eventually evaporates, leaving behind the minerals it has carried in solution. Such a dry lake bed at the center of a bolson is called a *playa,* the Spanish word for beach.

Little of the precipitation that falls in the desert ever reaches the ocean since most is either absorbed by the earth or evaporated. However, small amounts channeled into washes or dry river beds do ultimately join rivers which have arisen in wetter climates and which must traverse the desert on their way to the sea. Such rivers are called *exotic,* and can only exist if supplied with large quantities of water at their distant origins. In contrast to normal rivers, which are increased in volume by numerous tributaries as they travel toward the sea, rivers crossing deserts receive little

A bend of the Colorado River below Hoover Dam (*M. W. Larson*)

Hoover Dam impounds a portion of the Colorado River; the resulting body of water is Lake Mead (*M. W. Larson*)

or no moisture and actually lose water to the dry lands through which they pass. Examples of exotic rivers are the Colorado and Río Grande in our American deserts, and of course the Nile in the Sahara. Today, however, these exotic rivers are not depleted by the climate as much as by man, who has dammed and trapped their waters for his own use. The result is that even less of it finally reaches the oceans.

The pattern for much of our desert, then, is that of eroding mountain ranges gradually filling the intermountain lowlands between them with their own debris. Water is one of the most potent agents in this process and does a great deal otherwise to influence the texture of the desert's surface. It affects individual rocks by flowing into their cracks and crevices and weakening them, enlarging the breaks, and leaching out their more soluble minerals. It lays bare much of the rock structure of the mountains as it sweeps away loose material. It drops the larger, heavier materials it carries in the upper reaches of the bajada; intermediate-sized pieces further down the bajada; and the finest material last of all. This graded texture is readily apparent as one ascends from the center of a bolson and up the slope of the bajada.

Wind, too, is a powerful erosional force, especially where there is little vegetation present to protect the surface of the desert from wind and water. As the surface soil and sand is usually dry, frequent winds pick them up from one place and redeposit them in another. On still summer days, a common and striking desert feature is the "dust devil," "whirl-wind," or "tornillo." It occurs when air becomes greatly heated over the hot desert flats. As it rises, other air moves in from the sides to replace it and create a whirling mass of air. The dust devil circles, moving wildly across the surface of the ground and whirling about dust, sand, and debris, sometimes to great heights. Finally the momentum of the air is lost and the whirlwind dies, dropping the material it has transported.

Wind-born particles of dust or sand act as an abrasive against anything in their path. A tiny grain of sand appears fairly harmless, but not when it is joined with millions of others in a current of swiftly moving air. Extensive sand deposits lie along the highway between Yuma, Arizona and Palm Springs, California, and signs warn the motorist about the possible danger of blowing sand. When the situation merits, red lights may flash, advising him not to proceed until later or to take an alternate route.

Driving on this highway one night, we noted the lights flashing, but since we were in a hurry and noticed that the sand didn't seem to be blowing too hard, we continued on. The drive was interesting but eerie. Surrounded by the blackness of the night, our headlights pierced a layer of silver-white sand, constantly blowing and drifting in front of us at right angles to the highway. We were bombarded by it for about fifteen or twenty miles. Daylight revealed that the car, scoured by millions of grains of sand, had been literally sand-blasted. A new windshield, grill,

Lichens growing on rock (*M. W. Larson*)

bumper, and half a paint job were required to repair the effects of the abrasive sand. As with the car, so on the surface of the desert, blowing sand scours and gradually disintegrates objects in its path.

Wide fluctuations of daily temperature also have an eroding action on desert rocks. Stone surfaces may be exposed to terrific heat that expands them during the day, and to rapid cooling that contracts them during the night. The interiors of larger rocks remain relatively cool while their outer layers become very hot, resulting in stresses that cause outer layers to flake away or other dramatic changes to take place. Even more drastic temperature changes may take place when sudden cool rains fall upon sun-baked rocks or when freezing temperatures occur in many parts of the desert in winter.

The desert's basic rock structure is assaulted by mechanical, chemical, and biological forces—plant roots and lichen acids among them—that ultimately reduce portions of it to particles small enough to become the parent material of soil. Soil provides the base for desert life, supporting the plants that in turn sustain the animals. Although inanimate itself, soil provides the physical support for the plants that grow in it, and holds the vital minerals, water, and air that their roots require like a giant sponge. Man, however, has all too often taken soil for granted; not until it has blown or washed away has he learned how precious it is and what a difficult commodity it is to replace.

In addition to mashed or pulverized rock, good soil contains organic materials. Consider the great quantities of leaves, trees, and other plant materials in a forest that must die and decompose in order to enrich and build the soil. On the great prairies, countless crops of grass once grew and died to produce the rich, thick soils that the settlers exploited and damaged unbelievably in the period of a few short years. Animals also contribute to the soil when their bodies decompose at death, and through their droppings and urine during life. Earthworms serve to aerate and enrich the large quantities of moist soil through which they work. Ants—to say nothing of larger burrowing animals—also mix and loosen the soil materials when they build their nests.

One of the most important factors that goes into the building of soil—and one that is often forgotten by man—is time. The breakdown of rock, the addition of organic materials to this base, and the play of climatic forces upon it, all require decades or centuries. The climate in which the soil is formed also influences the end product. Heat or freezing cold, dryness or wetness, slope or plain, wind or calm—these and other similar factors in a variety of combinations are important in the type of soil formed.

The formation of desert soil is a particularly slow and difficult process; in fact, some desert soils have progressed very little beyond the point of fine rock containing as little as 0.25 percent humus. Plant cover over much of the desert is sparse—in some portions, plant cover may be entirely lacking, or if present may cover only two or three percent of the ground's surface. Even in death a plant's constituents may not be returned to the piece of desert earth on which it grew for water or winds may sweep them away.

Rainwater is pulled into this soil by gravity and capillary action, but in many desert soils the subsoil is dry. The only moisture available to plants lies in a layer not far from the surface. When winds and high temperatures evaporate moisture from the surface, some of this small water reserve is then drawn upwards by capillary action. Eventually, a temporary equilibrium is reached, the upper inches of dry soil serving to insulate the moisture just below. The next rain, dampening at least the surface of the ground, will encourage more capillary give-and-take. This is not to say that there are *no* extensive ground water reserves in the desert; however, a good many of them are what has been termed "fossil" water, deposited long ago when the climatic conditions were different.

Having recently drilled a well on the lower levels of a saguaro-studded bajada, we can attest that ground water often lies a long way down, 450 feet in our particular location. Since you pay according to the number of feet drilled, and then must pay to raise whatever water you do find (and there's no assurance that you will), fossil water is a valuable resource. Unfortunately, man depends upon this ancient, exhaustible resource to a frightening extent in his efforts to domesticate the desert lands.

Water dissolves soluble minerals from the rocks and soil and carries them along with it. In humid regions, the soaking water transports the minerals deep into the earth, where they may ultimately find their way into springs or rivers. This process therefore tends to leach out humid soils—flushing many of their minerals away—but it has the opposite effect in the desert. Here again, the water carries mineral salts as it seeps downward, but usually for only a short distance. They are often swept upward again as the water is pulled toward the surface by capillary action. On some heavily impregnated soils, such as those found in a bolson, thin layers of salts may even form on the soil surface. This buildup occurs readily when the soil has been irrigated for some time, particularly if the irrigation water is heavily mineralized and cannot flow away periodically, taking its salts along with it. A layer of hardpan composed of calcium carbonate often forms in the upper layers of the soil. This "caliche" may occur in successive thin layers down to a depth of several feet. Caliche impedes water penetration, and the unlucky desert homeowner may be forced to use a jackhammer to provide drainage for the trees he wishes to plant.

A certain amount of salts can supply a fertile base for plant growth, providing other conditions are favorable. Some desert soils are extremely productive for this very reason. Excessive amounts, however, are detri-

A crusty layer of caliche, here exposed along the bank of a desert wash (*M. W. Larson*)

mental to plant growth, particularly in the undrained playas. Rain water flowing into the area but never out, leaves behind a successively thicker crust of salts. In certain outstanding playas, mineral residues may be many feet thick and can be exploited commercially. The types of residues vary, depending upon the predominant minerals in the rocks and soil of the surrounding area. Thus some playas are known as salt lakes, borax lakes, bitter lakes, saltpans, and alkali flats—all of which are brutally inhospitable to plant life. When funneled into a salty playa, precious water is of about the same value to the living things of the desert as sea water is to a shipwrecked sailor.

Actually, a good deal of the desert is not covered by a soil mantle. Some of the surface is simply rock; other areas are covered by sand or gravel, and much of the desert's surface is veneered by various combinations of sand, gravel, soil, and rock. The amazing thing about desert soil is not its scarcity, but rather that there is as much of it as there is. Washed by brief, infrequent, but violent floods; blown by unimpeded winds; dried from a shortage of water; lacking organic matter; often suffering from excessive mineralization and little protected by vegetation, it is easily disturbed and disrupted.

One interesting—although not exceptionally common—type of desert surface is that known as "desert pavement." Such a surface is literally paved with small adjacent rocks with very little or no soil apparent between them. Desert pavement is caused by wind and water which erode the fine soil originally present around the rocks until they eventually settle and nestle against one another. Desert pavement may stretch for many acres in extent. Of course when finally completed this flat stone terrace precludes further removal of the soil beneath, and for the most part, it is barren of plant life. As the soil shrinks and is removed from the surface during the formation of desert pavement, there is apparently a corresponding, upward displacement of stones and smaller materials from below.

Some deserts such as the Sahara and Arabian have a greater percentage of their surface covered by sand than do others. A popular misconception has it that most deserts are largely composed of this material. Our North American Deserts have some areas of sand and sand dunes—some of the most outstanding lie west of Yuma, Arizona (they are called the Algodones—Spanish for "cotton"—Dunes), around the head of the Gulf of California, and in the White Sands National Monument in New Mexico. The type of sand varies from one location to another: that of many areas is largely quartz. The dunes of White Sands are nearly pure gypsum, and some dunes nearer the gulf are made up primarily of ground-up shells. But the extent of such areas and the size of their individual dunes are minor when compared to certain sandy wastes of the Old World.

As a growing medium, sand presents at best a difficult barrier to plant colonization. Fine, light, and usually dry, the individual grains are readily moved by air currents, so that any one sand deposit may be constantly

Desert wash and sand dunes, Sonoran Desert (*M. W. Larson*)

shifting. Even if plants germinate successfully, they are in danger of being buried in the sand which tends to drift about such small obstacles. Swiftly blown sand, too, is a danger to plants, scouring and abrading them. However, sand's permeability is high and it does absorb moisture quickly and deeply. Once received on a sandy surface, water is stored at some depth in the sand deposit, and due to the large size of the grains, it is less likely to return to the surface by capillary action. These factors help modulate sand's basic disadvantages, often making sandy areas interesting and distinctive plant communities.

Few things in nature are as simple and clear cut as the printed word would make them seem. The formation, erosion, and disintegration of some of the rocks of the earth's surface, the redistribution of their components, and their integration with other materials to form soils are all extremely complicated. Eons of time, reaching back to the genesis of the earth, have been invested in the production of what we finally see today as desert country. We can look at the desert and observe some of the results of the process but no doubt there is much yet to be observed and, we know, much yet to be learned and understood about the formation of the desert surface as well as about the precise relationship between the nonliving and living components of the desert community.

chapter four

Microclimates and Microhabitats

LIFE in the desert is a challenge, and those plants and animals that have best been able to meet that challenge have survived to reproduce and form the living core of the desert. Those that lived were often the ones which took advantage of any amelioration of its stringent conditions. The desert as a whole is a hostile environment, but even within one region, minute but highly significant differences exist that can create certain habitats that are quite favorable to life. Therefore, the term "microclimate" is being used increasingly in scientific studies of the desert. *Webster's* defines microclimate as "the local climate of a given site or habitat, varying in size from a tiny crevice to a large land area, but being usually characterized by considerable uniformity of climate over the site involved and relatively local as compared with its enveloping macroclimate, from which it differs because of local climatic factors (as elevation and exposure)." Microclimates often provide the slight but vital benefits necessary to sustain life in the desert. Man enjoys his own desert microclimates by building air-conditioned homes; but so does the termite within its nest, and the rodent resting in its burrow underground.

The study of microclimates is largely being promoted by a "new" type of scientist, the ecologist, who investigates the mutual relations between organisms and their environment. Ecology is a new scientific approach

45

different than that, say, of the traditional mammalogist, ornithologist, herpetologist, or botanist who operates within the specialized confines of his particular subject. Ecologists actually hark back to early writers and philosophers who displayed an interest in the interaction of literally every-thing under, and including, the sun. Modern ecologists also attempt to understand how all the varied types of living things relate to each other and to their total environment. Their efforts are of great importance today, for man is, unfortunately, continuing to disrupt the environment over much of the earth, and ecologists are helping to point out the often disastrous consequences.

It is not easy to study the maze of interrelated factors that determine a particular environment and the living things that are found there. For that reason, the ecologist often finds it convenient to break the environ-ment into smaller pieces and to study each individually. Thus where the climatologist may analyze deserts in terms of average temperature and precipitation, the botanist in terms of special plant ranges, and the geolo-gist in terms of topographical characteristics, the ecologist zeros in more closely, viewing a single desert environment as many small communities of living things, each the result of differing microclimates and other fac-tors and each reacting to these conditions in a different way. A particular microclimate may give rise to one particular type of habitat, or it may support several. Thus the north side of a hill may support a definite microclimate, but several other differing conditions on that one hillside may give rise to several distinct habitats or microhabitats within the microclimate. Going back to *Webster's,* we find a microhabitat to be "a small, usually distinctly specialized and effectively isolated habitat (as a decaying stump, a pat of dung, or the rhizosphere of a plant)." Ecology has emphasized that the desert is a mosaic of miniature worlds. Living things tend to "choose"—either by chance, heredity, or habit—the microhabitat best suited to their needs. The net result is that plants and animals in relatively close proximity may be living under very dissimilar conditions.

Deserts are notorious for their high temperatures. Since there is little cloud or plant cover to reflect the sun's rays, most of the solar energy is therefore expended in heating the desert's surface and the air immedi-ately above it. Official temperature records are taken five feet above the ground in shade, and with free air circulation around the thermometer. However, the soil surface in that same area in the desert may be as much as 50°F hotter than the air above. Therefore when we consider that the highest official temperature recorded in our North American Deserts is 134°F, it is obvious that the actual surface temperature must have been phenomenal. Although this Death Valley record is certainly extreme, very high temperatures occur regularly and for extended periods over large desert areas. In their monumental work, *Vegetation and Flora of the Sonoran Desert,* Shreve and Wiggins report that in parts of this desert, a temperature maximum of 100°F lasting for periods of ninety consecutive days is not unusual. A soil surface record of 161°F was made at Tucson, Arizona, at a depth of 4 millimeters (approximately .15 inch), and at the same time the official air temperature taken under standard conditions was 52.5°F lower. As we noted, the desert's surface readily cools at night, so both air and surface temperatures can fluctuate widely in twenty-four hours. In *Life in Deserts,* J. L. Cloudsley-Thompson and M. J. Chadwick report a diurnal range of 101.7°F at a soil depth of 0.4 centimeters (approximately .15 inch) in Arizona.

In midsummer, a man on the desert often imagines he is walking through an inferno. Even when protected by shoes, his feet feel as if they were on fire, but his head and most of his body are several feet above the ground and thus in lower temperatures than those prevailing about his ankles. Except for birds and some insects, most desert creatures do not share man's ability to literally rise above the hot surface. Therefore, the desert appears almost completely devoid of animal life at noon on a hot summer day. The animals, however, are there. Displaying more common sense than the human observer, they have repaired to various retreats or microclimates which afford protection and are waiting out the worst of the searing heat.

Soil is an excellent insulator, and although its upper levels may become superheated, extreme temperatures do not reach great depths. In *Desert Animals: Physiological Problems of Heat and Water,* Knut Schmidt-Nielsen reports that diurnal variations in temperature may be virtually lacking at a depth of 80 centimeters (approximately 31 inches), and that tests in Arizona showed annual fluctuations at a depth of one meter (3.28 feet) amounting to only approximately 12°C (about 53°F). Therefore, the protecting earth enables many creatures to survive the desert heat in microclimates within burrows and under or among the rocks. With the advent of night and cooler ground surface and air temperatures, such creatures emerge from their underground homes and become active.

Ringtailed cat in the Arizona-Sonora Desert Museum's under-ground tunnel (*Courtesy of Arizona-Sonora Desert Museum*)

There is a time lag in the heating of soil beneath the immediate surface, and thus only when the animals are preparing to leave their shallower retreats does the previous day's heat begin to warm the soil around their buried homes. In the same way, this time lag causes the night's cooler temperatures to begin reaching the burrows only in the early morning hours, about the time the animals are returning.

The desert covers a fascinating underground world, inhabited by life in every size from microscopic organisms to large ones such as badgers and foxes. It is a vital, busy world over which man walks although he is seldom aware of it. In order to help people understand the complexity of the desert's underground reaches, the Arizona-Sonora Desert Museum near Tucson has constructed an underground tunnel to exhibit the underground portions of desert plants as well as some of the animals that spend their days in underground retreats. This ninety-foot tunnel, its surfaces finished in simulated rock and dirt, is kept in near darkness. Along its two walls are numerous exhibits which appear to be carved in the rock and soil of the earth and in which reside numerous living animals such as kit foxes, ringtailed cats, rattlesnakes, pack rats, bats, prairie dogs, ants, mice, and badgers. (These animals have access to outside dens above the tunnel.) By pressing a button in front of each den, the visitor may illuminate it to reveal its occupant. Since daytime is the normal resting period for these animals and also man's time to visit the museum, the timing works out well. The visitor usually finds the animals in their underground dens as they would be when living in the wild. They have adapted to the lights flashing on and off and are no longer bothered.

Many other types of microclimates afford heat relief besides underground retreats. Animals may seek shelter in caves, in or around plants, in shade, in and around man's dwellings, in nests or constructions of their own making, or even in other animals' homes. Equally important is the alleviation of moisture stress that microclimates afford. Desert oases, fed by rare springs or seepage, provide a striking microclimate where numbers of typical desert animals and plants congregate to take advantage of the moisture supply. Such oases also attract other living things which need more water than the desert usually affords. Palm trees, fish, amphibians, and flocks of birds—including migrating species—make the oasis a distinctive community. Exotic rivers flowing through the desert support oasis-type communities along their banks. A wash collects and stores runoff beneath its surface and even a simple depression may collect sufficient water to support a plant in an otherwise barren area. Man's irrigated fields, ponds, and lawns provide similar microclimates. Roads shed water, and increased supplies of moisture are present along their edges and ditches. Whereas man is responsible for creating many microclimates in the desert which plants and animals can take advantage of, he has also destroyed or changed a good many by cutting down or stopping the flow of rivers, by bulldozing desert communities, and through other such activities.

Dew may provide a distinctive microclimate. During its rapid and excessive cooling at night, the desert air may reach the "dew point," at which time drops of excess moisture condense over the surfaces of soil, rocks, and plants. There is considerable controversy over just how much help such dew actually provides. Nevertheless, it is apparent that it provides valuable moisture for at least some plant species that we will be considering later. Dew is certainly of value to certain small animals who can lick or suck up the moisture directly or eat the foliage it dampens.

Dew may be widespread enough over a desert area to be considered a part of the overall climate, but it also may be more restricted or concentrated in certain places so as to cause definite microclimates. Significantly, in the Negev desert of Israel hundreds of gravel mounds laid out in grids have been discovered. Archaeologists speculate that these ancient structures were built to accumulate dew for the benefit of plants growing around the base. Indeed, investigators in the Sonoran Desert have reported that depressions in rocks occasionally collect as much as a few cups of water from dew falling on the surrounding rocks.

Temperature and moisture are interrelated in one microclimate. A burrow in the soil provides cooler temperatures for the animal resting there and also protects him from dehydration. The confines of the burrow retain the moisture the animal loses through respiration, and the humidity inside a burrow is usually higher than in the air above. Similarly, an oasis or irrigated field offers both water and the cooling effects of evaporation. Microclimates that differ significantly from the general desert climate often provide a life-sustaining advantage, as we will note numerous times as we consider the ways in which the desert's plants and animals survive. For the plants and animals that make the desert their home, a few degrees in temperature or a few drops of water, can tip the balance between living and dying. It is apparent that in the desert especially, it is the little things that count.

chapter five

Desert Ephemerals

G REEN plants are the all-important base upon which the animals of the world stand, literally and figuratively. Without them there would be no animals; and in the dawn of time the development of green plants was a necessary prerequisite to the development of animal life. Our human lives depend upon the green plants, yet we ordinarily take them for granted unless disaster strikes a particular crop, or some other happening jolts us to awareness. A number of years ago a novel was written based on the interesting theme of the destruction throughout the world of all plants classed as grasses. The ramifications of such a happening in the novel were stupendous, as they would be in reality. In the desert, as in the other environments of the earth, all life is basically dependent upon green plants, although these may be as varied in size as the one-celled blue-green algae or the giant saguaro cactus, and it is therefore with the plants that we will begin our survey of the living things that populate the desert.

Through the action of a plant's chlorophyll in the presence of light, carbohydrates are formed from water and carbon dioxide. This process is known as photosynthesis. The sun is the fundamental source of all energy except atomic, but animals cannot use the sun's energy directly for their bodies except for warmth. It is green plants which convert this fundamental source of energy into a form that can be used by plants and secondarily by animals. Plants are thus a vast reservoir of banked energy. This store is drawn upon by the plants themselves, by animals consuming the plants, and later by the consumption of these animals by others.

With the exception of certain bacteria, only plants laden with chlorophyll are capable of manufacturing their own food. Chlorophyll is also present in certain types of plants which are not obviously green; in their case, other pigments camouflage the green of the chlorophyll. (Such pigments produce the bright colors of trees in the fall, when chlorophyll production wanes. They also color portions of plants such as the flowers and fruits.) Some plants, however, contain no chlorophyll and thus being incapable of photosynthesis, have to derive their nourishment directly from other plants or from animals. Most bacteria and the fungi, such as the familiar mushrooms, are examples. Unlike green plants, these species have no need for sunlight and can grow in darkness, providing other conditions are propitious.

Photosynthesis is a complicated process. In very simple terms, however, water and carbon dioxide are the two basic raw materials. A plant's roots, of course, absorb water from the soil, and pores known as stomata (usually located on the leaves) admit the carbon dioxide. Within certain of the plant's cells are bodies called chloroplasts which contain the green chlorophyll. When powered by light, this pigment splits water molecules into their component elements of hydrogen and oxygen. The latter is released into the surrounding air through the stomata. Some of the hydrogen then recombines with oxygen from the carbon dioxide, forming additional water. The remaining hydrogen combines with carbon dioxide to form sugar. In this way, the sun's energy helps weld inorganic constituents into a basic food which provides energy and raw materials for life on earth.

Since water is an essential ingredient in photosynthesis, green plants cannot exist without it. It is necessary in other ways also: water soaks through the soil, is absorbed by the plant, and most of it is eventually transpired through the stomata into the atmosphere. Water acts as a solvent for the soil minerals that are important for the plant's growth. On its journey through the plant, water transports dissolved oxygen and carbon dioxide, minerals, and food from one place to another. Chemical reactions within the plant take place in a liquid medium, and protoplasm —the living material of the plant's cells—contains water as an essential ingredient. Water is capable of absorbing much heat with relatively little change in temperature, and during periods of heat, the water vapor lost in transpiration helps lower the temperature of the plant below the lethal point. Individual plant cells are kept turgid (swollen) by the pressure of the water they hold within; consequently, the strength of the entire plant is partially dependent upon the quantities of water it retains inside its cell membranes.

It is as though plants have in water a disposable circulation medium. On its journey from root to leaf, some water may enter into chemical reactions and be changed, but at any one time, a plant has only about 0.1 to 0.3 percent of its water content tied up in chemical compounds. The humidity of the surrounding air has a vital influence on transpiration. The evaporative pressure of dry air is one of the powerful factors that cause the water to flow upward through the plant. Finally, if measures are not taken by the plant to prevent it, the water is taken into the absorptive air and lost. In this sojourn the water has served a good many valuable purposes.

The stomata support two-way traffic. It is through these that carbon dioxide enters the plant and oxygen and water leave. The name stomata comes from Greek and means "little mouths." Each stoma is bordered by two bean-shaped guard cells. When water within these cells is present in sufficient quantities, they swell. The centers of the two are pulled apart, and thus the stoma is opened. Under this condition, exchange of materials between the plant and the air can take place and photosynthesis may be carried on. However, if the turgor of the two cells decreases, their centers are drawn together, closing the stoma. But even when the stomata are closed, some water loss must occur. Without some transpiration and resultant capillary movement, the plant's life processes would cease.

Obviously, a plant must rely for the most part on supplies of moisture around its roots. If the soil's moisture supply becomes insufficient for the plant's needs, then the plant will lose its turgor and wilt. Individual species vary in their needs and their ability to recover from wilting. Moisture loss can cause protoplasm to coagulate within an afflicted plant. Individual cells reduce in size, putting mechanical strain on the tissues. If not relieved by needed water, such wilting results in death; and even if a wilted plant is suddenly dosed with large quantities of water, the consequent rapid swelling of its cells may cause further tissue stress which may damage or kill the plant. To protect themselves from these possibilities, plants living in desert country have developed some of the most bizarre physical characteristics and highly adaptive living habits of the plant kingdom.

Plants may be broadly divided into hydrophytes (water plants), mesophytes (found in moist soils), and xerophytes. There are a number of interpretations of the term "xerophyte," but we shall consider it as signifying plants especially adapted or suited to arid conditions. Obviously, we will be dealing primarily with the xerophytes when discussing desert species. Many of these are so perfectly adapted to arid conditions that they would perish if transplanted to a more "favorable"—that is, considerably wetter—climate.

Xerophytes can be divided into at least two groups. One of these, which we will consider later, consists of plants known as "drought resisters." The second broad grouping consists of the plants known as "drought evaders," and it is these we shall deal with first.

Drought evaders do just that. They are annuals, but the life span of an individual plant seldom lasts an entire growing season and the term "annual" is almost too broad. Therefore, plants in this group are often referred to as ephemerals, from the Greek word for daily. The desert's ephemerals do last more than a single day, of course, but they are extremely short-lived, often completing an entire generation in six to eight weeks. They germinate only under the most favorable conditions the desert can offer, quickly flower, produce seeds, and die. For perhaps as much as ten or eleven months of each year these particular species exist only as minute seeds.

"Enjoy today, for tomorrow you shall die," would seem to be the motto of the ephemerals. Of all the desert plants, they seem to defy the usual sere environment most flagrantly by producing great extravagant, colorful masses of flowers. These ephemerals, however, never meet the desert head-on except in seed form, for they grow only following the rainy season or seasons of the desert when sufficient moisture supplies are present to support them. If the rains fail or are scanty in any one year, ephemerals fail to appear or are present only in reduced number and size. Authorities sometimes argue that the ephemerals are not really xerophytes at all since they avoid aridity. However the ephemerals may be considered xerophytes inasmuch as their avoidance techniques are in themselves an adaptation to the desert climate.

Certain locations provide particularly favorable temperature, moisture,

A stand of evening primrose (*M. W. Larson*)

or topography for the growth of ephemerals. Sandy areas often support exceptional stands. Whereas the ephemeral seeds are blown about on smooth surfaces such as desert pavement, they often lodge in sand and are drifted over enough to be held in place until growth starts. Sand absorbs and retains moisture well, it usually supports little perennial vegetation that would offer competition for space or moisture, and moreover, its surface heats quickly, providing the warmth ephemerals need to germinate in the winter or early spring. Very rocky surfaces may have localized collections of ephemerals that find a footing between the stones, but such areas do not produce the "carpets" of wildflowers for which sandy deserts are famous. Where small stones are abundant, numerous "lodgings" are provided and a better crop is produced. Disturbed soil often provides a good base for the growth of annuals, and this is particularly true along the edges of roads where not only has the soil been disturbed but extra water supplies—run-off from the road surface—are available. Certain annuals also tend to grow better under some large perennials, where shade from the larger plants may protect them from dehydration. The debris from the protecting plant or that which the wind blows against it provides a surface to catch the annuals' seeds, offers a source of humus, and retains a slightly increased moisture supply. Even a slight depression in the soil may favor the growth of ephemerals, as it manages to catch both seeds and a slightly increased water supply.

With the desert ephemerals it is often easy to note how microclimates may contribute to the success of a particular plant or plants at a particular time. The plant, especially if a perennial, may in turn contribute to this microclimate; for example by producing shade.

We tend to take it for granted that a seed will germinate when the proper time arrives, but that statement leaves a great deal unsaid. In the desert where climatic conditions tend to be extreme and erratic, how does the seed of a desert ephemeral "know" when to germinate? By germinating, it is betting on sufficient moisture. A mistake means death, and a species that places its entire future in its seeds cannot afford to lose the gamble too often. To investigate ephemeral seed timing, a classic series of experiments was carried out a number of years ago by Dr. Frits W. Went, now of the Desert Research Institute at the University of Nevada.

Dr. Went studied the vegetation of the Joshua Tree National Monument in the Mohave Desert of southeastern California. This area is characterized by creosote bush on the lower elevations, Joshua trees slightly higher up, and junipers above the 5000-foot level. Winter rains fall over the monument and summer cloudbursts occur in scattered localities, giving two peak precipitation periods in August and December. Dr. Went found four main groups of annuals growing here. One, the summer annuals, germinate, grow, and flower following the summer rains. A second group of plants germinates following the winter rains and blooms in the spring. A third germinates in summer or fall, following the summer rains and blooms the next spring, although they may flower earlier at times. The final small group of species has no specific germination time, but will grow whenever moisture is present and temperatures are not too low.

One apparent common factor for all groups is that germination follows rains. Small amounts of rain, however, will not produce germination; Dr. Went found that for some annuals, a rainfall of approximately 0.4 inch was not enough to cause germination, whereas a minimum of approximately one inch was. How can seeds discriminate between such small amounts? In some annuals, the seed contains a chemical inhibitor which must first be washed off or leached away thoroughly before germination can occur. Seeds with such inhibitors cannot therefore be misled by smaller amounts of rainfall which could ultimately prove inadequate to support later growth. Nor can they be misled by subsoil moisture rising by capillary action, for this moisture cannot carry away the chemical inhibitor as would water which was flowing downward. The duration of the rainfall, in addition to the amount, also appears to be important. A torrential rain causes far fewer seeds to germinate than does a slow, gentle rain that brings the same amount of moisture.

But since winter annuals do not germinate following summer rains, nor summer annuals following the winter, there are obviously important germination requirements besides moisture. One is the proper temperature. By collecting samples of desert soil and raising the seeds they contained, Dr. Went found that winter annuals will germinate only under a combination of cool days and cool nights. Summer annuals limited their germination to periods characterized by hot day plus high night temperatures. An interval of five to ten degrees separates the highest temperature at which winter annuals will germinate and the lowest temperature at which summer annuals will do so. This highly effective temperature difference results in two crops of annuals, each composed of its own distinctive species, with only a few species versatile enough to be found at any time of the year.

Even under optimum conditions, not all of the seeds of any one species will germinate. This serves as a reserve, should some sort of disaster annihilate the growing plants. It may be that when a large group of plants begins to grow, their vegetation inhibits the germination of additional seeds in the soil nearby. In one experiment, soil samples were taken from an area with a good growth of ephemerals already started on it. When these samples were subjected to optimum conditions, more of the seeds within them began germinating, even though no new seeds were sprouting in the area from which the samples were taken and which already carried a heavy growth. Also, some species of plants, and we will be noting examples when we discuss the perennial desert varieties, produce more than one type of seed, so as to spread germination over a longer period of time.

As would be expected, the distribution pattern of summer and winter ephemerals correlates closely with the east-west seasonal rainfall pattern in the desert. Summer ephemerals are most common in eastern deserts such as the Chihuahuan, and diminish in importance as one travels west until ultimately in some areas no summer ephemerals are found. Winter ephemerals are most numerous in number and species in the Californian desert and diminish in number and species as one travels eastward. Obviously, the biseasonal pattern of rainfall and the production of two distinct crops of annuals a year do not prevail over the entire North American Desert. Some areas have a single rainy season and consequently a single crop of annuals each; others with very cold winters have seasonal temperatures which limit the growth of annuals to warm seasons.

The seasons during which a plant grows influence it in various ways. The summer annuals have short lives, for growth is rapid under warm temperatures. Conversely, those that grow following winter rains tend to be slow in development due to the lower temperatures and are generally the smallest annuals. The third group, germinating after rains in the summer or fall but usually not flowering until the next spring, tend to be large, having had a longer period of growth than the first two groups.

The plants of an individual species may vary tremendously in size, depending at least partially upon the amount of water available to each one. A single cloudburst may be sufficient to trigger a plant's growth, but over the next few weeks that plant may be watered by several additional storms or it may receive none at all. An annual which germinates after a heavy initial rainfall can attain a large size for its species, as will one which receives a minimum initial rainfall followed by additional moisture soon after germination. However, if germination takes place under minimal moisture conditions which are not soon supplemented, the plant will attain only a very limited size. Nonetheless, it will flower and produce seeds, although seed production may be accordingly low.

Apparently, some annuals' ultimate size may be determined rather early in their growth, depending on moisture resources. It is sometimes theorized that, of two plants which germinate while moisture is still available in the topsoil, the fast growing main root of one may continue to find favorable moisture conditions. This plant will grow to a normal size. However, the root of the second hypothetical plant may soon encounter dry soil. Although some moisture is still available in the upper soil, this plant will immediately show diminutiveness. It is as if the root sent a message back advising the plant to husband its limited resources. Perhaps some change simply takes place in root development. From the start, the various parts of a plant remain in proportion with the very first leaves it produces. If these have been small, the plant enters the reproductive stage very quickly. Adverse temperature conditions—either extreme heat or cold—after germination may also cause a plant to attain only a small size. Different species vary in their ability to mature at a size smaller than normal, but the many that are able to do so have a better chance for survival as a species. Some species of annuals will ripen seeds when the "adult" plant is less than one-thousandth normal size!

Germination and growth in the annuals are directed toward only one end—the production of seeds, for the basic goal of all living organisms is the continuation of the species. And so it is with their seeds that the story of the ephemerals begins and ends. Seeds in themselves appear as mere fragments of matter, yet what else so nearly approaches the miraculous? Within each is contained life itself and the complex gene pattern that will, given the proper nurturing, produce one particular species of plant. These seeds are really the most basic way in which the ephemerals meet the challenge of living in the desert, for the seed is the only form of these plants that can survive the most extreme conditions of the desert environment. The seeds are exposed to soil temperatures sometimes in excess of 150°F, are desiccated to air-dryness, and can endure these con-

Evening primrose (*M. W. Larson*)

ditions for long periods. Not a great deal is known about how long seeds of the annuals can endure in the desert and still grow once favorable conditions prevail, but Dr. F. Shreve noted that especially favorable growing conditions brought forth the production of large crops of species of ephemerals which had not been common for the past ten to fifteen years. It therefore appears that the ephemeral seeds may lie low for many years if proper growing conditions do not prevail. With the protoplasm within it in a resting state, the seed's make-up is such that it can withstand, sometimes for many years, the prolonged severe conditions that would kill the vegetative form of the same plant in the matter of a few short days. The ephemerals produce vast quantities of seeds. These are blown, washed, buried, eaten and otherwise moved about and often destroyed, but if a few ultimately survive to germinate, grow, and produce more seeds for another season, success for the species has been achieved. Seeds are not, of course, a specific adaptation to aridity. These serve plants throughout the environments of the world as a means whereby the species can endure a variety of adverse conditions including heat, drought, and cold.

Having already been endowed with hardy seeds, the desert annuals developed three important abilities that serve them well in their desert environment. They are exactingly discriminating in their choice of conditions under which they will germinate. Once germination is initiated, however, they display rapid growth—seedlings are often apparent on the third day after a summer rain. And they also display a remarkable ability to mature and produce seeds even though environmental conditions may not allow them to reach more than a diminutive size. Of these three important adjustments to desert living, it is the remarkable germination requirements that are of greatest value. Dr. Went has succinctly expressed the amazing success of the desert annuals simply as "birth control."

chapter six

Desert Perennials

ANIMALS and man can retreat from the worst of the desert's heat, but plants must stand and take it. It is the rooted plants, much more than the mobile animals, which must find some means of dealing directly with heat and dryness. As we have seen, the ephemerals have met this challenge by shortening their life span into a brief, favorable period, and spending the remainder of the year in the dormant seed form. It is the desert perennials, then, which day after day, summer, winter and summer are subjected to the full effects of desert conditions, and it is these that we refer to as drought resisters. Desert plants can withstand the effects of heat providing they are supplied with sufficient water. In perennials' water procurement, use, and loss, we find interesting adaptations for desert living. Like modern man having trouble making his salary cover everything, the perennials are faced with a number of problems where water, rather than money, is concerned. They must attempt to get it, keep it, and make do with small amounts. Failing any one of the three requires increased effectiveness in one or both of the other alternatives.

It is sometimes difficult to draw a definite line between the perennials and certain desert annuals. In years of greater than average rainfall (or where water is plentiful) a few species of normally annual plants may persist for longer than a single season. These are known as facultative perennials. The desert marigold, *Baileya multiradiata,* is one of these "in-between" plants, described as biennial or sometimes a short-lived perennial by some authorities, and as an annual by others. This plant is commonly known as the woolly marigold, for its stems and leaves are covered by hairs. Each plant produces abundant, many-rayed bright yellow flowers resembling those of the garden-type marigold. These hardy plants may bloom any time from March to October, are found in a variety of locations including arid plains, and have a wide distribution from Chihuahua, Sonora, and Baja California, to southern Utah; and from western Texas to southern California.

Among the plants definitely classed as perennials we find some which would seem to be annuals at first glance. These can be seen only during favorable periods, and then die back to ground level. Only the underground organs such as roots and bulbs, persist until the next growing season. One showy root-perennial is the penstemon, *Penstemon parryi.* It is a graceful, light, beautiful plant which blooms only under favorable conditions in the spring. From the base it produces one or more erect stems which may reach as high as four feet. The upper third of each stem is adorned by flowers somewhat resembling small snapdragons in form, whose color varies from rose to magenta. This particular species is found in portions of Arizona and Sonora, but other members of the genus occur both here and elsewhere, as well as at higher elevations.

A desert plant which endures as an underground bulb from one year to the next is the desert mariposa lily, *Calochortus kennedyi.* In the early spring, stalks and long slender grass-like leaves appear, followed by large flowers in April, May or June. Approximately one-and-a-half to two inches in diameter, each cup-shaped flower consists of three small pointed green sepals below the three larger, colored petals that form the actual "cup." These petals are sometimes a bright yellow, but more often a deep, flamboyant orange-red with dark velvety centers. "Mariposa" is the lyrical Mexican word for butterfly, and like colorful butterflies, the mariposa lilies provide bright splashes of color against the normally muted tones of the desert. Also, their life-span, like that of a butterfly, appears to be short, but in reality both the flower and the butterfly represent the bright climax of their species, following long waiting or developmental stages. Other species of *Calochortus* thrive in the southwest, and one, *nuttalli,* with white to lavender-blue petals, is the state flower of Utah. *Calochortus nuttalli* grows at higher elevations than *kennedyi,* often in stands of sagebrush, and extends into mountain forests. Mormon pioneers reportedly ate the bulbs of the former, more commonly known as the sego lily.

The penstemon and mariposa and sego lilies are but three of the many desert plants which, like the annuals, actively grow and flower only under conditions that are optimum for their particular species. However, instead of surviving as a species only by dormant seeds, this type of perennial stores sufficient food and water within its underground organs to sustain life over a waiting period and to send forth quickly new stems and leaves when proper conditions prevail. This new foliage will die back to ground level once flowering is completed. These perennials have developed their own effective technique to escape from the heat and aridity of the desert.

Otter; like cottonwoods, these creatures live only where there is sufficient water (*M. W. Larson*)

In order to prevent death by overheating, a large plant standing directly in the sun's radiation must either tolerate high heat levels or be able to lower its temperature by the evaporation of transpired water from the leaf surfaces. Many perennials manage to grow in parts of the desert, not because they are especially adapted to desert conditions, but because they have found a particularly "undesert-like" microhabitat that allows them enough water to transpire as freely as need be. The palm tree is a good example. It must have rather large amounts of water available to it, for it transpires freely. Hence it is found where there are springs or seeps, or in canyons and similar locations where water collects and moisture is not too far underground. Palms are commonly thought of as a symbol of the desert, but actually they grow only near a source of water.

Where streambeds issue from high mountains bordering or within the desert, the large trees common to this streambed habitat may follow the waterway a distance out into the desert. Among these are cottonwoods and

Riparian Desert stream (*Courtesy of Arizona-Sonora Desert Museum*)

sycamores. In some cases these may be huge trees eighty feet or taller, luxuriantly green, cool, and shady. With other plants they trace a green meandering path outlining the watercourse across the otherwise dull-colored landscape. Such plants, like the palms, are not adapted for desert living; they have simply found a place where sufficient water supplies exist to support them. Water may flow in such a streambed a part of the year and stand in isolated pools later. Finally, when all surface water disappears, the trees will depend upon the moisture which earlier has soaked into and been stored in the ground. For the most part this is not even "desert" water which flows in the streambed, for its origin is to a large extent in the high mountains, which, because of their height, receive a great deal more moisture (sometimes including snow) than does the desert below them. Upon reaching the desert's floor the water is soon evaporated upward or sucked downward. Moisture available to the plants diminishes, large trees can no longer be supported, and their line of ad-

Desert wash (*Courtesy of Arizona-Sonora Desert Museum*)

vancement into the desert is halted, usually not far from the foot of the mountain.

The palms, cottonwoods, and other perennials like them do not actively resist drought—they merely escape it by growing only where enough water is provided. Such is not the case for the mesquite, the most successful tree of the southern deserts. It too must have access to water supplies and grows to a considerable size in thick stands along stream-beds where water is available underground, if not on the surface. The mesquite, however, is not confined to such habitats, as are the cottonwoods and similar plants. Also found on desert slopes and hills and across the arid grasslands, the mesquite is one of the most outstanding drought resisters. Its very long taproot is able to exploit even the deep sources of underground moisture. The mesquite is known to send its tap roots down forty feet after water supplies, but there is evidence that they can reach far deeper than that. In 1960, during the development of an open pit mine near Tucson, large numbers of roots were discovered in a gravel bed 175 feet below the ground surface. Ground water was located at 240 feet. Although the soil surrounding the roots was extremely dry, the roots themselves felt damp and were very limber. These were not ancient roots that had been buried, for a carbon-14 laboratory test indicated their age as less than six years. Microscopic examination determined that they were similar to mesquite roots, but positive identification was not possible. Dr. Walter Phillips of the University of Arizona reported this case as the deepest verified penetration of roots in the soil. It therefore appears highly probable that mesquite roots can reach down at least 175 feet.

But how does the young water-loving mesquite survive until its main root is long enough to reach a water supply? Researchers have found that mesquite seeds germinate only during wet seasons. Most of the food supply within the seed goes to nourish the rapidly growing root, rather than the leaves and stems. Only after the root has located a reliable water sources does the plant begin to show any significant growth above ground.

Other desert plants, with varying success, display an ability to probe deeply for water, although the mesquite is probably the most successful of these. Interestingly, Dr. W. G. McGinnes reports that Hopi Indians living in northern Arizona's dry plateau country have special varieties of maize admirably suited to semi-arid conditions. Its adaptations include a greatly elongated shoot (which permits deep planting of the seed) and like the mesquite, the rapid production of a long root which quickly grows to a depth where there is moist subsoil.

The mesquite is a water-spender, but certainly not in the sense the cottonwood is, for the mesquite is far more adjusted to desert living. It has emphasized the ability to get water, but it has other adaptations also helpful for desert living. We will be considering these in later chapters.

In the desert, water procurement is, of course, vital for all plants, and the various types of roots reflect the methods used by different species. Mesquites have concentrated on going to great depths and have therefore developed a long main tap root with shorter lateral roots. A second type of root structure is that displayed by creosote bush, which has both well-developed main root and lateral roots. But in this case, the main root does not reach to extreme depths. The third type of root system is one in which the lateral roots are primarily developed, lie in the upper layers of the soil, and serve to capture moisture quickly when it is present. Cacti use the latter method. The xerophytes often must produce large amounts of root growth to obtain sufficient moisture, and a characteristic of plants growing under dry conditions is a preponderance of root growth over shoot growth. Some xerophytes also show the ability to produce root hairs rapidly following a rainfall in order to increase water absorption. Growth of these may begin within three hours after a rain.

Where the water supply is precarious, some plants known as succulents store water in their tissues to maintain life and growth when dry conditions prevail. The cacti store water in both trunk and stems and are the most outstanding of the plants using this adaptation to the desert environment. The agaves—commonly known as century plants—store water in their thick, heavy, tapering leaves, which form a close, spiral rosette (like an artichoke) that issues from the rootstock at ground level. A single leaf may be two to three feet in length, three or four inches and tapering in width, and being succulent, is thick and heavy. The edges and tips bear stout spines possibly to discourage thirsty animals. After a number of years of growth, the plant produces a flower stalk many feet in height, topped by a panicle of showy flowers, after which the entire plant dies.

If desert plants cannot find water fairly constantly or store it, they must lose as little as possible to the dry air in order to prevent wilting. But if transpiration and water loss are cut to a minimum, the plant then must have some means of preventing or withstanding a dangerous rise in temperature. For a good many years, scientists studying desert vegetation

Agaves are particularly majestic when in bloom (*M. W. Larson*)

attributed such plants' survival ability to certain peculiarities of their anatomy and morphology. But recently, further study and better research tools have cast doubt on the value of at least some such modifications as adaptations for heat and aridity. Botanists and ecologists are far less prone today to state categorically that a cetrain plant structure achieves a certain purpose in meeting desert conditions. It had been generally accepted that the desert perennials were thrifty with water, able to get along with small amounts. It came as somewhat of a surprise then, to learn that hardy desert perennials use *more* water—when it is available—than do some plants which normally grow in moist habitats outside the desert.

Actually it is logical that desert plants should use moderate to large amounts of moisture when available if only to keep their temperature below that of the atmosphere and to allow their stomata to remain open so that exchange of gases and hence photosynthesis may be carried on. When a shortage of water does occur, however, then certain modifications of these plants' structure are of value in preventing water loss. Such adaptation is one of the reasons desert plants can survive where mesophytes cannot.

It is from the stomata, usually located on a plant's leaves, that the greatest water loss takes place. Plants regularly close them at certain periods, as at night when photosynthesis is not taking place; and certain xerophytic plants are able to close their stomata during hot periods. But even when the stomata are closed, minute amounts of water may escape from them or through the cuticle or covering of the leaf in a process known as cuticular transpiration. To cut down on even these slight water losses, the stomata of various desert plants are sunk below the surface of the leaf in pits or grooves that partially protect them from drying breezes. They may be guarded by hairs, partially plugged with a waxy or resinous material, or reduced in size. They may be located primarily where direct sunlight does not fall, as on the undersides of the leaves. In addition, the cuticle itself may be thickened or its surface may be covered by woolly hairs or a protective layer of resin or wax.

If a plant cannot afford to lose even small amounts of moisture through its stomata and cuticle, it may be of advantage to reduce the size of its leaves or do without them altogether, especially during the most difficult periods. A good many desert plants follow this course of action. The ocotillo has adopted a system of growing leaves after rainfall and shed-

Ocotillos (*M. W. Larson*)

ding them as soon as drought occurs. It may thus grow several crops of leaves in a year, each following a sizable rain. Quite distinctive in appearance, the ocotillo looks a little like a clumsy giant's attempt at flower arranging. Straight, largely unbranched stems bristle upwards from the plant's base. These thorn-covered shafts are all about the same length, up to fifteen feet or more in height, and spread out as if placed in a shallow, narrow-mouthed container, so that the whole plant attains the shape of an inverted cone. The tips of the branches bear bright red to orange flowers that often precede the appearance of the leaves; similarly, more than one crop of flowers may appear each year. The ocotillo's leaves are small but sprout along the entire length of each branch, from ground to flower. The petioles of the primary leaves become thorns as the leaves are lost, and thus the thorns too are distributed the length of the stems.

"Paloverde," literally translated, means "green stick" and is an apt name for several species of desert trees noted for the green color of their trunks and branches. They put out only very small leaves. The leaflets of one species are only one to two millimeters (.04 to .08 inch) in length; another's range from two to ten millimeters (.08 to .3 inch). Again, these minute leaves are produced only during favorable periods such as a rainy season. In these species the chlorophyll-rich trunk and branches have taken over most of the leaves' duty of photosynthesis, although probably with a much reduced effectiveness.

The crucifixion thorn is a grotesque, many-branched shrub whose sharply pointed short branches produce stout thorns. Seedlings develop leaves that are about 0.4 inch in length, but in mature plants the leaves

Paloverde tree; the feathery appearance is from frequent branchings, not from the infinitesimal leaves (*M. W. Larson*)

are reduced to mere scales so that the plant appears as a generally barren mass of powerful thorns. The cacti have carried the reduction of leaves to its ultimate degree. Those of the North American Deserts are entirely leafless, except for the seedling stage. A few species also develop small leaflets on their new growth.

To conserve water, some desert plants may drop more than just leaves. For example, one type of tree, *Parkinsonia microphylla,* has a chlorophyll-laden trunk and limbs, and drops its leaves at the onset of drought. If drying conditions continue, first twigs, then branches, and finally whole limbs die back, while life is maintained in the trunk.

The loss of leaves and shoots reduces the total surface of the plant exposed to evaporation. Needless to say, any plant which does away with leaves either wholly or partially, is also reducing its potential for photosynthesis and growth. Thus, plants such as the ocotillo, paloverde, or crucifixion thorn tend to be slow growing, and usually do not attain very large size (the paloverdes do reach a height of approximately twenty-five feet). All three plants, however, are extremely well-adapted to desert living. The paloverdes and ocotillos are particularly successful and are very plentiful in portions of the desert.

Some species' modifications appear to help prevent undue heating of their tissues. A covering of woolly, light-colored hairs over a leaf surface holds air within it, forming an insulating layer of air about the leaf and also probably reflecting radiation. A thickened or shiny leaf cuticle likewise reflects radiation. The loss of leaves and shoots reduces the total surface of the plant exposed to the heat. Many desert plants have the ability to roll their leaves or to turn them so that only the narrow edge of the leaf is exposed to the direct rays of the sun. Also, the form a plant takes may help it in temperature control. A compact shrub exposes less total leaf and branch surface to direct sunlight than does a more open, freely branched shrub—to some extent the outer portions actually shade those parts in the center. This is basically a principle followed by cacti, which have a large volume per surface ratio, valuable both from the standpoint of temperature control and prevention of moisture loss.

Thanks to the findings of modern research, it is now obvious that these adaptations do not explain fully the survival of desert plants. While anatomical and morphological modifications of some desert plants may help them conserve water and prevent undue heat rise, it is now obvious that these are not the complete story. It appears that a good many desert plants are also physiologically well adapted to desert living. In comparison to many mesophytes, xerophytes appear to be able to lose a greater proportion of water from their protoplasm, and to maintain a higher osmotic pressure within their cells. Higher osmotic pressure increases a plant's absorption of water from the soil and reduces its transpiration losses. It has been found that drought-resistant plants have greater cell sap densities. Annuals have low densities as would be expected. Those perennials whose leaves show special modifications such as thickened epidermis or hairs, tend to have lower cell sap densities than species lacking such protective coverings. Many xerophytes show a universal decrease in cell size, a thickening of cell walls, and an increase in mechanical tissue, which may help them endure and recover from longer periods of wilting. No one plant uses all of the modifications we have noted here and earlier, but a good many use more than one.

Besides heat and water stresses, the desert environment often places other imposing conditions on its perennials. One is the high amount of salts present in some of the soil. A well-developed playa is so salt-laden that no plant life can survive there. But around the periphery of the playa where the mineral deposits are less concentrated, various zones of vegetation can often be detected. The inner zone contains plants most tolerant to salt accumulations in the soils, and the plants of the zones further removed display decreasing tolerance.

Salt-tolerant plants are known as halophytes and their adaptations are primarily physiological. Such a plant may be able to withstand concentrations of mineral salts within its cells, it may actually excrete excess salts through special glands, or it may simply be able to keep from absorbing salts in the first place. Actually, though, it is difficult for any plant to absorb water from alkaline soils since, due to its concentration of salts, the high osmotic pressure of the soil solution opposes entry of water into the plant. In turn, halophytes are characterized by cell sap with a high osmotic pressure. Due to a general lack of leaching in desert soils, alkaline soils are rather common, though the amounts of salts vary. The plants that manage to grow in the more extreme alkaline soils are limited in the number of species and are highly adapted to this type of soil. Their ability to grow in such places is often apparent in their common names: species of the shrub *Atriplex* are commonly known as saltbush, and trees of the genus *Tamarix* (introduced into North America from Eurasia) are sometimes known as salt cedars.

The seeds of the desert perennials also show factors which are of value to the plants in their desert environment. We earlier noted that most desert ephemerals produce seeds in great abundance; the seeds are capable of retaining viability over a number of years, even under such severe environmental conditions. Their seeds are adjusted to germinate only under very specific moisture and temperature conditions; and not all of the seeds of a particular species in any area germinate in any one year. These statements apply in varying degrees to the desert perennials. Many of the latter also produce seeds in abundance, although probably not to the extent of the annuals, and the seeds of at least some retain viability for long periods. Mesquite seeds have been known to germinate after 45 years.

Germination requirements are evidently less specific than those for the highly specific annuals. In Joshua Tree National Monument Dr. F. Went noted that there were few seedlings of shrubs in the spring, and these were confined to species of a single genus. All other shrubs germinated in August and September following the summer storms. Winter rains in the area are quite reliable, summer storms sporadic. He reasoned that late summer germination following storms allowed the perennials to begin growth and then make full use of the winter rains when they arrived, achieving considerable growth before the hot, dry early summer. The perennials, however, rather than practicing birth control—that is, germination of seeds only under conditions that gave a rather good promise of survival—seem rather to practice infanticide. Large numbers of perennial seedlings appeared, but these were gradually greatly reduced in number by the deaths of those least able to survive the more extreme conditions that prevailed. Dr. Went concluded that "ultimately only one new shrub can become established for every one which dies." With the perennials, then, it would seem to be survival of the fittest and/or survival of the ones which manage (through chance or some specific method of seed dissemination) to grow in a particularly favorable habitat.

Some other perennial seeds have equally interesting germination requirements. The blue palo verde, *Cercidium floridum,* is normally found growing along washes. Its seeds germinate only after their seed coat has been broken, and this requires considerable force. The hard sheath is weakened by the tumbling action of sand and rocks in the wash bed following heavy rains. Germination thus takes place when moisture conditions are most favorable. Much the same is true for the smoke tree, *Dalea spinosa,* whose seeds must be freed from both the pod and seed coat. (It too germinates after being tumbled in washes following rains.) Other desert perennials seem to have seeds whose impermeable coat must first be destroyed by bacteria in the soil. Still other perennial seeds have dispersal units containing special inhibitors which delay the growth of the stem of the plant, but not the growth of the root. Not only moisture and temperature, but also the amount of daylight may help determine the proper time for germination—some seeds must be in darkness to germinate. Many seeds, desert and nondesert alike, require an after-ripening period, a period of cold, or other specific treatment before germination can occur. Like plants everywhere, the desert species have adopted many methods of dispersing their seeds; from those which sow widely on the basis that surely some of the many will find favorable conditions, to those that give a very narrow or specialized dispersal on the basis that the location or type of location of the parent plant proved to be satisfactory and should therefore continue to be a favorable choice.

As among the annuals, it is important that not all the seeds of a single perennial species germinate at the same time—that a reserve be left in the soil. This technique is often referred to as dispersal in time. For example, a study was done on the seeds of several Australian species of the genus *Atriplex*. (These are halophytes, known as salt bushes; different species of the same genus are common in parts of our North American Desert.) The seeds involved in the study are enclosed by bracteoles (small, modified leaves associated with the reproductive structures of a plant) to form a false fruit. In two species, one a perennial and one an annual, two colors of seeds are produced—a light brown, and a dark brown to black type. The lighter colored are smaller in size. Seeds with light colored coverings, described as soft, were freely permeable to water. Dark colored ones, described as hard, were impermeable to water when first shed from the plant. The bracteoles about the seeds retard germination; the reason is the presence of chloride in these bracteoles. This inhibitor serves to protect the seeds against germination during unfavorable conditions, but when sufficient rain fell, the chloride was leached away, allowing germination to take place. Soft seeds, being permeable to water at the time they were shed from the plant, could germinate once moisture conditions were propitious. Hard seeds on the other hand, not being permeable immediately, had their germination delayed until a later time. Dispersal in time for these two species of *Atriplex* is thus achieved by the production of two types of seeds.

It is interesting to note that all five species tested germinated over a wide range of temperature, but that only the seedlings produced in the winter did well. One inch of rain produced growth; two inches more than doubled it. The one-inch rainfall supported seedlings for one hundred days, although scientific calculations showed that under conditions present in the experiment, the wilting point of the soil should have been reached after a period of only eighteen days! Dr. N. C. W. Beadle, the scientist carrying out the experiments, therefore suggested the possibility —although this was only a possibility and not involved in this particular series of experiments—that these plants may have been obtaining moisture directly from the atmosphere, as from dew.

We referred earlier to the possible use of dew by ancient farmers who planted crops around rock mounds in the Negev Desert of Israel. Some scientific investigation of how plants in general utilize dew has been carried on sporadically over the last hundred years. Only very recently, however, has science regarded dew as a possibly important moisture source for desert plants. Fittingly, this interest has received much of its impetus from Israel. Faced with the problem of building an economy and supporting a population on limited natural resources, Israeli scientists have carried out a great deal of desert research, particularly on the possible uses of desert plants. It is known that dew is common in certain desert areas. In work done in Israel, dew was found to be present approximately two hundred nights a year in the study area. Moisture (such as dew) present on plants can be absorbed into them, although this is not true with all plants, and the amount of absorption varies among those which do possess the ability. As long ago as 1905, an experiment at Tucson's Desert Laboratory proved that the ocotillo can absorb water through its stem or bud scales. Cotton gauze was wrapped about the upper portion of an ocotillo stem and dampened intermittently so as to act as a wick. The portion of the stem above the cotton quickly produced leaves, as will the entire plant ordinarily, when water is available to its roots.

Research has even shown that some plants can successfully absorb water, move it through their stems, and ultimately discharge it through their roots into the soil, thereby storing it to some extent. In one experiment, tomato plants were observed to absorb water through their leaves and pump it out again through their roots which had been sealed in a dry, empty flask. Moisture available to the surface portions of a plant may be sufficient to prolong its life when the wilting point of the soil has been reached. Experiments carried out on a nondesert plant, ponderosa pine, showed that dew applied artificially at night to the seedlings helped them survive thirty days longer than plants of the same species not receiving the spray.

Dew is difficult to measure, since it is never present in any large quantities, nor is it deposited uniformly on all types of surfaces. Its absorption varies under different soil moisture conditions. In some cases, moreover, the apparent dew on a plant's leaves may not represent moisture derived from the atmosphere, but rather condensed water vapor that the plant itself has lost through transpiration. Because of so many variables, there is considerable scientific disagreement over dew's value, though it does appear that some desert plants are able to use it effectively. Even if water condensed on the leaves is that originally lost by the plant itself, it can be reused and thus represents a saving if not a direct gain. And even if a plant does not absorb the dew that is present, this moisture may be an important aid in delaying heating of the plant in the early morning, keeping its temperatures lowered until the dew is completely evaporated.

Dew forming on the soil is very likely of some value to those plants with roots located near the surface. Also, the interesting possibility exists that water vapor from deeper, moister soil levels may condense in the upper soil as it cools at night, and thus provide additional moisture for a plant's roots.

In North America, the fog characteristic of certain coastal deserts is a climatic factor only along parts of the Pacific coast in Baja California. Like dew, it may provide moisture, since the fog blowing across a landscape leaves tiny droplets behind on the vegetation in its path. Fog precipitation in the Vizcaíno Region of Baja probably waters a species of epiphyte known as ball-moss, *Tillandsia recurvata*. This plant grows on the branches of a larger plant or other object, but is not parasitic. Not in contact with the ground, it must obtain water and nutrients from the air and from the surface to which it is anchored. The familiar Spanish moss of the southeastern United States is another epiphyte, of the same genus as the ball-moss of Baja.

The uses and value of dew and fog (but particularly dew), will no doubt continue to be debated and studied for some time. Relatively little is positively known about it. Seemingly out of place, apparently present only in limited amounts, dew may however be proven to be rather important. Very possibly it is one of the many little things that some desert plants use in a big way to achieve success under difficult environmental conditions.

chapter seven

Creosote and Cacti

IT takes a while to learn to like a creosote bush. Newcomers to the
desert often consider it ugly in appearance; what's more (they say)
it literally stinks after a rain. But confirmed desert dwellers tend to view
the creosote bush differently; they at least respect it. Many go so far as to
say it has a certain beauty about it, and that its odor after a rain is refreshing and pleasing.

Most Americans have a heritage that decrees stands of tall green trees,
fields of crops, or at least thick prairie grass as the really "proper" type
country. The desert is none of these, except where man has changed it
artificially; and the small, hardy, ubiquitous, usually-green creosote bush
exemplifies the difference between lush green environments and the desert. It is when you accept the desert for what it is, rather than for what it
is not, that you can respect and even like the creosote bush, for this is
the most numerous widely-spread, best-adapted shrub of the hot southwestern deserts. That says a great deal for the creosote bush.

This plant can be found throughout the warmer deserts—the Sonoran,
Chihuahuan, and Mohave. (Interestingly, the same plant is also found in
South America.) Its northern limits rather well define the transition between the southern deserts and the cool Great Basin Desert where its
dominant position is taken over by sagebrush.

Creosote bushes (*M. W. Larson*)

Under favorable conditions, the creosote bush reaches a height of approximately twelve feet, but usually it grows from three to six feet tall. There is no main trunk, but rather several to many main branches which do not attain any great size. The creosote bush consists of a root crown from which arises, vertically or obliquely at ground level, many slender branches which then produce lateral branches. Along their outer portions, the branches and lateral twigs bear small, evergreen leaves, each made up of two leaflets joined at the base. Their leaves, although sometimes present in large numbers, are individually small, varying from .15 inch to (rarely) one inch in length. Normally they measure approximately one-quarter to one-third of an inch long, and are narrowly oblong in shape. The end result of these characteristics in a shrub which is light, airy, and seems to lack substance. The fact that the shrubs are usually widely separated, with bare ground and open space about each one, tends to emphasize the feeling and the fact that you can see right through each one. When beset by limited moisture conditions—which is frequently— the creosote bush loses many of its leaves. Those that remain become a dull gray-green to yellow, and the whole appears increasingly less substantial. Following rains the creosote bush produces small, bright yellow flowers. These are borne separately, but under optimum conditions are produced in large numbers. The petals are slightly turned, and the flower somewhat resembles a child's miniature pin wheel. This flower matures into an exceedingly white, hairy, round seed capsule, which ultimately splits into the five cells of which it is composed.

It is the creosote bush which, in its range, composes the common, almost ever-present covering of the desert landscape. It grows from below sea level in Death Valley up to approximately 8600 feet in Mexico. It grows on plateaus, intermountain plains, and rocky hills, and on a variety of soil types, with the sole exception of highly saline playas. In the desert's more favorable portions, the creosote bush grows in association with saguaros and additional cacti, desert trees, ocotillo, Joshua trees, yuccas, grasses and other plants; but where these and other plants admit defeat from aridity, the creosote bush continues to advance. It often occurs in almost pure stands over the hundreds of square miles where exceedingly few other perennials can survive the dryness and heat. Another plant often accompanying creosote bush, even into its drier ranges, is *Franseria,* commonly known as bur sage or sometimes as burro bush. This plant is a low and hemispherical bush, appearing gray and dry for most of the year. It is considerably smaller than the creosote bush and dots the open ground surfaces between its larger neighbors. It is also extremely drought-resistant.

Creosote bush does not survive the demanding conditions of the desert by means of any extreme modification of form. It has not completely abandoned leaves as have some plants, neither does it store quantities of moisture as do the cacti. Rather it survives by means of a number of less obvious adaptations which, in combination, explain its success. Creosote bush has a well-developed root system which is highly efficient at obtaining all possible moisture from the soil. Its roots spread far out about and below it, capturing moisture from a wide circular territory around the plant. This is the primary reason for the general wide spacing of the plants in a stand of creosote bush. Root competition for moisture is a common factor throughout the desert among all plants, causing desert vegetation generally to be well spaced with the percentage of the ground surface left bare varying due to long-range moisture conditions. Not only are its roots extensive, but it is believed that its cells are highly effective in extracting water from the soil. Spacing of creosote bush has been attributed by some scientists to this plant's ability to secrete a poisonous substance from its roots which prevents the growth of plants nearby. Whether this is true or not seems to be a matter of some question, but it is a possibility. Whether through poisoning of other plants or simply great efficiency in capturing the water supplies present, creosote bush is effective in limiting other growth about it under dry conditions.

Obtaining water is only part of the battle. Thanks to its leaves, the creosote bush also scores high on water retention. Its foliage is not winter-deciduous, and so it remains on the plant as long as it is of value. When the plant has a good supply of water, the leaves are a rather bright green. As moisture becomes scarce, its leaves gradually become a dull olive-gray color, the general tone of an area covered by creosote bushes. In periods of drought, the older leaves turn yellow-brown and are shed from the plant. Though some of the branches may be sacrificed to cut down on water loss in severe dryness, not all of the leaves are shed. The young, immature ones are retained, able to survive heat and desiccation by a remarkable kind of incomplete dormancy. Their growth is arrested until the drought is broken, at which time they again resume growth and activity. This ability of the immature leaves to stop development, endure drought, and then to resume growth is one of the most unusual attributes of the creosote bush.

As an additional adaptation, creosote leaves are surfaced with a resinous material, present in such quantities that it gives the greener leaves a shiny, varnished appearance. New green creosote foliage crushed between the fingers leaves them actually feeling sticky. This resin is of great value in cutting down on cuticular transpiration, and it partially clogs the stomata, reducing stomatal transpiration losses also. Embedded in the resinous material of each leaf is a covering of short hairs, which helps form the heavy protective covering of the leaf surface.

The creosote bush can blossom with several crops of flowers in the space of one year. When rain punctuates a period of drought, the plant quickly produces flowers and leaves and begins noticeably active growth. The ability to sustain life during unfavorable periods, but to initiate growth and seed production quickly just as soon as favorable conditions prevail—even if this means stopping and starting several times a year— is of great benefit to a desert plant. The seeds are produced in large quantities, and the capsules are lightweight and are easily distributed by wind and water. The fruit containing the seed capsules is reported to open in such a manner that some seeds are shed immediately after development, whereas others are retained for some time. This method would provide a kind of dispersal in time. There are also some indications that up to a certain point—perhaps as much as five or six years—increasing age of the seeds may result in their increased viability.

This plant not only can endure, but thrives under high temperatures. The seeds germinate under conditions of heat and sufficient moisture; in the Sonoran Desert, germination follows summer rains. While it can grow as a typical mesophyte (under which conditions it transpires freely), too much moisture is probably as lethal to it as prolonged cold weather. These limitations appear to be at least partially instrumental in setting the range of the creosote bush—its northern boundary is drawn by cold, the southern by excess soil moisture.

The creosote bush is remarkably versatile, and its tolerance is certainly a factor in its success. Dr. Shreve reports bushes growing where twelve months have passed without precipitation, as well as where the annual precipitation is approximately five hundred millimeters (about 19.7 inches). It is found where only winter or summer rains occur, where both are common, and in a variety of soil types and topographical locations. It can endure very high environmental temperatures and also brief periods of freezing. As a species, the creosote is capable of great variation in size, depending upon the conditions under which it grows.

Creosote foliage is eaten by very few animals. Rabbits may nibble on it, and a few insects depend upon it, but chiefly, desert animals use it only for perches or to provide light shade. On the ground under its branches, the wind drifts sand and soil into hummocks in which animals can burrow. The thing it does best, however, is to grow where little else will, and thereby hold the desert soil in place.

The Mexicans have a common name for this plant, *Hediondilla* which means "little stinker" or "little bad smeller." The odor of a creosote bush is a little like that of commercial creosote, but much more pleasant. When the air is still and the temperature is hovering around one hundred degrees Fahrenheit, one can catch the smell faintly when walking among the bushes. After a rain, however, it is much more pronounced. People who like the desert enjoy the strong characteristic smell, enhanced by dampness as a signal of newly-fallen rain.

Though the creosote bush has adapted to desert conditions without any drastic change in form, the cacti, on the other hand, have changed their shape greatly beyond that which is considered "normal" for most plants. The cactus family is wholly of the Western Hemisphere in origin, but some of its members have been transported to other parts of the world where they are now numerous. An outstanding example is the

Prickly pear cactus in bloom (*M .W. Larson*)

Liquid inside a barrel cactus (*M. W. Larson*)

introduction of the prickly pear cactus into Australia, where it has become, quite literally, a thorny problem. Cacti were tropical in origin, but
have since radiated into both North and South America and have adapted
to climates extremely different from those of their original home.

Primitive cacti of the genus *Pereskia* have well-developed, persistent
leaves; but these species are confined to the tropics. Among the desert
cacti, small leaves appear on the new joints of the stems of cholla and
prickly pear, but are soon lost. Essentially, the desert cacti have done
away with leaves almost completely, and their photosynthetic function has
been taken over by the surface of the stem and branches, which are green
with chlorophyll.

This drastic change is matched by other striking adaptations. The

Organ pipe cactus (*M. W. Larson*)

cuticle of the plant is heavy and covered by a waxy material, and the stomata are sunk into grooves or pits that are often filled with a woolly insulating material to further reduce transpiration losses. While the stomata of most other plants open during the day and close at night, the cacti have reversed the process, opening theirs at night when environmental stresses are less extreme, and closing them during the day. Their mucilaginous sap does not give up its water content easily. Their extensive root systems lie rather near the ground surface to capture moisture quickly following storms. They retain large amounts of this water in special cells within the trunk and stem—more than 80 percent of the weight of a giant saguaro cactus may represent stored water. Cacti have the strange power to expand and contract along with their water supply; like some other species, the saguaro is ribbed to allow for the change in volume. Others have tubercles to achieve the same effect. The form of the cactus provides a low surface-to-volume ratio which is of great value in reducing transpiration losses from the surface and, by sheer mass, in preventing the plant temperature from reaching a lethal point.

The net result of these modifications is a plant which not only captures but stores water efficiently. It has a very low transpiration rate, lower than for most xerophytes, and so makes economical use of its water supply. Cacti are thus capable of not only sustaining life during dryness, but of continuing growth—although slowly—through use of their impounded moisture. The real proof of the success of the cacti is the fact that they can remain alive for exceedingly long periods—even several years—without receiving additional water. In their contest to survive desert conditions, the cacti are as different from the ephemerals as the proverbial tortoise was from the hare. In this case neither loses the race, but each has its own unique talents for winning.

Certainly the cacti have developed an amazing variety of types. When mature, some species may be fifty feet in height; others a half inch. Some are simple unbranched stems, others may have stems branched at the base or high on the trunk like the saguaros. Some have branches that are erect, others prostrate. Most have a columnar form, but the prickly pear and chollas have stems from which arise a series of branching joints, flat in the case of prickly pears and cylindrical in the chollas.

An outstanding characteristic of the cacti is their covering of spines. Most species wear a veritable armor of spines; often so numerous and so arranged as to enclose the entire plant almost completely. On the cactus

An animal's-eye view of a cholla cactus (*M. W. Larson*)

Many-headed barrel cactus (*M. W. Larson*)

surface, spines arise in clusters from structures called *areoles*. Areoles, in turn, are arranged in a regular pattern, along the ridges of cacti with ribbed stems, or at the apex of each tubercle on cacti with this form. In addition to spines, the areoles of prickly pear and cholla cacti support numerous small, barbed bristles called *glochids*. These are particularly annoying to any unlucky person who rubs against them and finds them embedded in some part of his anatomy: they are very fine, hard to see, irritating to the flesh and troublesome to remove.

The true "purpose" of spines and the reasons for which they evolved in the first place are a matter of considerable debate; and not only in the case of cacti. Perennial desert vegetation in general is noted for its thorniness. Mesquite, ironwood, smoke tree, and paloverde trees are all adorned with thorns, and the names of various others—cat's claw, crucifixion thorn, desert thorn, gray-thorn—warn that they are equally well-endowed. The usual explanation is that a plant's spines protect it from hungry and thirsty animals. (In an area where plant growth is difficult to achieve and many animals get their moisture primarily or wholly from vegetation, spines may be a valuable asset.) However, this protection is clearly not complete, as we will note when we consider the desert animals

A close view of a cactus showing the arrangement of areoles (*M. W. Larson*)

The night-blooming cereus is a cactus with small, slender branches that usually grows under shrubs or trees and produces fragrant white flowers like these; it has a large turnip-like root in which food and moisture are stored (*M. W. Larson*)

who eat and/or live in even the spiniest of the cacti and browse on the other thorny desert vegetation.

Cacti are especially noted for the splendor of their flowers. Due to the plants' stored water supply, these blossoms are often lavish, large and showy and usually produced on schedule even if drought is the prevailing condition. The flowers' beauty is enhanced by the barrenness of the normally arid environment and by the harsh thorniness of the plants themselves.

By their unusual form, cacti add a most distinctive element to the desert landscape. It is in the Sonoran Desert that they reach the height

Hedgehog cactus in bloom (*Courtesy of Arizona-Sonora Desert Museum*)

of their development and diversification. They are far less common and varied in the other three North American Deserts, though the Chihuahuan supports a variety of smaller cacti and larger species like the barrel cactus and cholla. In the Great Basin Desert, cacti are relatively unimportant, primarily represented by low growing prickly pears. Nor are cacti well represented in the Mohave, where the most common species are certain chollas, the beaver-tail cactus, barrel cactus, and a few low-growing species. It is in the Sonoran Desert that such outstanding large cacti as the saguaro, cardon, senita, organ pipe, and others have developed, due to the Sonoran's combination of environmental factors. Cacti require warm soil temperatures for germination of their seeds. They absorb water

Beavertail cactus, common in the Mohave; it has no spines, only glochids (*M. W. Larson*)

primarily during warm periods, and therefore thrive where moisture and heat are concurrent. These conditions especially prevail in at least parts of the Sonoran Desert. In addition, cacti, by containing large amounts of water, are prone to damage by freezing weather and so are generally prevented from living in areas which undergo extended cold periods. Certain species of prickly pears do reach far out of the desert and into cold regions, but these are at least partially aided in their survival by depletion of their water supplies during the dry season preceding the freezing weather.

While large cacti cannot survive long periods of freezing, their low surface to volume ratio has been important in allowing the larger cacti to advance as far northward as they have. For example, the senita or "old man cactus," *Lophocereus schottii,* is a large plant that may reach fifteen feet in height. It consists of many columnar stems arising from ground level, which do not rebranch. The upper portions of these stems bear a heavy cover of very long, light-colored spines up to one-and-a-half inches in length, giving the plant a gray-bearded appearance and its "old man" nickname. Dr. Charles Lowe and Richard Felger of the University of Arizona studied this plant in northwestern Mexico as it occurs over a range of approximately four degrees of latitude. As one moves from the south, north toward the Mexican border, the climate of the area studied is characterized by decreasing precipitation and greater extremes of temperature. At the northern limits of this region, winter brings a few nights of freezing temperatures; the southern portion is frost-free. Drs. Lowe and Felger learned that old man cacti with the lowest surface-volume ratios, in other words the thickest stems, grew in the more northerly part of their range. The cacti produced a gradual increase in their surface-volume ratio, narrower stems, as they moved southward. The study included six other large, columnar cacti of the Sonoran Desert: the saguaro *Carnegiea gigantea,* cardon *Pachycereus pringlei,* lecho *Pachycereus pecten-aboriginum,* organ pipe *Lemaireocereus thurberi,* agria *Machaereocereus gummosus,* and sina *Rathbunia alamosensis.* These species also displayed the same gradual thickening of stems and trunks in the northern parts of their ranges. Work done on the saguaro showed that the larger stem mass provided definite advantages against low temperatures.

Cause and effect are often more apparent in the desert than elsewhere. The ephemerals, the creosote bush, and the cacti are examples of some of the more-or-less obvious but diverse methods plants adopt to survive the desert's demanding conditions. These examples also demonstrate the diversity of life forms that desert plants have assumed. Such diversification is not typical of most environments. The dominant plant growth in a tropical forest is composed of evergreen broad-leaved trees; a cold mountainside bears primarily coniferous evergreens. In those desert areas which show the richest vegetation, there is a number of important life forms ranging from stem succulents such as cacti and leaf succulents such as agaves, to desert shrubs and trees.

In comparing the desert to other environments, we find other important differences. Ecologists often speak of plant succession. If a forest is burned over, the first plants to return to the soil are not those same ones that composed the original forest. The new first growth prepares the way for later growth of the dominant species or "climax vegetation" that was present before the fire. There is an ordered succession of plant species typical for the environment, covering many years, before the normal plant community is once again restored. In the desert, however, the first species to repopulate a disturbed area are generally the same ones that were there in the first place.

Another obvious difference noted between the desert and wetter climates is the general spacing apart of desert plants and the large amount of bare desert surface. This is caused, as we noted earlier, by the underground root struggle to capture water supplies. The area required to obtain sufficient water for a plant is considerably larger than the area the plant covers on the surface. (In the tropics and forests the struggle is not so much for water but rather for space and sunlight among the dense mass of plants.) In the deserts where plants do manage to grow without wide spacing, there are obviously better moisture supplies—or the plants may be very unlike in their moisture procurement or habits, as mesquite and cacti, and can survive in proximity to one another.

Dr. Shreve estimated that about 12 percent of the North American Desert is occupied by vegetational communities of which only two or three species make up about 90 percent of the community. In these, only about 8 to 15 percent of the ground surface is covered by vegetation and the overall effect is one of vast areas sparsely covered by vegetation of a uniform height. Examples of such communities are those dominated by sagebrush or by creosote bush. He estimated that 60 percent of the North American Desert has communities composed of four to twelve species of large perennials, and with this enrichment of species the overall effect of the community is one of varied life forms, unlike the simpler communities. Surface coverage in such communities he stated as 15 to 20 percent. Finally, the rich communities contain fifteen to twenty-five species of large perennials with the percentage of surface covered by vegetation 40 to 70 percent. Due to the variety of life forms represented, the character of these communities is varied and there is a great diversity in height of the dominant plants present, as opposed to wetter climates where the dominant type of plant tends to form a community in which the uppermost layer is of uniform height (as, for example, the trees of a forest).

The Old World Deserts, especially the Sahara, have been in many parts worn down to a monotonous flatness. They are populated by a very limited number of plant species. But our North American Deserts are geologically young and provide interesting and highly varied topography. They are populated by a large number of species of plants, each of which has adapted to one or more of the many desert habitats available—these varied habitats formed not only by topographical characteristics, but also by soil types and climatic conditions.

Perhaps we should broaden our original statement and say it takes a while to like not only a creosote bush, but to like desert vegetation in general. It is usually spiny, seldom bright green, generally small in size, often dried, only occasionally bright with colorful flowers, and sometimes outlandishly bizarre in form. But understanding breeds appreciation. More than that, it often produces a fondness for this strange desert world and the plants which form an integral part of it. There are even a good many human inhabitants of this desert who feel that—like many of its animal inhabitants—they could not live so well nor so contentedly elsewhere.

chapter eight

Heat, Aridity, and Animals

I F, as modern science believes, the waters of the world's oceans were
the womb in which life first developed, then certainly the desert is one
of the environments farthest removed from that ancestral home. The environmental conditions the deserts present are among the most extreme
to which animals and plants have had to adjust. Plants, we have noted,
have developed numerous anatomical, morphological, and physiological
modifications to adapt to desert conditions. Animals as a group, however,
have concentrated more on *behavioral*, rather than structural, changes
to fit into the desert environment. Their primary means of adjustment
—both physiological and behavioral—are also used by animals outside
the desert, but are often intensified or carried to greater extremes among
desert-dwelling animals.

As a general rule, animals of the North American Desert are not
capable of surviving higher temperatures than their counterparts in other
environments. However, different species of animals do display differing
tolerances to heat. One species of lizard can stand body temperatures up
to 118°F, although this is higher than normal for most lizards. The most
body heat a snake can withstand varies from 98° to 107°F. Birds have a
normal daytime body temperature of about 105° to 108°F, but reach
their critical levels a few degrees above these. Man has a normal body

101

temperature ranging from 97° to 100°F. His lethal limit is a body temperature of approximately 110°F. Some other mammals have slightly higher normal temperatures; those of cattle, sheep, dogs, and cats are found to be between 100° and 103°F.

It is obvious that in the desert all animals run the risk of overheating and thereby, death. Their behavioral means of avoiding this risk include resting in cooler microclimates—as in the shade of vegetation, in caves, or in underground retreats. Animals also correlate their active period to the cooler parts of the twenty-four-hour cycle or to the most favorable season or seasons of the year. For this reason, the desert seems almost devoid of animal life during the hot daytime hours. Yet as the early evening approaches, animals begin their activities and continue through the cooler night temperatures. Bumbling man with his noisy feet and voice, poor night vision, man-smell, muffled senses, and natural aversion to stepping on a rattlesnake or sitting on a scorpion, finds it difficult to make himself a part of this nighttime world. By sitting quietly in undisturbed desert on a summer's night, however, he can catch indications of the large amount of life in a variety of shapes that has adapted its schedule to the dictates of desert temperatures. This is not a static thing. When cooler temperatures prevail at other times of the year, some animals will change their habits and become diurnal and/or crepuscular (active at dawn and dusk), rather than nocturnal.

Although microclimates are of great help to animals, they cannot always completely evade the heat. There are some large animals which cannot escape underground, such as deer in the Arizona Upland, and on them the heat strain in the meager shade of desert vegetation or heated rocks must be considerable. Neither can the birds—with only a few exceptions—retire beneath the insulating soil. Even small animals which are relatively well protected underground during the day are subject to at least warm or sometimes hot temperatures at night. We have driven across the Lower Colorado Valley subdivision of the Sonoran Desert when the temperature at midnight was 98°F. The hot, enveloping, blackness contributed to our claustrophobic tendencies and did only a little toward providing a cooler period for animal activity.

When an animal becomes overheated, it must attempt to lower its temperature. If behavioral adaptations, such as moving into shade or underground, are impossible or insufficient, the creature attempts to use the cooling power of evaporation of body water by way of the skin and res-

Fairy shrimp (*M. W. Larson*)

piratory tract. And so with the animals, as with the plants, water becomes the necessity, but also the difficulty, for heat—problem number one in the desert—usually goes hand in hand with aridity, problem number two. Animals too must concentrate on one or more of the three problems of getting water, keeping it, or doing with small amounts. In relationship to animals, heat and water cannot very well be separated and must be considered in combination.

Just as ephemerals reach their adult stage only when sufficient water is available, certain animals have developed the same technique. An example is the fairy shrimp, a crustacean whose near relatives include barnacles, crayfishes, crabs, and water fleas. The size of the adult shrimp varies according to species, but an average one measures about an inch in length. Its body is elongated and somewhat cylindrical, with a thorax of many segments plus a number of abdominal segments. Each thoracic segment bears a pair of flattened appendages which are used for respiration, locomotion and food procurement. Its mouthparts consist of a pair of mandibles and two pairs of maxillae. Two stalked eyes, two pairs of antennae, the digestive glands, and even the stomach are all located in the large head. The animal swims on its back with its appendages always facing the source of light, feeding upon detritus and microorganisms present in the water. It concentrates food material in a groove in the body and by means of a mucilaginous string, delivers the food to the mouth. In short, this shrimp is reasonably similar to its oceangoing cousins, except that it inhabits temporary rain pools in the desert which are bone-dry for the best part of the year!

The female bears an external ovisac arising just below the thoracic appendages, in which the eggs develop. She releases the fertilized eggs into the water, or she may retain them in the sac when she dies. When the pond dries up, these eggs may stay in the dry, baking mud where they've fallen, be carried away on the feet of animals, or may be transported by the wind. The eggs can endure extreme heat and resist desiccation; in fact, drying appears to be a prerequisite for hatching in many species. When rainwater once again collects to form a pool and other necessary conditions (such as warmth) are met, the eggs immediately hatch. Some of these hardy eggs have been known to hatch after a dormancy of twenty-five years in the desert soil! A complete life cycle from egg to egg may transpire in a period of three weeks.

Most fairy shrimp are found in temporary pools, for they cannot survive predation by fish. One species, the brine shrimp, *Artemia salina,* is unusual in being able to live in a saturated saline solution. This tolerant creature is found in the Great Salt Lake and similar saline waters, although not in the oceans. However, the fairly shrimp's egg hibernation is not a specific desert adaptation. Fairy shrimp of other species are also found in temporary pools formed by melting snow and ice; in this case, the freezing of the eggs is a stimulus which promotes increased ability to hatch during the later thaw.

Animals may wait out unfavorable desert conditions in forms other than the egg stage. Some of the amphibians endure periods of dryness in a waiting state, but as adults.

Amphibians have a moist skin. Water is readily lost from it, just as water may be easily gained through it when the animal is in water or a

Tadpole shrimp, also a denizen of temporary rain pools, is so named for its striking resemblance to a young frog (*M. W. Larson*)

Sonoran green toad (*M. W. Larson*)

moist place. The moistness of the skin is a necessary condition for respiration, all or part of which occurs through the skin. Most amphibians must lay their eggs in water, and the tadpole, the larval stage, must undergo its development there. Amphibians would therefore seem to be among the least likely candidates for desert living, but nonetheless, certain species of them are successful in the desert, such as the spadefoot toad.

The adult spadefoot spends much of the year hidden below ground awaiting more favorable conditions. It may bury itself by digging backward into soft earth with the "spades" or tubercles located on each of its hind feet, or may usurp a den made by some other animal. Once shut away from the drying air, the toad's skin secretes a gelatinous coating to guard against further moisture loss. In this condition, the adult toad's temperature approximates that of the surrounding earth. It waits as long as several months until sufficient moisture and optimum temperatures prevail for the proper development of its young. At that time, the toad and all its buried kin emerge to call, croak, feed, mate, and revel in temporary rain pools. The eggs soon hatch, the tadpoles undergo rapid changes, and the adults are developed and ready to leave their liquid environment by the time the temporary pools have disappeared, providing all goes on schedule.

The western spadefoot is active in California following the early spring rains. In Arizona and New Mexico, it lays its eggs following the summer rains, when warm temperatures can help the tadpoles develop rapidly. Once, while travelling in southwestern New Mexico, we were caught in one of the summer's first thunderstorms and were able to explore the muddy, drenched desert immediately afterwards. A low piece of land bordered by small, sandy hillocks was rapidly filling with run-off. All over the surface of a hill, we could see countless plugs of sand being pushed outward forcefully. Framed in each resulting hole were the face and peering eyes of a spadefoot inhabitant ready to emerge from its long, dry sleep and head for the water.

Many types of animals wait out unfavorable conditions. Reptiles retire underground to endure cold winter conditions, emerging when warmth and food are again available. Mammals do the same by hibernating during cold, or endure hot periods by estivating. (We will be considering estivation a little later as a physiological state of the mammals.) Many insects the world over also wait out heat, drought, or cold in egg, larval, pupal or adult phases. This period of waiting is often undergone in a state of diapause in the larval or pupal stages. Diapause is a dormant period—rather akin to standing in place or suspended animation—wherein further development is stopped for the time being, to be started again at a later date. Thus the spadefoots and other amphibians like them are by no means unique in their ability to lie low for long periods and to emerge when environmental conditions are at their optimum.

Like most human tourists, some species of birds visit the desert only during a part of the year when conditions are most suitable for them. Migratory species may pass through it briefly, while others come to spend a season. White-winged doves spend the summer in the Sonoran Desert to feed on the seasonal blossoms and the red-pulped, black-seeded fruit of the giant saguaros.

During the dry season, rare springs, seeps, or watering tanks for cattle become very important to many desert animals. Being the most mobile of the desert animals, a good many birds benefit from such sources; some, particularly doves, often range several miles from a water hole, yet return to it daily to drink. In the Arizona Upland, water is most scarce in the early summer, especially in June and early July before the summer storms have arrived and temperatures are still very high. The Arizona-Sonora Desert Museum has constructed a small water hole there, and beside it, a photographic blind. Every night in the hot, early summer, a variety of animals from toads to deer come to take advantage of this water, and pay for it by having their pictures taken. Once the summer storms arrive, however, business drops off sharply. Evidently the animals prefer water sources which are closer to home and certainly more private.

Mountain sheep have been pushed to the most inaccessible parts of the desert by the pressures of hunting and civilization. As partial compensation, the Arizona State Game and Fish Department is aiding them with watering tanks in parts of their Arizona range. During the driest parts of the year, water is hauled to the tanks by truck. In this arid area, what water is caught in natural cavities in the rocks would be sufficient to support only a small population of sheep. By providing greater water supplies, the department can maintain—and make available for hunting—a far larger population.

A great many desert animals have little or no need of free water supplies, receiving all they require from moisture in their food. In plants, a large percentage of total weight represents water, and many animals can thus survive on a diet of succulent vegetation. Insects feed on plants, pollen, and nectar. Some rodents feed largely on juicy cacti in spite of the thorns. Carnivorous, or meat-eating, animals obtain water second-hand from the bodies of their prey. Many birds and lizards dine on plant-eating insects; the coyote feasts on the rabbit, which has in turn consumed green vegetation. Even dead bodies provide moisture for vultures and other scavengers.

The most amazing water source with which some animals sustain themselves is metabolic water. Oxidation of carbohydrates within the body results in the formation of carbon dioxide, energy, and water. When oxidized, one gram of starch produces 0.6 gram of metabolic water; one gram of fat yields *1.1* grams of water! This metabolic water is produced in all animals. It is not unique to desert animals. What is unique is the fact that certain desert rodents—the most famous of which are the kangaroo rats—are in this way able to obtain water supplies, which (in combination with other physiological and behavioral factors that we will be noting) are sufficient to sustain them. This ability to survive on me-tabolic water alone is all the more amazing when you consider that the kangaroo rats can live solely on—and hence manufacture this water from—a diet of dry seeds!

Needless to say, desert animals need to conserve whatever moisture they can get. However, an animal's body has three very effective ways of losing water: through the skin (as sweat), through the respiratory sys-tem (as water vapor), and through the digestive tract (in the form of urine and feces). By avoiding heat, losses of water from sweat and breath-ing can be cut to a minimum. But when the creature must cool itself— by evaporating its own moisture—water loss through these two methods may be great and can eventually prove lethal.

Only man and certain large hoofed animals such as horses have sweat glands developed well enough to evaporate sizable quantities of moisture through the pores of their skin. A great many other mammals also have some sweat glands, but these glands are sparse and poorly distributed over the body. To cool themselves, such animals must depend chiefly on evaporation through their respiratory tract, hence the panting of a dog on a hot day. Even in the case of these animals, however, some moisture is inevitably lost through the skin surface, and this is known as insensible perspiration.

Amphibians, of course, lose great quantities of moisture through their skin. Reptiles, covered by scales or plates, are admirably protected, as are insects with their hard chitinous exoskeleton. The dry skin of birds and mammals retards water loss to a certain degree; fur and feathers act as insulation against moisture loss. In fact, the nomadic tribesmen of some Old World Deserts utilize the same principle by wearing light, loose, enveloping clothing. Their robes, like the fur of desert animals, is not so heavy or dense as to prevent air from reaching the skin surface, thus allowing evaporation of perspiration to take place on the skin while still providing a baffle against radiation and hot, drying air.

In their conquest of the land, mammals, birds, reptiles (and to some extent, amphibians) have developed internal lungs where air exchange takes place on moist surfaces. Moisture loss is therefore a correlate to respiration. Knut Schmidt-Nielsen reports that in man, air exhaled at 33°C—approximately rectal temperature—is saturated. If man is inhaling completely dry air, then moisture to bring this air to the saturation point is taken from his respiratory tract. Desert animals lose moisture in this same way. This loss is increased when evaporative cooling through the respiratory tract is necessary. Birds, reptiles, and many mammals use panting and moisture loss from the respiratory tract almost exclusively for evaporative cooling.

Panting, although necessary if heat cannot be avoided, is expensive in terms of water loss. Even respiration can be expensive if water stress is extreme, and certain of the smaller animals have ways of cutting down on such losses. Small mammals which spend the hot days in burrows underground often close off or plug up the burrow entrances. Much of the moisture the animal exhales is therefore retained in the air of the burrow, where it can be "stored" as humidity and re-breathed until night comes. The humidity also helps the animal cut down on moisture losses through its skin. Many small rodents also store seeds and other food supplies underground in their burrows. These caches absorb some of the moisture from the air, and sooner or later, the seeds are consumed by the animal along with their captured moisture. Kangaroo rats have evolved a further saving by maintaining their nasal passages at a lower temperature than that of the rest of their body. The air they exhale flows over these cooler surfaces, and some of its moisture condenses out, to be absorbed by the mucous membrane.

One of the most outstanding adaptations some small mammals make to the desert environment is that of estivation. Certain mammals' hibernation to endure cold periods is a familiar story, and even some small desert animals use it to survive winter in the desert. Estivation is a state similar to hibernation, but is used at high, rather than low temperatures, and primarily as a means of escaping drought. Reptiles, amphibians, and insects are *poikilothermic*—cold-blooded, or taking their temperatures from the environment. Birds and mammals however, are *homoiothermic,* having a relatively uniform body temperature. In hibernation or estivation, the mammal resembles the poikilotherms in that its temperature falls to a level approximating that of its immediate environment. As with the estivating spadefoot toad, the small mammal employing this avoidance technique repairs to a burrow underground when dryness and heat present trying conditions. With the drop in temperature, it enters a sleeping, lethargic state. Its metabolism is carried on at a very reduced rate, physiological processes are reduced, and its respiration rate is greatly slowed. Life is maintained on the energy reserves of fat stored within the body.

Great advantages are derived from such a state. No food, other than that stored within the body is needed. Nor is water needed, except that derived from the metabolic process. Loss of water from urine and feces is cut. The decrease in respiration reduces moisture loss from the respiratory tract. The animal shut in its burrow derives the benefits we have noted from the prevailing humidity levels. Even more importantly, the animal, having a temperature lower than its normal one, loses less moisture through its respiration. (Less water is required to saturate the cooler expired air than is the case when the expired air is at the animal's normal body temperature.)

Some desert ground squirrels that estivate during part of the summer often slip directly from estivation into hibernation as fall brings cooler temperatures. Schmidt-Nielsen reports that the Mohave ground squirrel, *Citellus mohavensis,* remains underground all year, except for spring and early summer!

Finally, the third way in which water is lost from the animal body is through the elimination of waste products. In mammals this elimination is in two separate forms, urine and feces. In birds and reptiles the urinary discharge which carries waste removed from the blood by the kidneys is a semisolid whitish material excreted from the body with the feces. In all—reptiles, birds, and mammals—the feces may be quite dry, all possible moisture having been taken from them by the body. (Particularly is this true of desert animals.)

The function of the urinary discharge is to carry urea, salts and other

Harris' ground squirrel enjoying a bite of cactus (*M. W. Larson*)

waste products from the body. Urea is a nitrogenous compound formed as an end product of nitrogen metabolism and is the chief solid component in the urine of mammals. In reptiles, urine as it leaves the kidney has a concentration of urea no higher than that of the blood. The urine is then moved to the cloaca—the chamber in which both the intestinal and urinary canals discharge in both birds and reptiles. Here the urine is held, and the urea precipitated out as uric acid. The fluid remaining then has a *lower* concentration of urea than the blood, and some of this water is reabsorbed. The reptiles therefore have an efficient method of removing waste products with a low moisture loss.

In birds and mammals, the urine is concentrated in the kidney, with a resulting higher concentration of urea in the urine than in the blood. In addition, in birds some of the urea is precipitated out as uric acid. Then birds, like reptiles, excrete concentrated, whitish urinary wastes in combination with intestinal wastes and obtain a distinct water saving.

In mammals, the excretory system is designed differently than that of the reptiles and birds and prohibits the precipitation of uric acid. To prevent clogging the urinary system, the urinary wastes must be kept in solution for elimination from the body. The amount of water necessary for discharge of these wastes is therefore much higher in mammals than in birds and reptiles. The ability to concentrate waste products in the urine varies greatly, however, between different mammals; some of those of the desert have the most powerful kidneys of all. (The star in this regard, again, is the kangaroo rat which can produce urine with the urea content almost five times as concentrated as in that of man, and with salts in twice the concentration found in sea water!) The food eaten by the desert mammals also has some bearing on the amount of water needed for excretion. Mammals which are largely protein eaters consume much greater amounts of nitrogen than do carbohydrate (*e.g.,* seed) eaters. Larger quantities of urea are thus formed, and must be eliminated from their bodies at greater water expense. (Being seed eaters kangaroo rats achieve a saving in this way also.) But conversely, the carnivores obtain much greater amounts of moisture from their food than do the seed eaters.

As a group, the insects are well prepared for desert life through the specific adaptations they made long ago to life on land. Adult insects generally have a chitinous exoskeleton which is nearly impermeable to water; moisture is not lost from the surface. Respiration take place through spiracles, small external openings of the respiratory system, but special valves limit the amount of moisture lost. Insect food consists of plants or animal prey, either of which provide water. Metabolic water is also formed. Almost all of the free water is removed from their waste products. Some advanced insects like ants store food when it is plentiful to carry them or their young through inhospitable periods.

Precise timing of insect life cycles to coincide with optimum moisture and food conditions; diapause in immature stages, and the ability of adults to endure long waiting periods are of great value to many species. The difference in requirements of the larval and adult stages is also sometimes of value to desert survival. For example, some desert insects spend much of their life history as larvae in protected locations where food is plentiful, while only the adults are exposed to extenuating desert condi-

Grasshopper (*M. W. Larson*)

tions. This latter stage may be a relatively short phase of the insect's total life.

The power of flight is also useful, allowing insects so empowered to fly well above the hot soil surface and to rest in cooler vegetation. Some insects simply climb higher on plants to escape extreme surface temperatures. Others burrow, and some are equipped with long legs with which they raise their bodies as high as possible from the surface. Certain insects seem to be able to endure high heat levels; some species being found in hot springs which may have a temperature of 120°F. Others can actually absorb moisture from the unsaturated atmosphere, and still others are covered with pilosity—light colored hairs which may serve to reflect light and retard heating.

Also important is the fact that insects are small—their needs can be met by meager amounts of food and moisture, and the smallest of many microhabitats are theirs to exploit. They are, indeed, some of the most successful inhabitants of the desert.

As a group, reptiles too are well adapted for life in a desert environment. Their dry scaled, or plated skin is heavy and resists moisture loss. Their elimination of waste products requires little expenditure of water. Most desert reptiles' diet consists of other animals, although a few lizards and the desert tortoise eat vegetation—both of which provide moisture. Retreating underground or into similar alleviating microclimates to relieve heat stress is of vital importance to their well-being. That they are poikilothermic also aids in their success, for when their temperatures are reduced, so are their metabolic functions. Like the estivating or hibernating mammal underground in its burrow, the cool reptile has reduced its need for food and water and loses less moisture through respiration.

The qualities that best adapt birds to life in the desert are primarily behavioral. With their mobility they can take advantage of microclimates over a rather wide area. They are without sweat glands and insulated by feathers, so moisture loss from the skin is retarded. When necessary, evaporative cooling takes place from the respiratory tract by rapid breathing and by gular fluttering—a rapid fluttering of the loose skin on the underside of the throat. The formation of uric acid reduces water losses in waste elimination. Meat-eating birds derive most or all of their moisture from their prey. Some quail are able to live on moisture derived from succulent vegetation, but for many birds, some free water is necessary.

That most birds are not adjusted to living underground where lower temperatures reduce heat stress, and that most of them are diurnal, would seem to be distinct disadvantages in the desert. But the first is largely compensated for by their ability to fly; the second by adjusting their activity during the hot summer to take place during the coolest part of the day, in early morning and late afternoon. One sure bonus factor the birds possess, however, is their normal body temperature, which is within a range of 104° to 108°F. (Their normal temperature is thus a few degrees higher than that of most mammals.) Birds can lose heat by conduction— from their bodies to the environment—up to a higher environmental temperature point than can mammals; and can sustain higher body temperatures than can the mammals before reaching their lethal limit. (Body temperatures within a range of 113° to 116°F are finally fatal to birds.)

Black vultures roosting on cardon cactus (*M. W. Larson*)

Mammals vary tremendously in their ability to endure desert conditions. In this regard, the sublime and the ridiculous are the kangaroo rat and man, in that order. Credit goes to Knut Schmidt-Nielsen for much of our knowledge about the physiological workings of desert animals. His studies of desert rodents, camels, and other creatures of the world's deserts are classic examples of scientific investigation.

It is physically impossible for small mammals to use evaporative cooling as the main means for regulating body temperatures. Such a method would soon prove fatal. Heat gained by the animal body is directly proportional to the body's surface area. Metabolic heat is also produced within the body, adding to the heat gain, and this heat production too is proportional to the surface area, not to the weight of the body.

The smaller mammals have a high surface to volume ratio. Their double heat gain is great, moisture resources low. A mouse attempting to cool itself by evaporation of moisture would so reduce its body weight within an hour as to die. Large mammals (like the camel) with a much lower surface to volume ratio have less heat gain and much greater internal moisture resources. They can afford to lose sufficient moisture for cooling over much longer periods than can small mammals.

For the kangaroo rat, loss of water for cooling is a prohibitive expense. Throughout this chapter we have noted some of the ways in which kangaroo rats are adapted for desert living. At the risk of repeating some of these, let us look at this animal's adaptation as a whole, as determined by Schmidt-Nielsen.

The kangaroo rat is first of all behaviorally adapted; he lives underground in a fairly constant and lower temperature range than that prevailing on the surface. In tests it was found that the temperatures of these burrows always stayed below 85°F; in winter they did not go below 46°F. It was also learned that the air of the burrows usually has a relative humidity of approximately 30 percent—or about two to five times higher than the outside air. The kangaroo rat emerges only at night into the cooler temperatures. When in his burrow, he closes the opening with a plug of dirt which keeps heat out and moisture in. In this more humid atmosphere, moisture loss from the skin (which lacks sweat glands) is very low. Losses from respiration are reduced, due to the moisture content of the burrow air—and the amazing lower temperatures of the nose which captures some moisture from the air being exhaled. Food stores in the nest absorb some of the moisture in the burrow. Water supplies

Kangaroo rat leaving its burrow in the sand (*M. W. Larson*)

consist only of the very small amounts contained in its usually dry plant food—mainly seeds—and of metabolic water formed from this diet.

The feces are very dry, little water being lost in them. Feces of the laboratory rat contain more than four times as much water as those of the kangaroo rat when the same amounts of food have been digested. The food eaten by the kangaroo rat is well utilized, and only relatively small amounts of waste need to be eliminated. In addition, the kangaroo rat often eats its own fecal pellets, in this way digesting portions that had not been digested the first time, gaining certain vitamins which were formed by action of bacteria in the lower digestive tract, and saving some water. There is so little protein in its diet that the need to eliminate urea is not great and the kangaroo rat need not urinate often. In addition its urine is highly concentrated—up to 23 percent urea. (This is almost five times as concentrated as man's.) When experimental animals were fed on a high protein diet unlike their normal one, they drank water—which was needed in order to eliminate the increased quantities of urea. The water given them, however, was sea water! Being able to concentrate salts in their urine to twice that of sea water, the kangaroo rats were able to thrive on this high protein, saltwater diet.

Kangaroo rats do not use water for heat regulation, nor do they drink water. They eat largely air-dry—not succulent—plant materials. Yet Schmidt-Nielsen's experiments showed that kangaroo rats can maintain their body weight on dry food (barley) when the relative humidity is kept just above the very low point of 10 percent. Theirs is a frugal, but fabulously successful water economy.

By contrast, man must use water lavishly to survive high temperatures. The human body cools itself primarily by sweating. On a hot day in the desert, a man may exude as much as twelve quarts of sweat! Moreover, he is also losing water from his respiratory tract and through the formation of urine. Water lost through perspiration is taken from the blood, which in turn gathers more moisture from the body tissues. By drinking water, a man can replace such heavy losses, but he is a slow drinker when compared to many animals. Schmidt-Nielsen found that the camel can actually ingest over thirty percent of its body weight in water at a single drinking session! When man's thirst is satisfied, he will often stop drinking before he has replaced enough water to make up for what he's lost. This dehydration is usually corrected later when he drinks liquids in conjunction with meals. However, if he continues to perspire heavily without being able to obtain water, he is doomed. After losing approximately two percent of his weight in water, he is exceedingly thirsty. By the time he reaches a ten percent weight loss, he is generally incapable of caring for himself. According to Schmidt-Nielsen, death occurs after a weight loss of somewhere between 15 and 25 percent. With increasing dehydration, the viscosity of the blood increases, placing added strain on the heart. With circulation thus impaired, metabolic heat within the body cannot be carried to the skin surface rapidly enough. An explosive heat rise occurs internally and death is the result. Moreover, body salts are lost in perspiration, and excessive water loss often creates a salt imbalance. When the water is replaced, the body fluids are diluted and serious cramps are the result. If sweating is prolonged, the sweat glands may become fatigued and stop functioning and a devastating fever develops.

Man has weak kidneys in comparison to many other mammals in their ability to concentrate waste products. Normal urine volume is approximately one to one-and-a-half quarts per day. If the body is dehydrated, this volume drops to approximately a pint a day, and waste products reach their highest possible concentration.

Man's body can make a few adjustments to heat; sweat glands may increase their output, and minor internal modifications occur to retard salt loss. But there is no circumventing this need for water. Man cannot "train" himself to get along on small amounts, or store it in advance in his body. Some authorities feel a man doing hard labor in desert heat must have a daily minimum of two gallons to maintain his health. The U. S. Army Quartermaster Corps recommends twenty-five quarts per day for anyone performing hard work in the sun at a temperature of 122°F. Under the same temperatures, a man resting in the shade should have sixteen quarts. If he is exceedingly careful, rests, and stays in the shade, a man without water in the hottest portions of our North American Desert has a life expectancy of two days at the most. In the summer of 1968, when the temperature exceeded 110°F, two girls bogged down their automobile in sand not far from Yuma, Arizona. They decided to hike ten miles for help, and leaving food, water, and ice in the automobile, they set out on foot. When near their destination they inexplicably turned back toward the car, and were found later that day by a passing motorist. One girl survived, but the other died within an hour after their rescue.

Anyone in trouble in the desert is advised to remain with his vehicle, to avoid exertion, and to rest in shade. If he must walk, he should do so only at night, realizing that the total distance he can cover cannot be too great. Man can make only very minor physiological adjustments to desert heat. He can make no adjustments that allow him to cut back on his minimum water needs. Man has, indeed, only one thing really going for him in the desert, and that is his brain.

chapter nine

The Saguaro Cactus

ELDER BROTHER, the ancient deity of the Papago Indians, created the magnificent saguaro cactus by planting a bead of his perspiration in the desert soil. From his gift, the people and the animals of his desert have gathered a bountiful harvest. In and around the saguaros revolves a community of living things whose interrelationships are extremely complex, often little understood and even largely unsuspected by man. As an example of one of many similar interrelated desert communities, let us survey the living things of the saguaro forests in some detail, beginning with the saguaro itself.

The saguaro is the largest cactus in the United States. Columnar in form, it can reach a height of fifty feet and weigh six or seven tons! At about a third of the way up, the trunk begins to send out the first of five or six primary branches, which only occasionally produce secondary branches. These grow out and then bend upward, in most cases parallel to the main trunk, reaching skyward in seeming supplication. A very old and prosperous saguaro may have as many as fifty branches, but this is an unusually large number. The surface of the trunk and branches

121

Saguaros growing in the Arizona Upland subdivision of the Sonoran Desert
(*Courtesy of Arizona-Sonora Desert Museum*)

has longitudinal grooves which aid the plant in expanding and contracting accordion-fashion depending on the amount of its stored water. Atop the entire length of each ridge are clusters of spines. Each cluster arises from an areole and contains approximately twenty to twenty-five spines of varying lengths up to two or three inches. Since the spines radiate from the central point, the cactus is well-armored with intermeshed spines. The plant's epidermis is a bright green, and when touched feels very firm and almost waxy. Internally, the saguaro is supported by a woody skeleton composed of small, long, individual, cylindrical rods arranged in a circle which stretch the height of the saguaro. Within and around this circle lies the softer, water-storing tissue of the plant. Seventy-five to ninety-five percent of the weight of a saguaro may consist of water!

As is true for cacti in general, the trunk and branches bear the chlorophyll that carries on photosynthetic activities. This giant has a system of primarily lateral roots lying a few feet below the soil surface. Stretching out for as much as one hundred feet beyond the base, they capture moisture quickly and efficiently after storms. Due to its vast water reserves, the saguaro is able to flower each year, even when environmental conditions are severe and other types of plants cannot flower at all. In May the flower buds arise, one from each areole, in a circle around the tips of the trunk and branches. Each bud produces a large, white, waxy flower from two to three inches in diameter. These frivolous, seemingly extravagant white halos appear incongruous above the spiny body, and give the whole plant the air of a slightly tipsy giant celebrating the coming of spring.

In speaking of flowers in general, we find they usually—though not always—contain both the male organs (stamens which produce pollen) and the female organs (pistils terminating in ovaries). Pollen must be transferred from the male organs to the female organs in order to effect fertilization and to produce viable seeds. This transfer is usually made by wind or animal action. In some cases pollen from a flower can pollinate the same flower; often, however, fertilization is effected only when pollen comes from another flower, or even from another plant of the same species.

This has proven to be the case with the saguaro. The individual saguaro flower is self-sterile. Flowers on the same branch are not cross-compatible, and flowers on different branches of the same plant have only slight fertilization success. To be effective, pollen must come from the flower of

Saguaro fruit and flowers (*M. W. Larson*)

one saguaro to the flower of a different saguaro, thus achieving cross fertilization.

Not all of the flowers on a saguaro open at the same time. Each flower normally remains open for less than twenty-four hours, opening at night and closing sometime during the following afternoon. Pollination must be effected during this brief period. Saguaro pollen is too heavy to be disseminated by wind and so has to be carried by animals visiting the flowers. In good Victorian birds and bees fashion, it has long been generally accepted that honeybees are important pollinators of saguaros. They are—as are probably a variety of solitary bees. The saguaros, however, are an old established family line in the Southwest, whereas the honeybees are not. "Domesticated" honeybees did not exist in the Western Hemisphere until the white man brought them here from Europe. Escapees from artificial hives eventually populated the land, and so there are wild swarms today—we know of one colony which is currently hive-keeping in a hole in a saguaro trunk.

It is estimated, however, that honeybees have been in the range of the saguaros for less than one hundred years. Obviously bees were not—and are not—the sole saguaro pollinating agents. That they are effective in this regard has been proven, however, by a team of researchers in Tucson, Arizona—S. E. McGregor, Stanley M. Alcorn, and George Olin. In experiments they found that the honeybee *Apis mellifera* freely visited saguaro blossoms in order to obtain pollen and nectar. Plant pollen, the male fertilizing material, is produced in abundance, so that even when freely eaten by animals or blown by the wind, there is still enough of it to fertilize other members of the species. Nectar, a sweet liquid produced by the flower, is the lure, the bait that brings the animals in, causing them to be dusted with pollen. This pollen is then carried on their bodies to the next flower, where the animal will accidentally rub some off onto the female portion of the flower, thus achieving fertilization. For bees, pollen is protein necessary for the body-building of the young; nectar is carbohydrate, the source of their honey—an energy food.

The investigators in this pollination study estimated that each saguaro flower contained as much as 125 bee-loads of nectar. (A bee-load is approximately .04 gram; it takes a little over 28 grams to equal an ounce!) The saguaro flower was estimated as containing about 25 bee-loads of pollen. Actually a saguaro flower is an excellent bee food source, for in some extreme cases (with other species of plants) a bee may find it necessary to visit several hundred flowers in order to obtain a single bee-load of nectar.

A bee may at times collect only nectar, at other times only pollen, sometimes both on a single trip. Collecting food, the bees move in and out among the flower parts sucking up nectar. Their bodies become dusted with the creamy-colored pollen, and this is partially cleaned from the body with the legs and packed into pollen "baskets" on their back legs, in which it is carried home. Due to their numbers, industry, small size, and constant moving about from one flower to another carrying pollen on their bodies, they are efficient pollinators of many plants including saguaros. In these experiments it was found that the percentage of fruit set on those plants pollinated by bees was 52 percent. Where the flowers were experimentally cross-pollinated by hand, the percentage was 71. On control plants the percentage was 54.

The white-winged dove was another possible pollinator investigated in this study. These birds winter in Mexico and migrate into the saguaro forests in the spring, feeding on the nectar and later on the fruit. A dove will light on top of the saguaro and push its head down into the center cavity of the flower to drink the nectar. It withdraws its head now well dusted with pollen, and eventually moves on to other flowers. Fruit set by doves in the experiment was 45 percent. Other birds visiting the saguaros may also be instrumental in cross pollination, but no other species were investigated in this study. The final subject of investigation was a night pollinator, the long-nosed bat. These bats enter southern Arizona in summer and are thought to migrate into Mexico for the winter. They are reported to feed generally on fruit juices, insects, pollen and nectar. Indeed, this strange creature has a pointed face highly suitable for reaching deep into a saguaro flower. Its long tongue is tipped with papillae forming a brush, and the lower incisors are absent to facilitate rapid tongue movements. Like the doves, it was found to push its head into the flower, drink the nectar, and emerge covered with pollen that is then carried to other flowers. It would appear that the bat may feed on saguaro pollen as well. The percentage of flowers pollinated by long-nosed bats was sixty-two.

The saguaro fruits are oval, two to three inches in length and spineless. While still on the plant, each fruit splits lengthwise into three sections and opens out, giving the appearance of a flower. The prominently displayed inner lining is a bright watermelon red. In the center is a large mass of sweet, juicy, red pulp; embedded inside are a thousand or more tiny, round, black seeds, each about .05 inch in diameter.

When in bloom and in fruit, the saguaros are a free smorgasbord open to the desert public. Bees, bats, and doves are only a sample of the many. When the fruits open, the moist pulp and nutritious seeds are eagerly

eaten by a variety of other birds and insects. When the fruits finally fall
to the ground, earth-bound creatures—from insects and rodents, to coyotes and man—eagerly consume the rest. The pulp is not only the color
of a watermelon, it also has a slight melon flavor. The numerous seeds
within it are crunchy and crisp, somewhat reminiscent of poppy seeds in
texture. These are spread during their fall to the ground, washed about
following storms, or carried around by animals. Some creatures who consume the pulp do not digest the seeds it contains. These seeds, still viable,
pass through the animals' digestive tract and are included in their feces
which may thus be deposited far from the original cactus.

Research on the germination requirements of saguaro seeds was carried
out and reported by Stanley M. Alcorn and Edwin Kurtz, Jr. They dem-
onstrated that saguaro seeds require daylight in order to grow; that is,
germination is most likely if the seeds are on the very surface of the soil.
In the experiments, seeds germinated if the temperature was kept in a
constant range of 68° to 86°F. Germination also took place, however, in
periods of alternating temperatures, such as will occur over a twenty-
four-hour period in the desert summer. A range of "day" temperatures as
high as 95°F and "night" temperatures down to 59°F allowed seeds to
begin their activity. Other influential factors included moisture and soil
conditions.

The saguaro seedling is exceedingly vulnerable. Without spines or
heavy epidermis, the young cactus is but a moist, green, nutritious bite
for any animal looking for such a tidbit. Consumed by rodents, rabbits,
or stock while still faced by overwhelming problems of heat and aridity,
very few seedlings survive. In one test carried out at the Saguaro National
Monument near Tucson, eight hundred one-inch saguaros were planted
in the desert. Six months later, only fourteen of those plants were still
alive. Eight hundred additional young saguaros were then planted within
a cage. Of these and the fourteen earlier survivals, only thirty plants remained after two years! (In other words, thirty plants out of 814 in the
second experiment survived.) Almost all the casualties were attributable
to rodents who eventually tunneled under the wire cages. The few saguaros which do become established are usually those that happen to
start growth protected under other plants or among rocks where they
are not found by hungry animals.

The growth of the saguaro is almost unbelievably slow. In work at

Saguaro National Monument, J. R. Hastings and Stanley Alcorn estimated that a nine-year-old saguaro is approximately six inches tall. It
might be five feet tall at 27 years, twenty feet at 83, and thirty-five feet
at the grand age of 157! The oldest and largest of the saguaros have an
estimated age of 150 to 200 years. According to Dr. Shreve, the saguaros
sometimes do not begin to branch until they reach a height of sixteen to
twenty-six feet. They do not bloom until eight to ten feet tall—and a ten-
foot saguaro is an estimated 41 years of age. Hastings, in *The Changing
Mile,* a thought-provoking book that details vegetative changes in southern
Arizona, draws the conclusion that a saguaro will produce something
like 12,000,000 seeds in its lifetime, of which only one will ever reach
maturity.

Saguaros are strictly residents of the Sonoran Desert, but do not occupy
even its full extent. They are found in the states of Sonora and Arizona
and across the Colorado River in only three small locations in California,
but are absent in Baja. Saguaros grow on the lower portions of the out-
wash slopes of the mountains and hills. They frequent generally rocky
areas where a firm anchorage can be obtained for their roots and soil
drainage conditions are suitable. Saguaros do not normally frequent the
flats, leaving these to creosote bush and other vegetation. Their growing
periods are limited to the summer rainy season, and the decrease in summer rainfall toward the western limits of the Sonoran Desert limits their
range in that direction. Their northern limits and how far they will grow
up mountain slopes (to approximately 4500 feet) are determined by the
length of freezing periods. While it snows occasionally in the saguaro
forests, freezing temperatures rarely last for more than several consecutive
hours. No type of arborescent, columnar cacti is able to survive in the
colder winter temperatures of the more northern deserts.

These giants often die when hard winds break off their arms or over-
turn the entire plant. Saguaros are particularly susceptible to toppling,
due to their dependence on lateral, rather than deeper tap roots. Ground
softened by rains sometimes does not provide adequate support, and a
high wind coming at that time may blow over some saguaros.

One of the mature saguaros' greatest enemies, however, is a tiny species
of bacteria. The bacillus, *Erwinia carnegieana,* causes portions of saguaro tissue to liquefy somewhat into a dark, rotten, soft mass which sloughs
off in time. If the necrosis progresses throughout the plant, it eventually
dies. Affected saguaros produce a hard bark-like callus about injuries,

walling them off from the uninfected tissues and often stopping the spread of the disease. *E. carnegieana* can travel from one saguaro to another through their adjacent root systems. The infected arm of one may rub against another plant growing near it, and the rotten exudate from a badly infected cactus can soak into the ground and spread for some distance, reaching other plants.

The chief carrier of the bacillus, however, is a tiny, unobtrusive moth, *Cactobrosis fernaldialis*. This insect passes its larval stage in the saguaro tissue, where food, protection, and moisture are all handsomely provided at the same time. Unfortunately, it carries *E. carnegieana* in its intestinal tract and on its body. (The bacillus has also been found on the adult moth and on the surface of the eggs.) A larva does not remain in one location, but moves onward into new portions of the plant, further spreading the necrosis. Eventually, it leaves the saguaros to pupate for approximately a month under rocks and debris. The small, brown, adult moth lives only about three days, during which time the eggs are laid on the ground. Within another month they hatch, and the resulting small larvae wander off in search of a saguaro. Those that are lucky enough to find one eat their way inward. They remain there, still eating, for perhaps as long as ten months, since larvae have been found in saguaros from November to August. It is thought that they may also feed on some of the other desert plants.

Stanley Alcorn and Curtis May reported that between 1942 and 1961, this bacterial necrosis destroyed 29.3 percent of a stand of saguaros near Tucson. During the same period, windfall destroyed an additional 2.4 percent. The stand is failing to repopulate, and Alcorn and May foresee that if nothing changes the rate of decline, this particular group of saguaros will become extinct between 1995 and 1998. The reasons why go back quite a way. In the 1880's, cattle were brought to the Southwest in great numbers. The Indians were dead or pushed onto reservations, the Civil War was settled, the east and midwest were getting crowded, but the for Southwest yet remained to be exploited. That was taken care of: soon the grasslands were overloaded and overgrazed. Cattle spread out into less desirable areas—including the lower slopes of the desert mountains— and when a devastating dry period prevailed from 1891 to 1893 and finished off a large segment of the cattle, it must have been the only time in history that desert plants ever had reason to welcome a drought.

Vegetative changes were begun then, which in combination with climatic and human factors since, have had (and continue to have) ramifications that spread like ripples in a pond. Some of these as they affect the saguaros have been enumerated by a trio of Tucson investigators—W. A. Niering, R. H. Whittaker and C. H. Lowe. They list as a result of the overgrazing and drought a disturbance of plant cover, increased run-off, floods of greater intensity, formation of new deep arroyos in valleys, and other forms of erosion. Grazing was reduced by the drought, but certainly not eliminated; it continues today. Overgrazing in areas led to fewer "nurse" plants under which saguaros could begin growth with some protection.

Grazing also reduces grass cover and promotes the spread and increase of cacti such as prickly pear and cholla. Wood rats, or pack rats, accompany an increase in these cacti, for they feed on the former and live in homes built of the latter. Overgrazing also leads to an increase in the number of rabbits which eat a variety of vegetation that might otherwise help protect young saguaros. Both rats and rabbits are fond of young, juicy, seedling saguaros; so, no doubt, are cattle. These investigators also report that the lack of young saguaros in parts of Saguaro National Monument is thought to be a consequence of grazing before 1938 and a program of coyote control that was carried out in the 1930's when (due to the lack of these predators) high rodent populations developed. It is in a part of Saguaro National Monument, that the saguaros are foreseen as disappearing about the year 2000. The trio of authors call this portion a "stricken community." They predict the saguaro population in this section of the monument could recover from the effects of grazing *if the cattle were removed*.

I have inquired whether grazing is still permitted in Saguaro National Monument. A new block of land was designated as part of the monument in 1961; a beautiful stand of saguaros west of Tucson where grazing is not permitted. But in the original portion of the monument to the east of Tucson (including the "stricken community"), grazing continues under permits issued by the Forest Service!

The saguaros are not being exterminated as a species. In parts of their range, where they are reasonably protected from grazing and other pressures, they are doing well. What the case may be in another few hundred years is only a guess, but not a very optimistic one. A local advertisement currently extolls the glories of the "expanding city" and the "retreating saguaro." Perhaps they do not mean it in exactly that way, but the saguaro, like many of our other valuable heritages, is indeed retreating against the onslaught of cattle, people, houses, and a changed pattern in the relationships of living things around it.

chapter ten

The Saguaro Community

D R. JOSEPH WOOD KRUTCH once wrote that the Sonoran Desert is one of the few places where a person could return from a walk carrying a hole! These "holes" are formed by the layers of callus which, as we have seen, a saguaro builds up to wall off injuries. So hard is this material descriptively called "traumatic tissue" by some authorities, that it remains behind as do the supporting "ribs," long after the plant is dead and the other watery main tissues have rotted away. Commonly known as "saguaro shoes," these "holes" range in size from mere scabs to gourd-shaped containers fifteen or more inches in length, with a diameter of several inches. Where insects have tunneled into a saguaro or chewed on the surface, or where a bird has gone after those insects or excavated a nest, callus outlines the wound. Weathering also gives rise to a similar tissue, and old saguaros often bear extensive, hard, bark-like coverings around their lower portions.

Two birds are responsible for excavating nest cavities in the saguaros. These are the Gila woodpecker and the flickers, the latter also being a member of the woodpecker family. Woodpeckers excavating nest holes in trees is a familiar story and excavating them in saguaros is just a variation on the same theme, although a rather unusual one. The bird usually excavates such a hole into the saguaro for a short distance, after which the

133

Gila woodpecker at its nest in a saguaro cactus (*M. W. Larson*)

cavity is extended straight down in the plant. The result is a hole that has the outlines of a crook-necked squash. Once drilled to bird qualifications, the hole is gradually lined with callus by the saguaro as a protection to its remaining tissues. The result is a bird home with several exceptional qualities. In a deep pocket of the spine-covered plant, it gives its occupant some protection, is high above ground, is usually dry, and most importantly, it is a home with excellent insulation. Just as the inner tissues of the saguaro are protected to a great extent from freezing or overheating by the volume of the plant, so also does the nest cavity deep within the plant benefit by the insulation. The cavity prepared within the saguaro thus provides a most effective microclimate in an area where ameliorating microclimates are exceedingly valuable.

Under the direction of Dr. Charles Lowe at the University of Arizona, Richard D. Krizman and Oscar H. Soule found that within a saguaro hole, minimum and maximum temperatures occurred later than they did in the outside air. Moreover, there was a less extreme range in temperature within the hole than in the air outside, and a higher relative humidity prevailed within. Obviously these saguaro holes afford many of the benefits of an underground burrow. The birds cannot close the openings to their homes, as do some of the small animals underground, but the saguaro holes provide effective microclimates nevertheless.

A characteristic and familiar bird of the saguaro forests, the Gila woodpecker is approximately eight to ten inches long. The head and underparts are a grayish-brown, and the back, wings, and tail are marked with black and white bars. Only the male sports a bright red round patch on the top of the head. Within their excavated holes, these birds may raise as many as three broods of young a year. They feed largely on insects, but also eat fruits, such as those of the saguaro. During the fall and winter they move about more, sometimes into adjacent areas, but the saguaros are important to them during their breeding season.

The flickers are brown and barred above; white spotted with black below; and with a black crescent across the chest. In flight they may flash yellow or red under the wings and tail. The one with red is commonly known as the red-shafted flicker; the one with yellow, the gilded flicker. The range of the gilded is closely allied to the range of the saguaros. The two forms freely interbreed where their ranges overlap. Flickers as a whole nest in a variety of locations and environments, the saguaros and saguaro forests being one example.

Elf owl leaving its nest in a saguaro
(*M. W. Larson*)

Elf owl returning to its nest with large scorpion (*M. W. Larson*)

These three members of the woodpecker family unknowingly benefit a large segment of the saguaro forest's bird population, for the holes they abandon at the end of the nesting season are usurped by other birds who are incapable of such handiwork themselves. In this way, the saguaros become avian apartment complexes. Older saguaros are marked with the openings of many nest holes, each of which is used year after year by a variety of occupants.

The elf owl, the smallest owl in the world, prefers to live in the largest cactus in the United States. This diminutive creature is five-and-a-half to six inches in length, about sparrow size, and reddish-brown in color with white above the eyes. Elf owls spend the winter in southern Mexico and migrate northward into the desert for the summer, which seems contrary to common sense. But during the warm period, particularly the time of the summer rainy season, the saguaro forests abound with the insects and other arthropods that compose these birds' diets. And what a diet it is! These miniature hunters catch and devour great numbers of the desert's most fearsome smaller inhabitants—the centipedes and scorpions. In the spring the elf owls set up housekeeping in saguaro holes; the young hatch

Elf owl with beetle (*M. W. Larson*)

A flycatcher at its saguaro apartment (*M. W. Larson*)

in June. The adults hunt by night and often return to the nest with scorpions, insects, or centipedes as long as themselves. Approaching the nest for a landing, the adult holds one end of the many-legged centipede in its mouth, flipping the other end up and into the hole for the young to devour. The elf owls are not strictly confined to the saguaros, being also found in different types of trees below approximately the 5000 foot level of elevation in southeastern California, southern Arizona, and southwestern New Mexico and Texas. However, they are strongly associated with the saguaros. The calls of the elf owls in the saguaro forests on a warm summer night while lightning distantly flashes and thunder mutters atop nearby mountains or out above the desert flats provide memorable and satisfying moments for the human observer.

Other owls, including the pygmy and screech owl, use the saguaro holes for nesting or resting. Their nocturnal hunting habits bring them in contact with a large variety of smaller creatures that emerge only in darkness. Their prey is thus largely different than that of the woodpeckers and flickers who do their hunting by day, often in the early morning and late afternoon.

The woodpecker-owl-saguaro association is a strong one, but other birds besides owls also make use of the woodpecker-drilled saguaro holes. These include the ash-throated flycatcher, the Arizona crested-flycatcher, and purple martin. An unfortunate new addition to that list is the starling.

Man has taken four vertebrates from Europe and spread them over the face of the earth. The brown rat and house mouse he took by mistake; the sparrow and starling with intent. Man has pretty well upset, shifted, and changed animal populations throughout the world, but the aforementioned four have been among the most successful from their own standpoint and most destructive from the standpoint of man and a good many other living things. The starling was intentionally and successfully introduced into North America in 1890–1891, when one hundred birds were released in Central Park in New York City. From a hundred came—and continue to come—millions. The starlings began to spread. Within twenty years they had spread over most of the New England and Middle Atlantic states. By 1930 they were in the Middle West and southern Canada. In the 1940's they made it to California. The starling was first reported in Arizona in 1946, and has since become established around Phoenix, Tucson, Yuma, and similar locations.

The starling is a short-tailed bird approximately the size of a meadow-

Wasp (*Polistes exclamans*) nest under the arms of a saguaro (*M. W. Larson*)

lark. It is black, but has white star-spots at the tips of the feathers when in new plumage—hence the name "starling" meaning little star. These spots gradually wear away during the winter, and the bird is all black by spring. The starling's bill is brown in the fall and winter, but bright ivory-yellow in the spring breeding season. These birds are gregarious and often gather in large flocks in winter and at night.

In their European home the starlings are useful, insect-eating birds. In the United States their population growth has been explosive. They have caused sanitary problems in cities where they flock and have taken over nesting sites of other birds. It is with human regret that they have recently been reported as nesting in saguaro holes in the areas adjacent to their present locations—in and around towns, ranches, and irrigated land. It is bad enough that they may be starting to use the saguaros near man's habitations; hopefully they will not ultimately spread out into the saguaro forests, for the native users of the saguaro holes would no doubt fight a losing battle with the highly successful, highly prolific starlings.

The use of the saguaro holes certainly does not end with the birds. Small mammals like mice may enter low holes at times. Snakes such as the racers, occasionally and amazingly ascend a saguaro and enter a hole in order to eat the young bird occupants. Insects may make a hole their home or simply drop in for a short stay. They may arrive independently or with help, as in the case of insects attached to birds. The invertebrate fauna in these locations includes such diverse items as mites, ticks, beetles, and colonies of honeybees. An interesting insect inhabitant has recently been discovered and reported by Dr. Charles Lowe of the University of Arizona. This is a new species of mosquito which undergoes its developmental stages in water which may be blown or drained into the bottoms of some saguaro holes with an exposure or angle that contributes to their catching water. Such unexpected water sources may even be important temporary water supplies for some animals—such as birds and insects—which can obtain them.

One of the interesting occasional occupants of saguaro holes is the big brown bat, *Eptesicus fuscus*. This common bat enjoys a wide distribution over almost the entire United States, southern Canada, Mexico, and most of Central America. It is really only a medium-sized bat, displaying chestnut brown fur in parts of its range but a pale brown in the deserts. It commonly passes the day in old buildings, or in caves, mines, crevices, and other sheltered locations. Evidently an abandoned saguaro hole is also acceptable. There may well be other species of bats which also inhabit the saguaro hole habitat, for bats are highly mobile and due to their nocturnal habits, a good deal more numerous than one would believe. Among the mammals of the world, only the rodents exceed the bats in the number of species. In the state of Arizona, alone, twenty-eight species of bats have been reported; not all of which, of course, occur in the desert.

Like most bats found in the North American Desert, the big brown bat is an insect eater, leaving its roost at sunset to feed. Actually, the insectivorous bats of the desert are not specifically adapted for desert life. But their way of life—hanging in dark, protected roosts by day and hunting by night—helps them avoid most of the heat, as does their ability to migrate or escape to other environments when necessary. Some mammals can glide such as the North American flying squirrels, but bats are the

Vampire bats (*M. W. Larson*)

only mammals that can actually fly. Their forelimbs and fingers are greatly elongated to form supports for thin membranes which enclose all the fingers (except for the short, clawed thumbs) and extend back and are attached to the hind limb at the ankles. Between the two hind limbs stretches another membrane that encloses most of the tail.

At dusk and after dark, these bats locate their insect food by means of echolocation. An insectivorous bat in flight gives out twenty to thirty or more ultrasonic cries per second. The sound waves bounce off solid objects ahead and travel back to the bat, advising him of obstacles to be avoided or insects to be caught. It has been found that the big brown bat and some other insectivorous bats also produce sounds when at rest. These cease when the bats are asleep. The insect diet of these bats provides them with a good deal of moisture. However, its high protein content also produces large quantities of urea, and hence a bat needs considerable amounts of water for elimination. It is also likely that the thin, membranous wings lose appreciable amounts of moisture, for in flight, the bat exposes large areas of surface to the warm air, and its body volume is slight. This no doubt explains why bats are common visitors at water holes. It is a familiar sight in the desert at dusk to see bats swooping low over water tanks, water holes, or swimming pools, drinking as they skim the water's surface. Like the birds, their ability to fly considerable distances to water sources helps them survive in a dry land.

Nectar-feeding bats like the long-nosed are usually confined to the tropics and semi-tropics where flowers are more readily available. Another tropical group of bats feeds mainly on fruit, and still another small group containing three species feeds on fish. But the most notorious tropical group—and certainly the one with the most gruesome eating habits—is that of the vampire bats. One species of vampire can be found in Northern Mexico, just adjacent to the deserts.

So far as we know, the vampires live on an exclusive diet of fresh blood. They scoop out a small wedge of skin from their warm-blooded victim, usually while the animal is asleep, and lap up the blood from this cut. The vampire places its tongue over the wound and turns the edges downward, forming a concave surface. In conjunction with a groove in the middle of the lower lip, this forms a tube through which, by moving its tongue, the vampire can draw liquid into its mouth. The victim of such an attack usually does not suffer any great loss of blood, but the bite itself is dangerous, since the vampires carry several diseases including rabies. With the permission of the United States Government, the Arizona-Sonora Desert Museum displays approximately a dozen of these bats in a simulated cave environment. The vampires obligingly hang, head-down, behind glass and are not disturbed by the light that is flashed on them by visitors. They successfully raise young in their "cave," and live on a diet of "whipped" or defibrinated blood obtained from a slaughterhouse.

Not in, but *on* the saguaros, birds like the red-tailed hawk may build their nests. These hawks are large, with bodies twenty to twenty-four inches in length and with broad wings and tails. They soar in wide circles high in the air in search of prey such as ground squirrels, which they swoop and catch. Various races of red-tailed hawks have a wide distribu-

The dead saguaro in the center of the picture will remain standing for some time (*M. W. Larso*

tion. Those in the Southwest nest in a variety of locations—from tall trees to the crotches of saguaros where they build large, obvious nests. They are reported as nesting even on the ground at the base of low shrubs in extreme desert areas in southeastern California.

Whereas the red-tailed hawk is active diurnally, another large bird which nests on the saguaros—the great horned owl—is active nocturnally. This is a large owl, nearly two feet in length, with conspicuous ear-tufts or "horns" of feathers. The species is widespread, being found in many different habitats. These owls feed on rodents, rabbits, skunks, and other mammals.

For their 150 or 200 years of life, the saguaros continue to provide food and shelter for a good many of the animal inhabitants of the saguaro forests. Even in death their usefulness lingers for a considerable time. A fallen saguaro harbors within its slowly rotting tissues a large number of living things devouring it, and others in turn preying on these. The flesh once rotted away, the hard woody skeleton and the saguaro shoes persist for a very long period; and under these, small creatures live, or hide, or eat. The saguaro is a long time growing, a long time persisting, and a long time dying. Through all, its uses are multitudinous.

chapter eleven

The Cholla Community

WITHOUT a doubt, the spiniest thing that grows in the desert is the cholla cactus. Considering the quantity of spine-covered vegetation present there, that is to say the cholla is indeed well endowed. Yet within and among the cholla, some of the desert animals make their homes and derive partial protection from predators. Cholla cacti—several species of them—are plentiful in the saguaro forests and spread out beyond there into other types of desert country, some extending into the desert grasslands. Just as the saguaro cactus acts as a focal point around which the lives of many desert animals revolve, so also do the chollas scattered among the saguaros or in other areas outside the saguaro forests serve as important centers for the lives of other animals.

Cholla cacti and the familiar prickly pear cacti are very close relatives in the same genus, *Opuntia*. Each is composed of numerous joints which are flat in the prickly pear and cylindrical in the chollas. On the prickly pears the areoles that bear spines, glochids, flowers and fruits are spaced about the flat surface of the joints; on the chollas they occur on tubercles. Chollas produce branches from a main trunk and the individual joints, dependent on the species, vary in diameter from pencil size to two or more inches; the plant as a whole varies in height from a small shrub size to an arborescent form.

147

Cholla cactus (Mohave Desert) (*M. W. Larson*)

Common names of the various species are descriptive—pencil, stag-horn, cane, teddy bear, and jumping cholla. The teddy bear cholla must certainly be the most misnamed of all the earth's plants—the most heavily spine-covered of all chollas, it is hardly something to hug and carry off to bed. The teddy bear cholla is usually from two to five feet tall, and well-branched. The spines are about an inch long, and a light yellowish-white in color. When backlighted, they give the plant a soft luminous glow, and seen from a distance, can lend the cactus a soft, furry appear-ance. Certainly this is not true on closer inspection!

Best known (and least liked by anyone who has brushed against it) is the jumping cholla. One of the largest cholla, this species occasionally reaches twelve feet in height. Its main trunk may be eight inches in di-ameter at the base and produces several branches arching up into an irregular, rounded crown. The individual joints may be as much as two

Cholla cactus; note the "chaining" of the joints (*M. W. Larson*)

inches in diameter with a heavy armature of inch-long spines intermeshed about each one. The flowers are rather small, pinkish or whitish streaked with lavender, and produce green, spineless fruit. Strangely, these fruits usually remain on the plant until the following year, when they themselves produce new flowers and fruits. Long chains, as many as twelve or fourteen fruits long, often form and are a characteristic feature of the plant.

The terminal joints of this cactus are very easily detached. By barely rubbing against one, an unknowing person or animal may cause it to become dislodged; and due to its spines the joint immediately attaches itself to fur, clothes, or flesh. Cattle blunder into them at times, and are occasionally seen with joints stuck about their faces. These joints almost seem to "jump" at the passerby, hence the name. Once embedded, these joints present a painful problem. Attempting to pull them loose with the fingers simply transfers the spines to the hand. Trying to rub them off with a stick usually just rolls them onto adjacent skin. One of the successful ways to remove them is to take a pocket comb, insert the teeth of the comb among the spines between the joint and you, and then pull up with the comb, flipping the joint out and away. Broken-off joints are often thickly scattered about the ground under the plants and "jump" onto the boots, shoes, and ankles of the unwary. Tennis shoes with their cloth tops are definitely not recommended for hiking in cholla country.

The fruits produce relatively few seeds; some in fact are seedless. The plants' main method of reproduction is by vegetative means. Joints or fruits lying on the ground will, with favorable moisture and temperature, produce roots and shoots and establish new plants. Since jumping cholla joints become easily detached from the plant and attached to passing animals, the species enjoys a satisfactory mode of distribution. As with the saguaro, growth of the jumping cholla seems to be largely dependent on periods when warmth and moisture coincide, and the jumping cholla's peak of distribution is centered in the Sonoran Desert.

Despite the cholla's murderous spines, a number of desert creatures find shelter and protection in its bristling branches. Measuring approximately eight inches in length, the cactus wren is the largest wren in the United States. The top of the head is dark brown, and a white stripe runs over the eye. The back feathers are black to brown with white streaks, and the underparts are lighter but heavily and darkly spotted. The bird has a long, pointed, curved bill. The cactus wren lives permanently in the southern desert areas, dining on insects, spiders and larvae, and is the state bird of Arizona.

It would seem impossible for a bird to build a nest in the cholla cactus, but these wrens are experts at the task. Built of twigs and grasses, the nest is an enclosed one, more or less globular in shape and nestled deep among the spiny branches of the cactus. The bird enters it through a projecting tunnel which may be up to several inches in length. Alighting on the cholla stems, the bird enters the sloping tunnel and drops into the larger nesting area, which is usually feather-lined during the breeding season. The entrance is the only opening and it, too, is protected by encircling spines. Cactus wrens live in these nests the year around, and each fledgling builds its own sleeping nest after the conclusion of the breeding season. In fact, there are usually more nests constructed than there are birds to use them. Some of these may simply represent "busy work" or some phase of courtship activity on the part of the male; building of extra nests, often poorly or flimsily done, is a trait of male wrens as a whole. Cholla is a favorite nest site but other plants, particularly spiny ones like catsclaw, are also used where cholla are scarce.

The two sexes look alike, and produce one or two broods of four to six chicks each year. The male often sits atop a cactus and sings to advertise his ownership of the area; his song is a familiar sound on early spring mornings when the desert is cool and refreshing. These wrens spend a great deal of time foraging on the ground, poking here and there with their long bills. They are reported as being able to turn over or push away small rocks in their search for insects and as having learned to pick dead insects from car radiators. The three ornithologist-authors of *The Birds of Arizona* report that they have never seen one drink. The cactus wren, from cactus home to insect diet, has obviously found a successful pattern for desert living.

We have noted the white-winged dove, which pollinates the saguaro flowers and feeds on its flowers and fruit. A second very common dove in saguaro-cholla forests is the mourning dove, which is widely distributed from Canada to Panama. When in the desert, these doves make their nests in the cholla cacti, and occasionally in the crotches of saguaros. In order to live in the desert, they have had to follow an entirely different pattern than have insect eaters like the cactus wren. Doves are exclusively fruit and seed eaters and must have frequent (some authorities believe twice daily) access to drinking water.

Two mourning doves in their cholla cactus nest; the second dove is in the fore-ground, flattening its body to appear inconspicuous (*M. W. Larson*)

Doves and pigeons are the same general type of bird, the domestic pigeon belonging to the same family (Columbidae) as the mourning dove and the white-winged dove. Members of this family are distinguished by two traits. They drink by sucking up water, immersing their beaks in a pool, and they are able to drink their fill without taking their beaks from the water. Other birds immerse their beaks, but must then raise their heads to imbibe. Also, doves produce crop milk to feed their young. Both male and female produce the milk and regurgitate it as the young poke their beaks inside the mouths and throats of the parent birds. The "milk" consists of a thick material produced by the lining of the birds' crop which sloughs off like curd.

The mourning dove is approximately twelve inches in length and distinguished by its pointed tail. It is brownish and gray with some white on the outer tail feathers and has an iridescence on the back of the head and neck. Its nest, whether built in cholla or any other location is a rather flimsy, flat affair. Two or three is probably the average number of eggs, but a single pair can produce more than one brood per season, as many as six, according to one report.

An interesting study of mourning doves was made by George A. Bartholomew, Jr. and William R. Dawson at the University of California in Los Angeles. They learned that the dove's body temperature normally fluctuates over a range of several degrees centigrade—it does not attempt to maintain a constant temperature level. The mean daytime body temperature in this study was found to be 41.5°C, but varied from 39.4°C to 43.3°C. At night, the dove's temperature is approximately 2°C lower than during the day. The bird's temperature rises rapidly with activity— as much as 2.2°C in four minutes. These birds can thus withstand a wide range of temperatures, but cool themselves by panting and fluttering of the throat when their deep body temperature reaches 42.6°C (approximately 108°F). In addition to the respiratory tract, another site for the dissipation of heat is the thinly feathered skin under the wings. While birds do not have sweat glands, as long as the air temperature is lower than that of their skin, they can lose some heat when the wings are held away from the body or when the bird is in flight.

Experimental birds kept at 39°C (approximately 104°F) drank four times as much water as those kept at 23°C (approximately 73°F). Those kept at 39°C for twenty-four hours lost up to fifteen percent of their body weight through dehydration without ill effects. (At a twelve percent body weight loss by dehydration, man can no longer swallow and cannot recover without assistance.) Amazingly, the mourning doves were found to be able to drink water equivalent to over seventeen percent of their body weight in ten minutes' time. Experimental doves kept at 23°C were able to survive four or five days without water or succulent food. The investigators concluded that the mourning dove meets the demands of desert living through its abilities to endure elevated body temperatures and dehydration, and to make up water deficits quickly once water is found within flying range.

Every animal community has its special character, and the desert's is the roadrunner. Roadrunners are large birds, approximately twenty to twenty-four inches in length; about the size of a pheasant but with a more slender appearance. Their plumage is a heavily streaked mixture of

Roadrunner, having just killed a sidewinder rattlesnake (*M. W. Larson*)

browns, gray, and white, with a naked blue and red skin patch behind the eyes. The tail, bill, and legs are long, and the top of the head is adorned with a ragged, uneven crest of feathers. This bird nests low in trees or shrubs, and frequently in cholla.

The roadrunner seldom flies. It is basically a walker, prefers running, and can hit fifteen miles per hour. To facilitate such a pace, it has strong, sensibly designed feet. Its number two and three toes point forward; numbers one and four backward. The result is an X-shaped footprint in the desert dust. At the takeoff for his run, the roadrunner lowers his crest, stretches his neck, body and tail into a horizontal line, and streaks away with a surprised expression. This bird wanders about in search of its food, which consists primarily of insects, lizards, and snakes. A quick pounce secures the insect, and stabbing blows with the powerful two-inch beak

Roadrunner nesting in a cholla cactus (*M. W. Larson*)

stuns or kills reptiles, including rattlesnakes. The bird bolts its food down whole. When it catches a large snake, the roadrunner swallows the head first and begins digesting it, while the tail dangles outside the beak until the roadrunner's stomach can accommodate it. This slow swallowing process may take the roadrunner several satisfying hours. It occasionally goes after young birds and small mammals, as well as a small amount of plant material.

The roadrunner is a loner except during the nesting season. It is a member of the cuckoo family; however, it is only the European cuckoos which lay their eggs in the nests of other birds and then shed their parental responsibilities by leaving their young in the care of the unsuspecting nest owner. The roadrunner has none of the parasitic habits of some of its relatives. Its nest is a rather course, bulky, stick affair. As soon as an egg is laid the female begins incubation and the young are thus hatched sequentially, not simultaneously. This tends to drag out parenthood to rather monotonous lengths and produces large and small young in a nest at the same time.

The adult roadrunner goes his way with a somewhat preoccupied, arrogant, ungraceful, and very important air. He obviously enjoys exploring the world of people, for individual birds often get in the habit of visiting yards and looking things over. His crest and tail are the barometers of his moods, always raising, lowering and bobbing. The name roadrunner comes from the bird's habit, observed many years ago, of racing along the road beside horses and early automobiles, apparently just for the fun of it. Roadrunners are independent, self-satisfied individualists. Occasionally they condescend to admitting that human beings share the desert with them—but only when they feel like it, on their terms, and in their own inimitable ways.

Inhabiting arid and semiarid regions from north central California, Utah, and Colorado south into Mexico, the roadrunner is obviously a bird that does very well in deserts. William A. Calder, working in conjunction with Knut Schmidt-Nielsen at Duke University, recently published the results of their research on this species. They found that roadrunners, in terms of metabolism, temperature regulation, and evaporation of water, are just normal, ordinary birds. Their urine concentrating abilities are no greater than those of the chicken. When temperatures become uncomfortable, they begin panting, and their respiration rate increases from twenty-nine breaths per minute to as high as 356. These scientists noted that the waste matter of the young is enclosed in a membranous sac. The adults feed one end of the chick, then wait briefly until a sac is voided at the other. The adult swallows the sac. This aids in nest hygiene, and since the fluid in the sac is less concentrated than that of the adult urine, the adult may gain small amounts of moisture from reprocessing the material. The roadrunner combines a moisture-filled diet of meat with water-conserving behavior, such as resting in shade during heat and hunting in the cooler parts of the day. And so he lives in the desert with aplomb.

Old wives' tales say he kills rattlesnakes by placing a ring of cholla joints about them and letting them starve, but the truth is much more remarkable. The bird feints and prances around the snake with wings outstretched, then dashes in, striking the snake's head with a sharp blow of its bill. If a snake represents the Evil before which Eve fell, then perhaps there is some psychological factor deep inside the human mind that feels a glimmer of revolted delight when a small, feathered, seemingly ill-equipped creature causes the downfall of the serpent, and then—gorily and primitively—proceeds to devour it as well! Nevertheless, the road-runner presents not only drama but a good deal of comedy in the desert. The Mexicans call him *paisano* or fellow countryman, and he is viewed with real affection by all desertophiles.

No animal appreciates the cholla as much as the pack rat, for whom the cactus often provides both room and board. Various species of these animals of the genus *Neotoma* are widespread, found in western North America from Northern Canada to Guatemala and ranging across the southern United States. They are known by other such common names as wood rats, cave rats, brush rats, mountain rats—but mainly as "pack rats," because they spend a great deal of their time packing things around, or "trade rats" because they often leave what they are carrying, "trading" it for something else they pick up in its place. They are often attracted by bright manmade objects and carry them off from cabins or camps, sometimes leaving a stick, pebble, or cactus joint behind simply because they cannot carry both. Wherever they live—in mountain, brush, cave, or wood—they use locally available materials for their house building. Several species inhabit various sections of our North American Desert. As an example, we will be discussing the white-throated wood rat which ranges over Arizona, New Mexico, parts of Texas, Utah, Colorado, southeastern California, and a large part of northern Mexico.

The white-throated wood rat is approximately twelve to fifteen inches in length, about five to seven inches of which is tail. Large males can weigh a half pound. The wood rat resembles the house rat except for its hair-covered tail. The animal is tannish on its back with white underparts and feet. It has rather large, rounded ears, and big dark eyes. A soft-looking, clean, shy creature, it is unfortunately saddled with the name "rat" and the connotation that word carries from the house rat, with whom it has little or nothing in common.

The pack rat (as it is more commonly known in this part of the country) is justly famous for the home it builds, a great mound of debris which the rat piles up over its rest chamber. Such mounds are usually constructed under shrubs, trees, or cacti, although they may lie inside small rocky caves or similar locations. The living quarters under the mound

Pack rat (*Courtesy of Arizona-Sonora Desert Museum*)

are at least partially below ground level; the rat either prepares this exca-
vation or uses a preformed cavity of some sort. Beneath the covering
mound is an open trench which forms the main part of the nest. From
this, there may be side tunnels beneath the ground which sometimes lead
up to the surface. Off the main trench is usually found the rat's bedroom
—a branch or pocket with a diameter of about eight inches, lined with
soft plant material. Inside the main entrance to the nest, a rather large
chamber often serves as the dining room. The protective mound of various materials is placed over this basement apartment and is honeycombed
with tunnels leading into the shelter beneath. In the larger mounds, some
of the tunnels may be also used for eating and food storage areas.

The mound itself is something to see, for it is often constructed primarily of joints of cholla and can attain gigantic proportions, three or
more feet high and several feet in diameter. One author has reported
accumulations of up to fifty bushels of material in some nests. In their

study of the white-throated wood rat, Charles T. Vorhies and Walter P. Taylor reported a partial count of the materials in one mound. It included over 4000 sticks from mesquite and catsclaw, 208 pieces of dried cow dung, cactus, and the skull of a fellow pack rat! Before dissection, this nest measured six feet by five feet, and fourteen inches in height. Strange objects are often reported in similar structures; everything from cigarette packages, to tobacco cans and false teeth. But even if composed only of sticks and the like, a mound is a first-class deterrent to such predators as coyotes, foxes, hawks, owls, and badgers. When also fortified with cholla joints, it is indeed a fortress. These animals live alone; each mound is constructed by a single individual. Small, clear runways lined with cholla afford entrance for the rat, but heartily discourage most predators. There may be two to six entrances into a mound, and along the sides of the aboveground trails to these entrances, the rat often arranges cholla joints and loose clumps of cactus spines. Radiating from the nest are well-worn trails that the rat follows in its nocturnal foraging. These often lead to cacti where the rat can rest, eat, or perhaps meet other rats during the breeding season.

Pack rats are almost wholly vegetarians. Not only that, in cholla and prickly pear country, they are to a large extent cactus-arians. In a study of pack rats in southern Arizona Vorhies and Taylor found that over a year's time, about 44 percent of the pack rat's diet consisted of cactus. Another 30 percent was of mesquite. Only 0.82 percent was animal matter and this included ants, beetles, and termites. In the driest times of year, cactus may constitute 90 percent of the diet—this cactus diet consisting mainly of cholla and prickly pear. The flesh of these plants is admittedly succulent and evidently nutritious, but to reach this the rat must first breach the spiny armor. This it does successfully, biting into the flesh between the spines, but even in watching one it is hard to determine how it manages.

Prickly pear pads would seem to be the easier of the two. Here the spines are not so closely set as in the chollas, but the small glochids are numerous and formidable. A start once made, however, the rat enlarges the hole and eats away. Their mouths do not seem to be especially toughened for this diet, nor are their soft feet, which carry them scurrying up and about the cactus plants and over the (to the human mind) murderous joints on the ground. To transport the cholla joints back to the nest for eating or building, the rat uses his mouth. A joint may be three or four inches in length. The rat grasps it in his teeth at the less spiny stem end,

Harris' ground squirrel eating a prickly pear (*M. W. Larson*)

holds it horizontally, or almost vertically, and carries it away. Or it may grasp a spine or spines and drag the joint backwards.

In studying the pack rat's physiology, Knut Schmidt-Nielsen made a comparison between the laboratory white rat and the pack rat in their ability to deal with the spiny cholla. He found that an experimental white rat, upon approaching a cholla joint, immediately became impaled on the spines. The animal's efforts to free itself were unsuccessful, and it became wild with pain. A pack rat, with the spines of a cholla joint experimentally placed in its leg, turned its head, broke the spines by biting them, and freed itself from the cholla joint without apparent agitation.

Schmidt-Nielsen also found that the pack rat needs a great deal of moisture. Yet it does not require drinking water, since its succulent cactus diet is about 90 percent water and its other food, fresh, green mesquite leaves and beans, also contains much moisture. When both were given the same diet of only dry food, the pack rat died sooner than the laboratory white rat. The pack rat can live on cactus while the white rat cannot;

in fact a white rat died sooner on a pure cactus diet (the spines had been removed) than it would have without any food at all. Its moisture-filled diet of a type of plant in little demand by other members of the desert community is one of the finest adaptations the pack rat has made to desert living.

Being crepuscular and nocturnal, pack rats largely avoid heat and consequent moisture stress, and their nests afford equitable microclimates. The mound itself provides shade and in addition the nest is almost always built around or under a plant like a mesquite tree, cholla, or prickly pear cactus, which also provides shade and some cooling. Schmidt-Nielsen found that temperatures in a nest did not exceed 31°C (approximately 88°F), although temperatures on the nearby open desert surface ranged as high as 75°C (167°F).

Although usually quite secure within its spiny home, the pack rat is troubled now and then by snakes which manage to enter. Its nest also plays host to a number of smaller creatures such as insects, spiders, and lizards. Outside its home, the pack rat is prey for a good many animals from coyotes to snakes and as such, represents a nutritious bridge from plant to animal food in the chain of desert life.

The young pack rats are usually born in litters of two. They are blind, naked, and helpless. When danger threatens, they cling tightly to their mother's teats and are carried away with her as she makes her escape. Even when dragged roughly and bounced over cholla stems, they retain their grip.

Certainly the pack rats' ability to live from birth onward and to eat among the cholla spines makes them some of the most interesting and least understandable of the desert animals. To the desert pack rat, however, spines are evidently a very important part of life. There is one pack rat who has lived in the tunnel at the Arizona Sonora Desert Museum for a number of years. Although he has a cozy, clean, cool den in the tunnel, is protected from all predators, and given an adequate and free diet, he is without cholla and evidently—in modern human terms—thereby disadvantaged. His den opens off another whose occupant is a porcupine. Lacking cholla joints, the pack rat has gathered the closest thing available—shed porcupine quills—and lined his den with these. I suspect he simply wished to fortify the periphery of his den with them, but his accommodations slant toward the center. The result is a bed of quills on which he rests, quite evidently satisfied.

chapter twelve

Reptiles

BY physical or behavioral adaptations, living things radiate outward to take advantage of whatever niches nature affords them. Some birds, such as the cactus wren, and some of the mammals, such as the pack rat, have found in the spiny cholla and similar plants valuable material to exploit for homes and—in the latter's case—for food also. It serves them well, but not perfectly, for some other animals have found ways of in turn exploiting them, even in the almost impregnable fortress in which they live. One of these is a snake, the racer.

This is *Masticophis flagellum*, which under the guise of several subspecies ranges from the Joshua tree country of the Mohave Desert, through the sagebrush country of the southern Great Basin Desert, to New Mexico and Texas, the Sonoran Desert, and out of the desert entirely. The subspecies have more than one color phase, the two most distinctive being a black and a red form (hence one often hears references to red racers and black racers). The racer in general is a large attractive snake: three, four, or exceptionally six feet long. It is active during the cooler parts of the day, unlike a good many desert snakes which are nocturnal. Particularly in the cool of an early summer morning, the racers can be seen moving swiftly and alertly through the desert. As their name suggests, these snakes are quick—they attain about eight

The same black racer entering the nest of another cactus wren in an organ pipe cactus (*M. W. Larson*)

Black racer looking for eggs in the nest of cactus wren in a cholla cactus (*M. W. Larson*)

miles per hour when pursued, and bite vigorously if picked up. Racers have a healthy appetite for rodents, lizards, other snakes, birds, and bird eggs and are able to climb plants like the cholla in order to consume the contents of birds' nests. Like the cholla residents themselves, the racers seem to move over cholla with impunity. Recently, we observed a racer moving about the desert going from one large cactus to another. It appeared to examine the heights of these plants from its terrestrial position, then finally ascended one of the cholla and there advanced upon the nest of a cactus wren. The bird owners fluttered and scolded from a short distance away, as they will do when they see snakes about. In this case the nest was empty. The snake departed and continued his search in other nearby cacti.

Another snake often seen on the desert during the early morning hours is the bull snake or gopher snake, *Pituophis melanoleucus*. Actually it enjoys a wide geographical range and fits into a variety of habitats. Its various subspecies range over much of the United States from the Pacific to the Atlantic, and are found from the seashore to at least a 9000 foot elevation. These reptiles grow to six feet—exceptionally eight feet— in length, and are light brown or cream color with an overlaying pattern of darker blotches. These snakes are fond of rodents which they kill by constriction, and are sometimes found in pack rat nests, where they may have been seeking either shelter or the original occupant. Probably snakes are the main predators that can breach the pack rat nest, being of a size and shape that could use the rat's entrance tunnels.

Like some other snakes, the gopher snakes have the disconcerting habit of vibrating the tip of their tail when alarmed. The sound, particularly if the snake is lying in dry leaves or brush, is alarmingly rattlesnake-like. The gopher snake forages during the day when desert temperatures are moderate, and becomes crepuscular and nocturnal when summer heat prevails. This seems to be the extent of its modification for desert living, except for perhaps a lighter color in the desert. As its range would suggest, the gopher is an exceedingly adaptable snake, found from mountain forest and chaparral to grassland and desert. It is also a good climber, reaching birds and their eggs in shrubs and trees; and a good digger, able to remove the earthen plugs some rodents place in the openings to their underground burrows. It will retreat underground to avoid extreme heat and cold, and is satisfied with a variety of food. (As we earlier noted, reptiles are already well adapted as a group for desert living with their water-conserving epidermis, carnivorous water-filled diet, ability (through behavior) to keep their temperature within an equitable range, and conservation of their resources through a lowered metabolism as their temperature approaches that of their environment during the winter months.)

A good many of the desert's other snakes are strictly nocturnal. Some, like the gopher snake, may emerge from hiding during the day in spring and early summer, but generally come out only at night when daytime temperatures are at their peak. Rattlesnakes will bask in the sunlight on early, warm, spring days, but in midsummer they will likely emerge from their retreats only at dawn, dusk, and during the night. Strange as it may seem, one of the best ways to observe desert snakes is to drive about at night, for these reptiles can be easily seen as they cross the open pavement and are often attracted to the dark black-top of a road for the warmth it has retained from the previous day's sun. This can be fatal to the snake but convenient for the human observer. In fact, a small fraternity of amateur collectors and herpetologists regularly drive the roads on summer nights to collect specimens or simply to see what's crawling. Certain species of desert snakes were thought to be very rare until herpetologists began collecting by automobile. In many cases, the snakes had been there all along, and it was only the experts who had been "rare" at the right places and times. The best roads for this kind of activity, however, are the old-fashioned, two-lane, slow-traffic kind, which are themselves becoming rather rare. Built-up highways with embankments, ditches, four or more lanes, and high speed traffic are, to say the least, discouraging to snakes and leisurely observers alike.

Rattlesnakes, of course, are not found exclusively in the desert, but are

Rattlesnake (*M. W. Larson*)

certainly plentiful there and are represented by a variety of species. A great deal of human interest centers on these animals, a good deal of it morbid and often with little actual knowledge on which to base it. There are four families of snakes whose venom makes them a potential danger to man. These are the Hydrophidae, or sea snakes; Viperidae, true vipers found in the Old World; Elapidae, such as the cobras and coral snakes (one of which is found in the Sonoran Desert); and the Crotalidae, which include the rattlesnakes, water moccasins, copperheads, and other snakes of both the Old and New World. Crotalids are known as pit vipers, due to the sensory depression or pit they possess between the eye and the nostril. This pit is well supplied with blood vessels and nerve endings and is a specialization for detecting, through their heat, the presence and location of nearby animals that may serve as prey or as dangers to be avoided.

The rattlesnakes are limited to the New World, being found in North,

Diamondback rattlesnake (*M. W. Larson*)

South, and Central America. They are renowned for their rattles, the only group to have evolved such a remarkable organ. Its purpose is considered to be protective—a warning device to frighten or notify predators or larger animals, such as grazers, of the snake's presence.

In addition, the rattlers are justly famous for their venom. The venom is produced by certain remodeled salivary glands which in these snakes have been converted to venom producers. Venom production is a specialization for obtaining food. Thus where some types of snakes constrict to kill prey, or others specialize in prey that cannot escape (such as eggs) the rattlers concentrate on killing theirs through the action of their venom. In locating the prey they are aided by their sensory pits. They are aided in tracking the dying but still somewhat mobile prey through the Jacobson's organs—chambers inside the mouth. The familiar forked tongue of the snake picks up odors from the environment and transfers these to the Jacobson's organs, which have sensory cells connected to the olfactory lobes of the brain. Thus the rattlesnake is able to track the prey to the point where it drops. Rattlesnakes, like other snakes, are capable of engulfing seemingly large objects, for their jaws are arranged with a "double hinge" feature at the back, allowing the lower jaw to be dropped greatly. Nor is this jaw rigid at the center; its two sides being connected at the center front only by muscle. These two features allow wide distention of the mouth, so that the snake can engulf prey of a larger diameter than its own body. Once swallowed, the prey is slowly dissolved by the snake's digestive enzymes, and in addition, the venom the rattlesnake injects into the animal also serves to break down the tissues of the prey.

The venom, produced by the glands located along the outer edge of each upper jaw, is conducted through ducts to the fangs in the upper jaw. The two fangs normally lie folded back against the upper jaw. As the snake opens its mouth widely to strike, the fangs are lowered until approximately perpendicular to the upper jaw or are even advanced slightly farther. The venom is forced through a hollow tube within the fang and is ejected into the object bitten through a hole near the tip of the fang. In effect the fangs are long, efficient, hypodermic needles, stabbing and envenomating at one and the same time.

It is obvious that the rattlesnakes are specialized to obtain prey in a particular way. They are highly efficient. In the desert they obtain a satisfactory livelihood, for the deserts in general support a goodly number of species of small mammals in large quantities. These in turn are able, often by rather extreme abilities (like those of the kangaroo rat), to survive and find sustenance in the plant life produced in the desert. So in the darkness of the summer desert night the rattlesnakes join the myriad animals that emerge in the coolness, and there they obtain the mice, rats, rabbits, and other such creatures on which they feed.

The rattlesnake will, of course, also use its bite for defense, and it is here that man—and fear—enter the picture. A rattlesnake bite is serious, and occasionally fatal. Laurence Klauber, author of a monumental two-volume work on rattlesnakes published in 1956, came to the conclusion that each year approximately 1000 rattlesnake bites occur in the United States. Of these, thirty cases are fatal. The resulting mortality rate from snakebite is about 0.02 per 100,000 population per year. In other words, the odds are excellent that you will never be bitten, and even if you are, the odds still greatly favor your recovery. Klauber lists the sixty-five species and subspecies of rattlesnakes which are found in North and South America. These vary widely in size and other characteristics. The severity of a rattlesnake bite to a human is dependent upon many factors: the species, the size, the virulence of the venom, the amount of venom received, the site of the bite, the physical condition and age of the person bitten, the care received, and other factors. Most interestingly, it has been found that a rattlesnake does not always inject venom when it strikes! This, however, you cannot depend upon.

Their venomous bites do not give rattlers complete immunity from enemies such as the roadrunner and the king snakes. None of these animals goes out of its way to kill a rattlesnake, as some stories would have you believe, but if hungry and faced with a moderate-size rattlesnake, they will probably eat it as readily as they would any other suitable thing that came along. The common king snake has a wide range over the southern and much of the mid-United States, as well as northern Mexico. It is an attractive creature, up to five feet in length, sometimes jet black, but more often black to brown. White or creamy crossbands on the dark background give it a banded appearance; some display merely light spotting. The subspecies and patterns are numerous, as are their habitats—from the everglades, to pines, grass, chaparral, and deserts. King snakes commonly feed on other snakes, killing them by constriction, but also indulge in lizards, amphibians, birds, and rodents. They are immune or practically so, to rattlesnake venom. Klauber reports experiments during which captive king snakes were offered rattlers to feed on. In subduing their prey, the king snakes were bitten numerous times, receiving sufficient venom to make a man 300 times their weight dangerously ill. The bites had no apparent effect. King snakes have died, however, after receiving large experimental doses of rattlesnake venom.

Rattlesnakes can recognize a characteristic odor in the skin of the king snakes and they display a characteristic behavior pattern when confronted by these predators. The rattler usually tries to retreat with his head and neck close to the ground. He arches the center part of his body and uses it, if possible, to deliver a heavy blow to the king snake. The king snake in turn attempts to seize the rattler with his mouth and throw several coils of his body about the rattler. The king snake then gradually works his mouth toward the rattler's head, during which process he may be bitten several times. This does not seem to deter him. He eventually swallows the rattler's head and, controlling its still somewhat active body by constriction, gradually consumes the rest until the rattles disappear. The rattler is usually not dead before it is swallowed. Klauber reports one king snake that disgorged a rattler it had been in the process of eating. The rattler was alive and evidently unhurt, although its neck had been well stretched and its anterior portions had spent a good ten minutes inside the king snake's stomach!

Some other snakes, too, show a degree of apparent immunity to rattlesnake venom. Klauber states that rattlers are resistant to their own venom, and only slightly less resistant to that of other species of rattlesnakes. In other words (all tall tales to the contrary) a rattler cannot commit suicide by biting himself. Other snakes such as the racers and indigo snakes are known to feed on rattlesnakes occasionally, and larger animals are also sometimes reported to kill and feed on them, including coyotes, badgers, eagles, and red-tailed hawks.

In saguaro country, the types of rattlesnake include the western diamond, blacktail, tiger, and Mohave rattlesnakes. Of these, the western diamond attains the largest size up to five-and-a-half feet, with one record of seven-and-a-half feet. Because of its size and the amount and potency of its venom, it is potentially quite dangerous. The tiger is a considerably smaller snake, only two to two-and-three-quarters feet long, but its venom seems to be more potent than that of the large western diamond. Of the rattlers in this desert range, the Mohave rattlesnake is considered to have the most highly potent and dangerous venom. This snake is from two to four feet long and is of an olive green or green-brown color on its back.

The tail is ringed with bands of black. The Mohave rattler covers a wide geographical range including parts of California, Nevada, Arizona, Sonora, and a number of central Mexican states. In parts of its range it is found up to 8000 feet elevation. We have found them too close for comfort near sea level, in sand dunes close to the head of the Gulf of California.

In considering the animals such as the rattlesnakes that are found in the saguaro forests, we do not mean to infer that these animals are restricted to this one rather typical, rich desert habitat. Certainly in almost every case, they are not. Thus the western diamond rattlesnake has a geographical range covering parts of Texas, New Mexico, Arizona, southeastern California, Sonora, and Mexican states in the Chihuahuan Desert. The tiger is limited to portions of Arizona and Sonora. And where

172

one species or subspecies of animal meets the limits of its range, a close relative or another creature which fills approximately the same niche in the community usually takes over. A look at common rattlesnake names gives you an idea—Grand Canyon rattlesnake, Great Basin rattlesnake, western pygmy rattlesnake, Mexican pygmy rattlesnake, southeastern pygmy rattlesnake; or with the sidewinder rattlesnakes—Mohave Desert sidewinder, Sonoran Desert sidewinder, Colorado Desert sidewinder. These sidewinders are special rattlesnakes which we will be discussing with some other reptiles which like the sidewinders, have a special affinity for sandy areas.

One other type of poisonous snake occurs in southwestern deserts: the Sonoran coral snake, which is of a different genus than the corals found in the southeastern United States. The coral snakes, like others included in their particular family (the cobras, kraits and mambas) have a potent neurotoxic venom dangerous to man. Unlike the rattlers, whose fangs are so long they must be folded back within the mouth, the corals and the members of their family have shorter, rigid, hollow poison fangs. Whereas one good stab is sufficient for a rattler to inject venom, the corals and their relatives may chew or bite several times to obtain best results. The Sonoran coral snake is a very small creature, approximately twelve to sixteen inches or occasionally up to twenty inches in length. Sporting bright rings of glossy black, yellow, and red, it is somewhat slender, with a slightly flattened head and body, a blunt snout, small eyes, and only a slight constriction between the head and body. The Sonoran corals have broad red bands bordered on each side by light-colored ones, and can be distinguished from the similarly colored Sonora mountain king snake (not the common king snake we have been discussing) by this arrangement. Three other species of snakes have the same colors in the same series as the coral, but the red bands completely encircle the body on the coral, whereas they do not do so on the other three snakes.

The Sonoran coral is seldom seen. It is secretive and unaggressive in its habits, and probably spends much of its time underground. Its food consists of small snakes and lizards. There are no published records of Sonoran coral snakes having bitten humans. This is no doubt due to their small size—including a small mouth—and their retiring habits. This coral is nonetheless a snake for which one should show all due respect for its potentialities.

The Sonoran coral snakes kept at the Arizona-Sonora Desert Museum

Leaf-nosed snake (*M. W. Larson*)

feed almost exclusively on worm snakes. These are strange, innocuous members of the snake group, brown to pink in color, and reach only nine to twelve inches in length and about 3/16 inch or less in diameter. They have merely vestigal eyes, and only a few teeth. There is no constriction between the head and body, and the snout is rounded and blunt, no doubt to assist the snake in its burrowing habits. The worm snakes live underground, burrowing efficiently in loose sand and soil. There they feed primarily on termites, ants, and ant pupae and larvae—with which the deserts are rather abundantly supplied. On warm summer nights they often appear aboveground and we (or more likely, our cats) often find them in our yard or in the nearby desert.

A variety of generally small snakes occurs in the deserts which like the worm snakes are rarely seen by the average desert resident. These are nocturnal reptiles, and since they pose no threat to man, they are not popularized like the coral snake and rattlers. Nevertheless, they are often quite lovely in their colors and patterns and fascinating in their habits. One member of this group, the lyre snake, is of a ground color with a slightly darker pattern—its name is derived from the shape of the pattern on the back of the head. It is two to three feet in length and active at night or early morning. It feeds on lizards and small rodents that it kills by means of venom delivered through grooved teeth at the rear of the mouth. Its venom must be "chewed" in. Due primarily to its rather ineffectual venom injection mechanism, this snake is not considered dangerous to man. A near relative, the spotted night snake, has saliva that is toxic to its prey but has only slight grooves on its rear teeth. This, again, is a small snake twelve to eighteen inches long, active at night or dusk, that feeds on small creatures like lizards.

Another small, interesting snake that emerges at night is the leaf-nosed snake. Twelve to twenty inches in length, generally a ground color with a pattern of darker blotches (although one species may be creamy or flesh-colored), this snake is adorned with a much enlarged rostral scale which covers the "nose" or front portion of the face. When the snake's head is viewed from above, this scale is triangular in shape, with the apex of the triangle pointing toward the top of the head, and the broad base tucked under the forefront of the upper jaw. This scale may be of value when the snake burrows in loose sand and soil from time to time. It appears to feed mainly on lizards and lizard eggs.

It is obvious that lizards come in for a good bit of wear and tear where the snakes are concerned. Lizards are among the most numerous of the desert inhabitants, present in far greater numbers than the snakes. A very few eat some plant materials, but most are carnivorous, living largely on the insects which are particularly plentiful at certain times of the year.

Eric R. Pianka of the University of Washington recently published an account of his studies on the ecological relationships of some common desert lizards. Four of these lizards are widespread and also occur in the saguaro forests: *Uta stansburiana,* the side-blotched lizard; *Crotaphytus wislizeni,* the leopard lizard; *Phrynosoma sp.,* the horned lizards; and *Cnemidophorus tigris,* the whiptail lizard. Let us survey briefly something of these lizards, and then return to Pianka's observations of their relationships.

The side-blotched lizard is found in all four North American Deserts, and it may occur in sandy, rocky, or gravelly places from below sea level in Death Valley to 7000 feet in the mountains. It is about two inches long, plus not quite that much tail. It is diurnal, and being small, warms quickly and may be active when larger lizards are not. It feeds on all sorts of small things from beetles to bees, scorpions to sowbugs. It is plentiful, and falls prey to a good many of the other desert animals.

Collared lizard (*M. W. Larson*)

The leopard lizard is approximately four inches in length, plus tail. It is generally grayish, with darker spots and whitish crossbars on the back, and capable of changing color from a lighter to a darker phase. In the light phase its darker spots are often quite prominent, hence the common name of "leopard." Leopard lizards also forage during the day. They are alert, wary, and pugnacious if captured. These lizards, too, feed on insects and the like, but also prey on other lizards including the aforementioned side-blotched and the western whiptail, next on our list.

The western whiptail is a streamlined, slim lizard two-and-a-half to four inches in length, plus a tail about two-and-a-half times as long as its body. Its back is of varying brownish, olive, and yellowish hues, arranged in a somewhat transverse striped pattern which adds to its sleek appearance. It is an exceedingly swift runner, appears to be nervous, and feeds on insects, spiders, scorpions, and termites. It may dig a burrow in the soil or dash down a tunnel belonging to another animal.

The last of these four ubiquitous types of the study is the horned lizard. These appear to be spiny lizards unfortunately mashed by a passing steam roller. They are, in fact, just naturally flattened lizards endowed with short flattened tails, a halo of sharp horns about the back of the head, and some rather sharp-pointed scales scattered over the back. They are of a ground color with a mottled pattern on the back. Flattened, usually resting quietly in place, slung low to the ground, and matching it well in color, horned lizards are models of protective coloration. They are docile, the most likable of all lizards, and affectionately known by small boys as "horned toads" or "horny toads." Horned they are, toads they are not. Due to their popularity as pets both in their natural range (and out of it through pet dealers) but their general failure to do well in captivity and the rate at which they were being exploited, the state of Arizona a number of years ago passed a law protecting them.

These members of the genus *Phrynosoma* are found from British Columbia to Guatemala, and range from the Pacific coast as far east as Arkansas. Common in the saguaro country is the regal horned lizard. This is a large species, up to six-and-a-half inches or more in total length. Its range is rather limited, and it is found only in Arizona and northern Mexico. The desert horned lizard is a slightly smaller species with a wider territory that covers parts of Oregon, Nevada, Utah, California, Arizona, Sonora, and Baja California. Other horned lizards include the coast, round-tailed, flat-tailed, short-horned, and Texas horned lizards—all of various ranges and sizes, but of basically similar appearance and habit. Horned lizards have the rather startling ability to squirt blood from their eyes when alarmed, probably as a defensive gesture. The blood is released by the rupturing of a sinus at the anterior corner of the eye, and a considerable amount may be projected, one-and-a-half feet or more! As a more practical protective measure, horned lizards readily bury themselves in loose sand by rapid lateral movements of their bodies. They also seek protection in rodent burrows or under stones. The sharp head spines are a protective measure deterring to some extent hungry snakes and other animals. That the spines do not always stop such predators is shown however by cases of dead snakes having been found with the horns of one of these lizards projecting through their sides.

Horned lizard; this one has just squirted blood from his eye (*M. W. Larson*)

Horned lizard and young (*M. W. Larson*)

The horned lizards display an interesting range of reproductive habits. Reptiles, as a group, represent an advance over the amphibians in that they produce an egg enclosed in a material that retards its desiccation— hence reptiles do not need to repair to water to lay their eggs. Amphibians generally still must do so. We find some horned lizards which lay eggs, and these require several weeks for their development. Other species of horned lizards (and other types of lizards and some snakes as well), how- ever, retain the eggs within the body of the female. These hatch just be- fore, during or shortly after laying. Retention of the eggs within the body would afford increased protection during this helpless phase of the rep- tile's life; those which retain the eggs are called *ovoviviparous.* Some lizards and snakes have gone even farther: they have a placenta-like ar- rangement between the mother and the young. But even in these, the yolk is still present and is the main source of nourishment, unlike the case in mammals. The night lizards, genus *Xantusia,* which we will consider later, have this latter arrangement between mother and developing young.

Returning to Pianka's study, we learn that the small side-blotched liz- ard and the larger leopard lizard exploit their environment by a process of "sit and wait"—sitting under shrubs and waiting for food to wander by, at which time they advance upon it. The smaller lizard goes after the smaller insects; the larger lizard after the larger insects and lizards also. The whiptail, on the other hand, hunts actively, being rather constantly and nervously on the move: digging, pausing, or climbing. Pianka says its exploitation of the environment is more like that of a bird than a "typical" lizard. The horned lizards have developed a food specialization —ants—and have a body well developed for this specialization. They will also eat other small creatures, but obviously have a fondness for the ants which are abundant, but are a food item little in demand by other animals.

We have had pet horned lizards which we fed by herding them about anthills. Some of the desert ants are nothing a human cares to become deeply involved with, for they are well endowed with stings. One type of these—a large black harvester—was a favorite food of one of our pets. The lizard simply flicked out his tongue among the milling ants, as quickly pulled the tongue back in, and swallowed each ant, evidently before it had an opportunity to do anything about the situation. With what seemed like—anthropomorphically—almost audible gulps and a pleased expression, he ate 63 in thirty minutes.

Pianka concludes that horned lizards have a large stomach in proportion to their body, which allows them to eat quantities of ants at one sitting (this may be necessary since a large percentage of the ant's body consists of an indigestible chitinous covering). The horned lizard is able to stay out near sunny anthills due to its relaxed thermoregulation, which permits it to undergo a higher variance in body temperature than the other lizards in this study. In addition protective coloration and horns help protect it from predators while it hunts in open areas.

There is another way to divide the environment besides horizontally—that is, vertically. We have been surveying a very few of the lizards that live on the ground. Other lizards take advantage of the upper levels of the desert, by means of its vegetation. One of these is the desert spiny lizard, *Sceloporus magister*. This lizard, too, Pianka found, has a sit-and-wait attitude but often carries it out by perching on the side of a tree, yucca, or similar plant. Here it waits, head down, surveying and obtaining its insect food from the ground area immediately below it. This technique is carried even further by a small lizard which does not occur in the saguaro forests, but rather is limited to southern Nevada, southeastern California, northeastern Baja California, western Arizona, and northwestern Sonora. This is the long-tailed brush lizard *Urosaurus graciosus*. It is a small lizard with about two inches of body length but with a tail twice as long; is gray or beige, and slender. This lizard is almost completely arboreal, spending its time in shrubs or trees, most often in creosote bush. Here the lizard aligns itself with a branch, the body flat against it, the tail sometimes appearing to be a twig connected to the branch. (Here it sleeps also.) It can alter its color to harmonize with the background. If startled it may shift to the opposite side of the branch or drop to a lower branch or to the ground. Occasionally it will descend to the ground to move to a new plant or to hibernate, but is essentially arboreal, and there obtains its insect food.

There is yet another way in which the resources of the environment can be divided—that is, between night and day. Most lizards are diurnal. One of the few nocturnal exceptions is the small, delicate-looking gecko. The western banded gecko occurs in southern Nevada, southeastern California, western and southern Arizona, and portions of Lower California and Sonora. Further east, its place is taken by the Texas banded gecko. These lizards are approximately two-and-a-half to three inches, not counting the tail. They are flesh-colored, creamy, or yellowish with brown crossbands

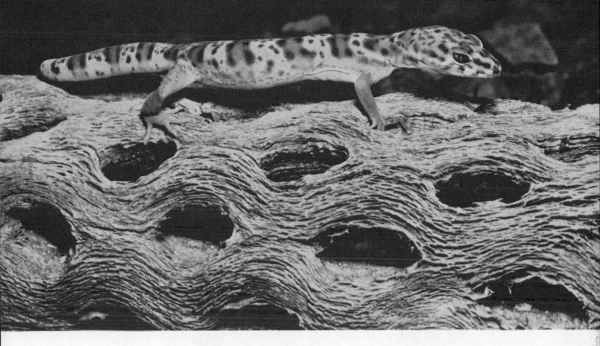

Gecko (*M. W. Larson*)

on the back of the body and tail. Their thin skin is easily torn. They have a soft, almost velvety appearance which in addition to their light color makes these lizards appear almost translucent. They sometimes carry their tail curled up over the back or held to one side.

This lizard (as is the case with most, but not all, lizards) is capable of easily losing its tail—as to a predator who grabs the disposable end—and of then growing a new one in its place. This ability often allows a lizard to make good its escape while the predator remains fascinated and fooled by the wildly twitching tail. Lizards possessing this ability have a preset point for the separation of tail from owner. At that location, there is a crack in the vertebra, and the muscles are arranged for an easy parting.

The geckos live under and among the rocks and under plant material. At night they emerge and may sometimes be seen on the roads after dark. These lizards and their soft-shelled eggs form tasty treats for a good many reptiles. The geckos themselves feed on small insects and spiders. These lizards are particularly noted for their ability to emit a noise. They are

Gila monster (*M. W. Larson*)

the only lizards which have a voice—they make a small, squeaking sound. They are, all in all, most improbable lizards.

The creature that stands at the opposite extreme in the lizard group is neither small nor delicate, but improbable, too, in its own way. That is the Gila monster, the only poisonous lizard in the United States and one of the two poisonous ones in the world. Gila is the name of an important Arizona river, a woodpecker, and the name of the first white child born in what was later to be Arizona—his mother was floating down the Gila River on a raft at the time (or perhaps the raft was tied along the bank—at any rate the child was so christened). For the lizard, "Gila" was combined with the descriptive term "monster," and so we have one of our most colorful common reptile names.

The Gila monster is a large lizard. Exceptional specimens reach two feet in length, including tail. The body is almost cylindrical, the head more flattened, with a rounded snout. The legs are short and appear to be set too far apart to support the long, heavy body. Its strangely formed dorsal scales bear a close resemblance to Indian beadwork. The animal's colors are equally decorative—a most irregular pattern of spots, bars, and dots of orange, buff, or salmon in combination with blackish-brown. The blunt, thick tail usually displays definite bands of light and dark colors, and the sides of the face and the feet are primarily dark. In this species, the tail is used as a storehouse for fat which the lizard lives on during hibernation.

Add to this bizarre appearance the fact that the creature is venomous, and you can understand how the nickname "monster" originated. Actually, the Gila monster is to all intents and purposes quite a gentleman, for the most part going his own way unobtrusively. This lizard remains hidden much of the year in pack rat nests, in rodent burrows, under rocks, and in similar locations; and is most frequently seen in midsummer, when it is active from dusk to dawn. The Gila's range is limited to Arizona, northwestern Mexico, and very small parts of southern Nevada and extreme southwestern Utah and New Mexico. Its food consists of rodents, fledgling birds, and small mammals. Apparently eggs are one of its favorite foods, for captive lizards do well on a diet of raw chicken eggs.

The Gila monster does not have a highly refined means of envenoming its prey or enemies, as the rattlesnakes do. The lizard's neurotoxic venom is produced by glands located at the sides of the lower jaws. These empty their poison along the outer side of the lower anterior teeth, which are nearly concealed by the gums. The teeth of both the upper and lower jaws have grooves in them. In biting, the Gila monster clamps onto its prey and chews, working into the wound whatever venom has managed to seep into the grooves of its teeth.

There are no records in Arizona of any healthy human beings dying from the bite of a Gila monster. These animals are usually rather sluggish, although they can move quickly if provoked or alarmed. They must get a grip and chew on a person before doing any damage, and this is not easy unless they can clamp onto a finger, hand, or toe. They cannot strike like a rattlesnake, which can direct its bite to any part of the human body. Seldom seen and unaggressive, they pose no serious threat to the hiker who uses common sense and a little caution in the desert, as he should where rattlesnakes and even cactus spines are concerned. Gila monsters are actually protected by Arizona law. They cannot be killed, possessed, sold, given, or exchanged by any group or individual without written permission from the Arizona Game and Fish Commission. This specific statute, which protects the horned lizards as well, was passed in 1952. It must represent some sort of milestone, for *Homo sapiens* does little enough to save that which is beautiful or useful or economically valuable in nature. The Gila monster is interesting and colorful, but not exactly beautiful. It is useful in nature's schemes, but not directly and obviously useful to man. It is economically valuable perhaps only from the Chamber of Commerce viewpoint (and this is open to some question) or from a collector's viewpoint, if it were to be exploited. Basically—and importantly—the Gila monster has been protected for its intrinsic value, and this in spite of the fact that it is both a reptile and venomous.

The only other poisonous lizard in the world is the Mexican beaded lizard, the second member of the Gila monster genus. Very much like the Gila monster, the beaded lizard attains a slightly larger size. The head is usually all black and the body color is predominantly black or dark brown with scattered blotches of yellow, rather than the richer salmon shades characteristic of the Gila monster. Not a desert dweller, the Mexican beaded lizard occurs along the west coast of Mexico as far north as the southern part of the state of Sonora—which represents the approximate southern limits of both the Gila monster and the Sonoran Desert.

It appears that even the scientists were inspired to give showy names to the Gila monster and its Mexican cousin, although their enthusiasm is cloaked in Latin. The beaded lizard is *Heloderma horridum,* the Gila monster *Heloderma suspectum. Heloderma* breaks down into "nail-skinned," and *suspectum* means "to be regarded with awe" or "suspect," *horridum* is self-explanatory.

One expects snakes and lizards in the desert, but not turtles; yet two species belonging to the order Testudinata—that of the turtles—are represented in the North American Desert. These are the land tortoises, a subfamily within the turtle order whose members have adapted to life on land and who seldom enter the water. The desert tortoise, *Gopherus agassizi,* is present in the saguaro forests and in other parts of the desert, including some very arid sections. It ranges over the western portion of Arizona, much of the state of Sonora, southeastern California, and small areas of southern Nevada and Utah. Another similar species occurs in southwestern Texas and northeastern Mexico.

As a group, turtles have been wearing their shells for the last 175

Desert tortoise (*M. W. Larson*)

million years, proving that nature's better experiments are not soon forgotten. The shell certainly has its drawbacks in terms of weight and limited maneuverability, but it serves the desert tortoise well in its desert environment. His shell has two parts: an upper section known as the carapace, and a lower called the plastron. The two are joined by a bridge on each side. Both sections are composed of fused plates of bone, over which is laid a cover of hard shields arranged in a definite pattern. The desert tortoise's dome-shaped, yellowish-brown carapace is approximately thirteen inches in length and eight inches wide. Each shield exhibits a pattern of geometric lines as a record of previous growth. When disturbed, the desert tortoise withdraws its head and legs into the perimeter of the shell. He cannot close his shell about himself, however, as is the case with some turtles, and where portions of his legs remain exposed between the two shell portions, they are covered by hard, heavy, protective scales. His legs and feet resemble those of a miniature elephant, stocky and club-shaped, and adorned with projecting nails. When walking, the tortoise appears to go on tip-toe on the front feet, the weight falling on the nails. The round, flat bases of the back feet are placed squarely on the ground. His head is typically turtle-like in appearance, with small eyes. The tortoise has no teeth; its jaws are simply covered with a horny sheath.

Desert tortoises are vegetarians, spending a good deal of their time grazing on a variety of plants such as grasses and annuals. In summer, they are particularly active in the early morning and late afternoon. When daytime temperatures reach high levels, they may become mainly nocturnal. In order to escape the midday heat, the tortoise digs a burrow three to four feet in length that slants downward at a 20 degree to 40 degree angle. While digging such a burrow, one tortoise reportedly excavated the dirt with his front feet and pushed it out of the burrow opening by using the front of his shell as a bulldozer. A tortoise may have several such holes in its territory, which may cover anywhere from ten to one hundred acres. For winter hibernation, the tortoises prepare more permanent retreats known as dens— horizontal tunnels often excavated in the bank of a desert wash to a length of eight to thirty feet. Often a number of tortoises spend the winter months together; as many as seventeen have been reported holed up in one den. Once dug, these retreats are used year after year.

During its active summer, the tortoise stores within its body the fat that will provide the energy and the metabolic water necessary to sustain it through its hibernation period. The tortoise also appears to be the only desert animal which can store water in a fashion reminiscent of the cactus. It has a large, bilobed urinary bladder where it retains sizable amounts of nearly pure water. Wastes in the bladder, mainly uric acid, are deposited in granular form and thus can be held in the body for long periods. Only occasionally does the water reserve need to be used for elimination. A freshly caught tortoise frequently voids its bladder, and whether or not this bothers the reptile's natural predators, it does discourage a good many human captors. However, it has been suggested that this liquid might be a possible water source for a desperate person in the desert!

Tortoises do not become sexually mature until twelve to twenty years old. In the spring or early summer, the females lay between two and nine eggs which are buried three or four inches below the ground surface. When the eggs hatch in the fall, the young tortoises are approximately one-and-a-half inches in length. Their shells are soft and will not become completely hardened for about five or six years, by which time the tortoises are about four inches long. No doubt the young fall prey to a good many animals during this relatively defenseless stage.

The adult tortoises, however, are remarkably well-adapted to desert living. Their shell and armored skin are excellent means of protection against moisture loss and animal attack. The tortoise is able to take advantage of plants growing out in the open and has no need to be secretive. Its plant food provides much moisture, only a little of which is lost in elimination of waste products. Retiring to burrows during the heat of the day, the tortoise guards against overheating. It also serves to reduce water loss through respiration, for as in the case of rodent burrows, a higher level of relative humidity prevails within the burrow than in the outside air. Although they can go for long periods without drinking, tortoises often drink freely whenever they have the opportunity. It has been found that a tortoise can drink 41 percent of its body weight in water in a single drinking period! Lastly, the tortoises' secluded winter dens provide stabilized temperatures; temperature fluctuations were found to cease at approximately seventeen-and-a-half feet inside a den.

By pulling in its head and legs when startled or attacked and holding its legs rigidly in place, the tortoise can foil most of its predators. Coyotes, bobcats, and badgers may at times kill them. Mexicans and Indians have been reported as eating them, and the Anglo may take them home as pets, where they often die. If they escape, they are often run over by cars or fail to find an area in which they can support themselves. They are now wisely protected by California law.

The tortoise dens are popular with a number of other desert animals which take advantage of the microclimate within these excavations. Angus M. Woodbury and Ross Hardy carried out a detailed study of the desert tortoise and listed some of its houseguests: ant lions, beetle larvae, silverfish, spiders, ticks, fleas, geckos, desert scaly lizards, spotted night snakes, rattlesnakes, cottontail rabbits, burrowing owls, roadrunners, quail, and mice. The tortoise, though, is anything but thin-skinned and probably is little bothered by most of these—except for perhaps the ticks. So calm is he in fact, and so long does he rest, that mold has been found growing on some tortoises in humid dens.

There is one creature that often moves into these dens, however, that must severely try the patience of even the tortoise. This roommate is the pack rat. A tortoise den provides a perfect cave for a pack rat, and these litter-happy creatures often make their nests and imposing collections of debris in the entrances or deeper within these dens. Woodbury and Hardy found that in several instances, tortoises had been completely covered with the pack rat's debris while taking their long winter sleep. It is easy to imagine a quaking and crumbling rat house on a warm spring day, with a sleepy, dinosaurish, Disney-like tortoise emerging through it, expressing his feelings about guests who overstep the bounds of propriety.

chapter thirteen

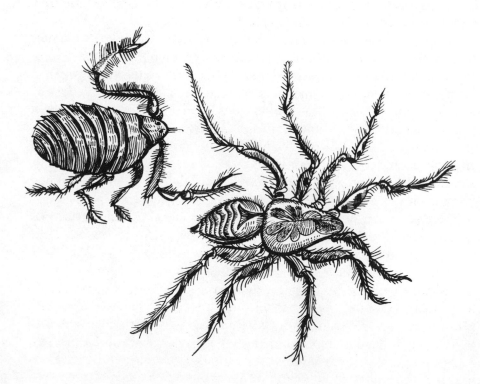

Insects and Other Arthropods

THE nicest time of year in the desert's saguaro forests is July. This, of course, depends somewhat on your viewpoint—a good many people feel that all of June, July, and August is a good time to leave the desert. June tends to be long, hot and exceedingly dry, but in July the summer rains arrive. They seldom make it by the Fourth of July, but usually do so by mid-month. Before any moisture actually falls, several days are passed in preparation: white, voluminous clouds build up over the mountains each afternoon, becoming heavier, darker, increasingly widespread, and more pregnant with each passing day. Finally the rains arrive, usually accompanied by impressive lightning and awesome thunder.

The desert comes to life. For many of the desert plants and animals this is really their spring. It is the time when both moisture and warmth are present together. Plants prosper, and so in turn do the animals. Particularly is this true for the insects and other arthropods. Beetles, moths, and other insects flock to the porch lights. Impressive palo verde wood borers—three inch long, black beetles with exceedingly long antennae—come zooming and land with a thud on the ground under the lights; their larval stage on the roots of the paloverde trees completed, the reproductive stage now about to begin. Out in the darkness of the desert, scorpions, centipedes, tarantulas, and an unnumbered group of other small creatures

189

These clouds build up over mountains in the Sonoran Desert just prior to the annual rainfall in July and August (*M. W. Larson*)

Sun spider (*M. W. Larson*)

Cactus beetle (*M. W. Larson*)

pursue their hunting, eating, and procreative activities. By day others of these small creatures shift into high gear, to make the best use of this brief favorable period. It is an interesting time.

Of the very small things that crawl in the desert by night, best-known, least-liked, and most often feared, are the scorpions. Even if they could care—which they certainly cannot—it is doubtful if scorpions would be at all concerned about any human opinion. To them, human beings would be but another creature dominating the earth, and perhaps destined to go the way of the dinosaurs—whom the scorpion family line watched both advancing and retreating. In fact, the ancestors of the scorpions (and these ancestors looked about the same as their descendants of today) date back an impressive 400,000,000 years! It is not by brain power that they have endured, however, for they are little endowed in that regard.

Scorpions are not insects, but arachnids. They have four pairs of legs (insects have three), large pincerended pedipalpi (appendages that originate at each side of the mouth), and a long, very thin postabdomen carried curled over the body and bearing a sharp terminal poison claw. The base of this sting is enlarged and contains a pair of poison glands which open near the tip of the sting. In stinging, the "tail" is flashed forward over the body and the prey stabbed. In obtaining food, prey is grasped by the crab-like pincers of the pedipalpi, and stung. The chelicerae, a pair of short appendages above the base of the pedipalpi, mash and shred it. Digestive enzymes produced by glands in the first two pairs of legs are injected into the torn flesh, which is liquefied and pumped into the mouth of the scorpion. Further digestion of the material takes place within the body.

Scorpions have eyes, but probably can only perceive the difference between light and dark. A pair of comb-like structures on the underside of the abdomen are probably tactile sensory organs, as are the fine hairs on their pincers. Scorpions are loners except at the brief mating time when male and female meet, join pincers, rub "tails," and move to and fro in a kind of dance. After mating, the female often eats the male unless he manages to make good his escape. The fertilized eggs develop inside her body, and the large numbers of young are born alive. They are delivered in thin sacks which they soon break through, and they clamber up on their mother's back for an extended piggyback ride, often completely covering the surface. At birth, the tiny scorpions are light-colored miniature replicas of their parents. Their midgut is filled with embryonic yolk

Tailless whip scorpion with prey (*M. W. Larson*)

which supplies their food for some time. They have their first molt while still on their mother's back, and when their inner food supply is depleted, they drop off and strike out on their own. Only during mating and baby-hood do scorpions tolerate any proximity to one another—except when one occasionally makes a meal of his neighbor. This latter catastrophe occurs readily enough, at least in captivity. Left overnight, two scorpions in the same container often condense into one well-fed scorpion.

In all the world, there are more than 700 recognized species of scorpions, varying in size from one-half-inch to almost seven inches in length. The state of Arizona alone hosts more than twenty species. All scorpions

Scorpion with young on her back (*M. W. Larson*)

are somewhat venomous, but only a few species are potentially dangerous to man. In the North American Desert, the only so-called "deadly" scorpions are *Centruroides sculpturatus* and *C. gertschi*. These thin, two-inch, yellowish-tan scorpions do not share the fearsome appearance of the large hairy scorpion, *Hadrurus arizonensis,* which reaches a length of three inches or more. But the hairy scorpion's sting is similar to that of a wasp or bee and causes only local pain and swelling (according to those unlucky enough to have experienced it). *C. sculpturatus* and *C. gertschi,* however, inject a neurotoxic venom which affects the entire body and can reportedly cause convulsions and cardiac or respiratory difficulties. Reaction to a sting varies greatly. A healthy adult member of our family and a friend have both been stung by *Centruroides,* and neither suffered much beyond a mild upset lasting a few hours. Nevertheless, these small scorpions should definitely not be underestimated. Their stings can be fatal to the very young, the aged, or those in poor health. Between 1935 and 1949, the state of Arizona reported fifty-four deaths caused by scorpion stings. Since then, there have been only nine. Antivenom is now available; and no doubt the greater use of insecticides, particularly in suburban desert homes, has considerably reduced the scorpion menace in homes and yards.

Scorpions normally live in small burrows they dig or under rocks and debris in the desert. In slightly higher elevations, they often hide under the bark of trees; in fact, the dangerous *Centruroides* is sometimes known as a bark scorpion. When exploring in the desert and surrounding terri-

Black widow spider (*M. W. Larson*)

Wolf spider, showing six of its eight eyes (*M. W. Larson*)

tory, the wise human never puts his fingers under rocks or bark without looking first.

Another impressive inhabitant of the saguaro forests and other habitats is the centipede. *Scolopendra heros,* the desert centipede, emerges from under rocks or similar hideaways to prowl the desert floor for the insects on which it feeds. This is a large creature reaching six to eight inches in length. The head bears two long antennae, and the mouthparts consist of a pair of mandibles and two pairs of maxillae. The body of the centipede, dependent on species, is made up of fifteen to 173 somites, or segments. The first of these bears a pair of poison fangs. All the others (except the final two) each have a pair of legs. Centipedes obtain their prey by injecting it with poison through their poison claws, after which

A female wolf spider carrying young on her back (*M. W. Larson*)

they chew it with the mandibles. The bite of this desert centipede can be painful to man, but usually causes only local swelling. Contrary to some stories, its many legs are not poison-tipped.

The wolf spider is a miniature ogre that roams the desert on summer nights. Certain parts of the desert, including the saguaro country, are spotted here and there with small nickel-sized holes that seem to drop straight down into the ground. Around each of these holes is built a low turret composed of bits of plant debris, pebbles, and similar materials. At the bottom of the tube, as much as a foot or more below the surface, dwells the wolf spider. He is small—only about an inch across—but has long legs, eight eyes, and a covering of hoary hairs of various shaggy lengths. This miniature predator spins no silky webs to trap his prey;

nor does he need any for he simply emerges at night to dash after any proper-sized insect that passes by. Female spiders carry the young on their back for a period after hatching, as do the scorpions.

Misnamed and often misunderstood is the tarantula, the largest spider of the desert. Hairy and dark brown or black, these spiders may have a legspan of six or seven inches; the body alone of a heavy female may weigh two-thirds of an ounce. Actually the name *tarantula* rightly belongs to a wolf spider of southern Europe, named after the city of Taranto, Italy. Supposedly long ago the bite of this European spider caused fainting, trembling, weeping, dancing, and crying; ending sometimes in death, sometimes in relief. The antidote was music, to which the sufferer danced and in so doing sometimes forced out the venom. Scientifically, the venom is nothing. Explanations of the "disease" vary from nervous disorders to a heathen religious rite (masked with the spider excuse to prevent persecution by believers in the more accepted Christianity). The erroneous name "tarantula," however, is now a firmly entrenched one for the large American spiders.

These tarantulas are not restricted to the deserts. There are approximately thirty species of tarantulas in the United States, although their eastern limit is the Mississippi River. They are especially plentiful in the Southwest. Tarantulas dig their own burrows or appropriate old rodent burrows. They are home-loving, hunting within a small area about their burrow and retreating into it if possible when danger threatens. Tarantulas primarily hunt insects and other arthropods, although in captivity they will also kill and eat larger animals as mice and lizards—so these may occasionally be taken in the wild. They spring on their prey and strike with their fangs, injecting venom. Digestive juices are poured into openings in the body of the prey, which is thus liquefied and drawn into the mouth of the spider.

These spiders are amazingly long-lived, not reaching sexual maturity until about ten years of age. Male tarantulas often do not last long after that because of their mates' cannibalistic habits. Males also easily fall prey to other creatures in their search for females, who have been reported as living to the venerable age of twenty-five years!

In the hot summer, tarantulas often hunt by night. If in the vicinity of a house, they may approach areas where insects are drawn by an outside light. They can also be seen moving along roads in the beams of a car's headlights. In mid or late summer, large numbers of them are some-

Tarantula (*M. W. Larson*)

times seen singly by a person driving some distance as these spiders are crossing the road during the day. We have seen them following a summer rain while the heat was somewhat dissipated and the sky still cloudy. These travelling tarantulas were probably all males searching for the stay-at-home females.

Before beginning his search, the male fills his palpi (portions of a pair of appendages on the spider's head) with spermatic fluid he has deposited in a small web. In mating the male transfers the sperm from his palpal organs to the female's epigynum, located at the opening to her internal reproductive organs, where she will store it. The female then spins a large sheet of silk in her burrow and on this deposits her fertilized eggs. She places another silken layer over them, and the two edges are bound together forming a bag. She will watch over this sac for approximately six

Tarantula hawk bringing a paralyzed tarantula into a burrow (*M. W. Larson*)

weeks, sometimes bringing it close to the burrow entrance, presumably to warm it. Upon hatching, the young remain in the burrow for a time and then leave to establish their own burrows.

In spite of a good deal of opinion to the contrary, no species of tarantula found in the United States has a bite dangerous to man. The spider can produce a painful wound, but the poison is not dangerous. These big spiders are mild-mannered, and if kept as pets, will often crawl about over their captor's hands and arms without biting.

Tarantulas are eaten by rodents, birds, lizards, and some snakes. If startled, the tarantula will tilt its body backward, elevating its head to show its fangs in a defensive attitude, or it may elevate its abdomen and stroke its sides with its hind legs. This latter action sprays loose a cloud of very fine abdominal hairs which are highly irritating if they come in contact with the eyes or mucous membranes of small mammals. The diversion may allow the tarantula sufficient respite in which to escape.

Among its more serious enemies is the tarantula hawk, which is neither spider nor bird, but a wasp of the genus *Pepsis*. Of all the solitary wasps that are common in the desert, the tarantula hawks are probably the most impressive. There are several species of these large wasps, some as much as an inch-and-a-half long, all of a striking blue-black metallic color with a bright, fiery red sometimes present on the wings. Females lay eggs from which emerge worm-like larvae or grubs that eat and pupate before finally emerging as adult wasps. Tarantula hawks secure trapdoor spiders or tarantulas as future "baby food." The female wasp cruises about the desert until she locates a tarantula who has temporarily left its burrow, preferably a female, since they are heavier-bodied. Approaching the spider, she usually grabs one of its legs with her mouthparts and proceeds to sting the tarantula's body. Very shortly afterwards the spider becomes paralyzed. The wasp then drags the heavy body into a cavity in the soil, lays a single egg upon it, emerges from the hole, and fills in its entrance with dirt.

Underground, the tarantula is paralyzed, but not dead. Eventually the wasp larva will emerge from the egg and begin to feed on the still living (but soon to die) tarantula. In this unique manner the tarantula hawk—and other wasps which use the same successful formula with other spiders

Praying Mantis (*Lane Larson*)

Cicada (*M. W. Larson*)

Creosote bush lac scales, attended by ants who "harvest" the reddish lac (*M. W. Larson*)

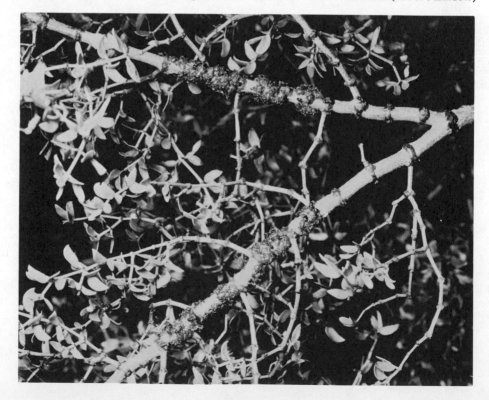

—are able to provide in advance fresh meat for the young they will never see or further provide for.

The desert abounds with other interesting insects. The mantids wait in a prayerful pose for the insects on which they feed. The larva of the ant lion lies at the bottom of its funnel-shaped depression in the sand, ready to kill and suck dry any ant or other tiny creature which falls in and cannot scramble up the crumbling, sandy walls. Male cicadas sing their continuous, shrill songs in the desert heat, while the cicada killer (another solitary wasp) goes about paralyzing them as food for her future young. On the creosote bushes of some regions, a tiny insect known as the creosote bush lac scale surrounds itself with a clear, reddish lac that the Indians once used for mending pottery. Solitary bees stock their underground larders with a combination of pollen and nectar on which they lay their eggs and on which their young will eventually feed. Velvet "ants" hurry about, fuzzy, often brightly colored, and wingless. These are actually yet another species of solitary wasp thought to be parasitic in the nests of ground-dwelling wasps and bees; only the males have wings.

It would be impossible to honor any one insect as being the best adapted to desert life, but in any such competition, the ants would be among the top contenders. Ants are newcomers compared to the ancient scorpions, but old-timers when compared to man. Two recently discovered fossil ants are considered to have lived 100 million years ago! Since then, ants as a group have traveled around the world and have adapted to almost every environment. In the beginning, ants were hunters, living on animal prey, and many species remain so today. Outstanding examples are the army ants of the tropics. Although blind, these insects have a keen sense of smell and hunt in large numbers. They have no permanent homes, being rather constantly on the move, and living in the largest colonies of any ant, one African species having colonies of 20 million individuals. Other groups use the sweet exudates of plants or of certain homopterans (small insects with sucking mouthparts feeding on plants) for their food. Some grow their own—a fungus—deep underground. Others harvest seeds.

In the deserts the harvesters have prospered. Insect hunting can be precarious during parts of the year in the desert; nor can this food be stored in times of plenty for times of want. Seeds are plentiful; they are also storable. From a meat to a vegetable diet is a radical change, and it must have been a very hungry or a very unusual ant that first made the switch.

Walking stick, one of the classic examples of insect camouflage (*M. W. Larson*)

Army ants returning from a raid with booty, the young of another ant colony (*M. W. Larson*)

Leaf-cutting ant carrying seed (*M. W. Larson*)

The harvesters still use some insect food, not bypassing a tasty termite or other tidbit that comes along, but by and large these ants are reapers, not hunters.

When the summer rainy season begins in the Sonoran Desert, winged ants stage their nuptial flights. This is the means whereby new colonies are established. Man cannot say definitely just what dictates when these demonstrations will take place, but temperature and humidity factors are evidently important. In most ants the male and female reproductive forms are winged. They emerge from their nest, mill about, and fly away. These forms fly from different nests of the same species in an area at the same time, effecting cross fertilization. Following mating, the males soon die; but life for the females is just beginning, if they are successful in avoiding predators, which are numerous.

A female loses her wings, secludes herself in a small hole in the soil, under a rock, or in a similar location. There she lays her eggs and tends them and the resulting larvae; in most species without venturing outside. The large muscles that moved her wings are no longer needed and are broken down within her body to provide the nutrients for her and for the larvae, which she feeds by regurgitation. Eventually the young—all females—having undergone their larval and pupal stages, emerge as adults. These are sterile workers who will carry out the duties of the nest, leaving the queen-mother to produce all the eggs and hence future members of the colony. Once the colony has reached a certain size and prosperity, it too will produce winged reproductive forms.

The harvesters live in the soil. Their nests are often very obvious, for they build a crater of small gravel about the entrances. Beyond this they may keep the ground quite clear of plant material in a large circular area. There is often a ring of chaff about the outer perimeter of the crater, this consisting of husks and waste material from the seed supply stored underground. Some of the harvesters have special workers different in form, known as soldiers, with greatly enlarged jaws and heads. The big heads enclose the muscles, needed to move the large jaws. The jaws may serve a dual purpose with emphasis on one or the other dependent upon species —the owners may protect their colony with their heavy jaws, or use them for breaking and working with the seeds.

Some harvesters develop very large colonies—some are estimated to consist of as many as 90,000 individuals. In various chambers of their underground nests, they store the supply of seeds gathered from the soil

Novomessor colony showing workers, larvae, and naked pupae (other species' larvae spin cocoons) (*M. W. Larson*)

Harvester ant nest (*M. W. Larson*)

Pheidole soldier and worker on stored grain (*M. W. Larson*)

and the plants around the nest. If you dig into such a nest, you will find several of these caches of seeds, sometimes a half cup or so in each. An ant allows saliva to flow out on a piece of seed, works it with her mouthparts, finally reduces it mainly to liquid, and imbibes it. This goes into her crop. She may allow it to continue on into her digestive system, or she may regurgitate it, feeding it to the larvae or other members of the colony. The mutual exchange of food between members of an ant colony is known as *trophallaxis*. Pheromones (chemicals produced within their bodies or licked from the bodies of other ants or from the bodies of guests they may keep in the nest) are also passed with this food, and the whole provides a convenient chemical communication system for the colony, helping to bind it into a cohesive whole.

Ants are exceedingly numerous in the deserts; not all are harvesters, but a good many are. One is led to wonder how they can find enough seeds to support themselves. An interesting study in this regard was carried out by Lloyd Tevis, Jr., who studied the harvester ants, *Veromessor pergandei,* which were living in an area of sand flats and small dunes near Palm Springs, California. This is an arid area, and at the time the study was begun, it was, in addition, in the latter stages of a twelve-year drought. The previous year's rainfall had been so scanty that the seeds of the ephemerals had not germinated. The only other vegetation of the area was creosote bush and saltbush.

This particular ant is known to live in the most arid portions of the North American Desert, including Death Valley and the area at the head of the Gulf of California. In the study area Tevis found an average of six *Veromessor* colonies per acre. The average number of seeds collected by one colony in a day was approximately 7000. For each acre that would be 42,000 seeds daily; 1,260,000 per month; and finally 15 million seeds per acre each year! Later, working from the other direction, Tevis sampled the annual seed production of the vegetation when rain was sufficient to cause ephemeral growth, and found that it was in the neighborhood of 1½ *billion* seeds per acre!

When rain finally did arrive after this drought that had been superimposed on an already exceedingly dry land, Tevis reported the density of resulting seedlings as "little short of astounding." In other words, even in drought with consequent reduced seed production for a number of years—and despite the constant gathering of seeds from the soil by these ants and other animals during this long period—there were still sufficient seed resource in the soil to produce a bountiful crop of ephemerals when moisture was available once again.

For the most part these ants are not particularly adapted anatomically or physiologically for this hot dry environment, but their food habits and some behavioral adaptations help them live in the desert. Their nests reach to extreme depths, and deep within the ground they are protected from heat and dryness. Tevis excavated some to a depth of eleven feet and had to give up before reaching the final levels. The ants' activities above ground are strictly regulated by temperature, he found. When the surface temperature was 13°C (approximately 55°F), the ants were able to walk about six inches per minute; at 33°C (approximately 91°F), they were moving eight feet per minute. At 44°C (approximately 111°F), all the ants had retired underground. If caught out at 50°C (approximately

Craters of leaf-cutter ants in a desert wash (*M. W. Larson*)

122°F), ants died within seconds. In summer Tevis found the ants outside foraging from before sunrise to about 8 A.M. In the spring and fall they foraged in the early morning and late afternoon; in the winter, at midday.

A study of another harvester, *Pogonomyrmex barbatus*, in south Texas by Thadis W. Box disclosed that in August these ants were most active from 10 P.M. until 5 A.M. Soil surface temperatures at that time were approximately 85°F, while daytime soil temperatures in the same area ranged up to 150°F. This was in a prickly pear-short grass community, and there was an average of 8.4 mounds per acre. The bare area around each nest varied from two to seven feet in diameter; an average of approximately 128 square feet per acre was denuded by these ants. These harvesters collected the seeds of both the grasses and the prickly pears.

Earthworms have long been reputed to be great soil builders, as they move through the soil digesting material within it and serving to help aerate it. Earthworms, however, are not desert animals. They may occur in some flowerbeds around desert homes—having been introduced into these moist areas with plants or special soil—but in the desert proper they are absent. In the desert their function is carried out by the ants who move, mix, and change the character of the soil to a certain extent in the underground areas in which they live and work. They do remove some plant cover about the nest (especially at slightly higher elevations in the desert grasslands where there is more cover—particularly grass—to remove), but their activities are far more beneficial than detrimental.

In one way, some of the ants found in the desert are physically adapted for dealing with the dry, fine sand and soil of this habitat. Certain species have fringes of long hair about the lower portions of the head. These are collectively known as the *psammophore*. In *The Ants of North Dakota*, George and Jeanette Wheeler observed and described the use of the psammophore as a means of carrying sandy soil, as used by the harvester *Pogonomyrmex occidentalis*. An individual ant packed the psammophore with sand by thrusting her head into loose soil, pressing her head back against the thorax, and pushing the grains of sand into the psammophore with her front feet. A pellet of soil as big as the ant's head resulted, held under the head by the psammophore. The pellets were carried outside and pushed out of the psammophore with the feet. *Pogonomyrmex* actually means "bearded ant." These are interesting ants, capable of inflicting a first-class, uncomfortable sting, and are reputed to be one of the species of ants over whose craters Indians sometimes staked their prisoners.

One other type of ant is especially suited for arid and semiarid living— these are the honeypots. We mentioned that some ants rely on sweet juices primarily for their food, these derived directly from plants or second-hand from homopterans which suck juice from plants, use some of it for their bodies, but excrete a great deal of it little changed, and on this the ants feed. All ants have a crop or "social stomach" in which they store liquid food. This is shut off from the rest of the digestive system by a valve which can be opened as necessary to allow food to flow on through. Oftentimes the crop is kept filled rather constantly, and much of the material is re-gurgitated to others of the colony.

The honeypot ants have specialized in the use of the crop for food storage. The bees can produce wax and hence a comb in which to store their liquid food supplies. The ants are not so endowed, and so these particular ones use themselves. Among the species of ants known as

Honey pot repletes in their underground chamber; note the normal-sized worker to the left, standing on a replete's abdomen (*M. W. Larson*)

honeypots, the workers collect sweet exudates of plants in their crops, return to the nest, and regurgitate this liquid to other members of the colony. Eventually the crops of these stay-at-home members become greatly bloated with the stored liquid. Before they become immobile, they climb to the tops of their underground chambers and hang there as living pots of honey. Evidently the sweet juices are stored within the pots during cooler, moister periods when the material is available, and the honey, as needed, is passed back to the normal members of the colony for food during warm dry periods, when outside food sources are reduced.

These fat ladies (all worker ants are females) are amazing creatures. So distended do their abdomens become with the greatly enlarged crops, that the sclerites or hard chitinous plates which ordinarily cover and protect the surface of the abdomen are completely pulled apart. The golden

Close-up of a replete, showing the abdominal scales (*M. W. Larson*)

honey held within the crop shows clearly and translucently through, giving these ants the appearance of small-headed amber marbles. Called
honeypots these members of the society are scientifically known as repletes. They hold up to eight times their own weight in honey, and if they
loosen the six footholds by which they hang from the ceiling and fall the
inch or two to the floor of the chamber, they are in danger of bursting
and thereby dying.

These ants, too, live in the soil where temperatures are moderate.
W. S. Creighton and R. H. Crandall excavated one Arizona colony and
found the queen and repletes at a depth of sixteen feet. To do so, they
had to remove an estimated fifteen tons of soil! We have found the repletes
at the depth of approximately two feet in the early spring on the Papago
Indian Reservation in Arizona, in a creosote bush community traversed

Honey pot repletes (*M. W. Larson*)

by a desert wash supporting paloverde, ironwood, and mesquite trees. Near the head of the Gulf in extremely dry country we found a small species of ant which was evidently disadvantaged, compared to some of its relatives elsewhere, for these ants had only small amounts stored. To judge by their actions, it appeared they may have been storing juices derived to some extent from insect food. In northern Arizona we found beautiful honeypots about a foot below the surface hanging in red rock galleries. Like a good many native people have done for centuries, we ate some of the honey and found it sweet, flavorful, and delicious.

Of all the insects present in the desert, perhaps the least expected ones would be the termites. This insect group reaches its height of development in the moist tropics; and the termites are usually popularly considered to live in enclosed earthen nests or wooden tunnels where rather high levels of humidity prevail. Like the ants, termites are social insects, but belong to an entirely different order. The ants, wasps, and bees are members of the order Hymenoptera; the termites, of the Isoptera. Termites are—at least in the case of most species—thin-skinned and soft-bodied. In addition, most are blind; and the average termite, except for the soldiers, are defenseless. As with the ants, when the summer rainy season arrives in the Sonoran Desert winged male and female termites leave the nests and engage in a dispersal flight. Here again, scientists are just beginning to learn what factors cause the flights. Species vary in this regard, but evidently temperature, moisture, and light are controlling factors. Some species fly at night and are often seen about electric lights; others fly diurnally. Mating does not take place during the flight. The winged termites drop to the ground, their wings are lost, a male follows a female, and off they go in search of a homesite. Depending on the species, this may be in the soil or in wood. The pair prepares living quarters, and when these are finished, mating takes place. Unlike the ants, the "king" lives on to reign with the queen. Also, termites do not develop as do ants from egg to larva, to pupa, to adult; but instead move from egg, to nymph—a smaller modified version of the adult, and not a grub-like larva—to adult. In the termite society there are almost always soldiers; there may or may not be workers, depending on the species. Where there are none, the work is carried on by the nymphs, who may remain arrested in this form or may later continue their development to soldier or reproductive forms. Both males and females are present on all levels. (Among the ants the males are present in only the reproductive form and here only briefly, one mating sufficing almost all ant queens for their lifetime of egg production.)

Termites are noted for their strange diet of wood, which they are able to digest thanks to the presence of symbiotic protozoa within their intestinal tract. The termite provides living quarters for them; the protozoa break down the cellulose in the termite's diet so that both termite and the protozoa can make use of the nutrients. Not all termites, however, rely on protozoa. Some of the more highly evolved species eat materials with less cellulose, such as grass; and need not depend on internal inhabitants to do their work for them.

Most termites live and work within enclosed areas. The entrances to their nests are kept closed to prevent drying air from desiccating them and to prevent enemies—foremost among which are ants—from reaching

Soldier termites and workers in dead boojum (*M. W. Larson*)

them. If termites wish to reach wood or other material away from their nest, most of them build earthen tubes through which they move. If such walls are broken, soldiers gather at the edge of the break, guarding the colony while the workers repair the damage. Soldiers, depending on species, are armed with oversized jaws or an elongated head which squirts or discharges a chemical towards enemies. These are called nasutes— "having a large nose." Other termites feed the king, queen, the very young, and oftentimes the soldiers. Food may be given them from the mouth of the worker or nymph, or from the anus. Waste materials in turn may be discarded, used to line the chambers of the home, or used as a building material.

At certain times, a conspicuous feature in desert areas are small plants (or plant materials) covered with a coating of soil. This covering may almost completely enclose a plant, duplicating its outlines, so that the plant appears to be made of mud. This is the work of termites who have constructed it in order to eat the plant beneath in safety from drying and predation. The covering material may be built up some distance from the ground on the surface of saguaros or ocotillo stems. Beneath the protective cover, the termites have stripped off dead plant material.

Most of the other desert termites are not so obvious in their workings. Some live in and eat away at dry wood. Others nest in the soil, where their tunnels can descend to cool, moist depths, and can go directly to wood beneath the soil or resting on the surface. Just how deep these nests descend, no one seems to know with any certainty, but the insulating soil gives the termites protection and a measure of choice in their living conditions.

Ocotillo with termite "sheath" along the lower portions (*M. W. Larson*)

W. L. Nutting of the University of Arizona found that of the eighteen species of termites in Arizona, six are desert species, and that some of the others of widespread distributions enter the desert also. He investigated one of the desert species, *Pterotermes occidentis,* which is a dry wood termite and is apparently endemic to the Sonoran Desert. These termites have been found living in dead palo verde trees, in the woody skeletons of saguaro cacti, and in the dead flowering stalks of yuccas. We have recently collected them from the skeleton of a boojum tree in Baja California. The two reproductive *Pterotermes* enter wood which will provide both home and food and prepare a chamber. At the end of the first year, one colony was found to contain the original pair plus eight nymphs and five eggs. Eventually a colony may number three thousand or more individuals. These are large termites, with fierce-looking, dark-headed, big-jawed soldiers. The tunnels in the wood are rather large. Nutting reported that in their nests, semi-liquid fecal material was used to wall off old galleries or tunnels.

Living in small, dry stems in the desert climate would appear to be hazardous for termites, most of whom are quite moisture-sensitive. Nutting found that temperatures within the central galleries of this termite nest in a palo verde trunk sometimes exceeded 38°C (approximately 100°F), and one day reached 41.8°C (approximately 107°F). The lowest temperature recorded during the study—and this in the early morning—was approximately 24°C (approximately 75°F). One investigator has found that the larger nymphs of this genus have a comparatively low rate of water loss, probably due to a well developed body covering. Nutting suggested that this termite may be limited in its distribution by higher moisture levels of the area surrounding the desert. That is, it may be so desert-oriented that it is unable to live under what we would consider to be more ideal termite living conditions!

217

chapter fourteen

Mammals at the Waterhole

THE desert is full of surprises—rats that never drink, mice that live on insects, honey-storing ants, quarter-century old spiders, wild pigs, carrot-shaped trees, even a few rattlesnakes without rattles, and deer among the cacti. A good many animals like the deer—which would seemingly not be adjusted to living in a hot, arid environment—are represented in at least parts of the desert. Particularly is this true in the saguaro forests, which are favored with two rainy periods each year which are well-timed and provide, for a desert, rather generous amounts of moisture.

The waterhole the Arizona-Sonora Desert Museum maintains among the saguaros is a good place to observe some of the larger animals of the desert. The musuem and waterhole both lie in a thickly-studded saguaro forest on the upper portions of a bajada. In back of the museum rise the craggy, gray, rough peaks of the Tucson Mountains. These are not high mountains; their upper limits never leave the desert vegetation behind. From their base flows the bajada on which the museum rests. It continues on past the museum, past the western section of Saguaro National Monument, and finally disappears into the valley floor a few miles further on. Among the saguaros live a host of smaller plants: foothill paloverdes, ocotillos, chollas, prickly pears, barrel cacti, smaller cacti, and bur sage

219

Ironwood tree in the Sonoran Desert (*M. W. Larson*)

cover much, but by no means all of the ground surface. Dry washes gully the bajada surface, and along these grow larger trees; but even these are not large by moist-country standards. The gray-green ironwood—its core so hard it dulls cutting tools and so heavy it will not float—blooms with pale, dusky purple flowers in the late spring. Mesquites mingle with the blue palo verde trees and grow to larger proportions than do their kin on the drier foothill slopes. Both species bloom gloriously with yellow flowers in the spring.

From the height of the bajada one can see across the lower valley, its edges rimmed here and there by other mountain ranges. Down its center one can see to Mexico some sixty miles away. On the valley floor, creo-

Desert mule deer at a waterhole in the Sonoran Desert (*Lewis W. Walker*)

sote bush, bur sage, and some of their associates prevail. About the valley are dotted fields growing rich green crops, watered by wells sunk deep to tap ancient supplies of groundwater. Beyond the fields stretches the vast desert Papago Indian Reservation, the land of the "Desert People."

We once lived in the desert near the museum's waterhole and visited it on warm summer nights, particularly in May and June. After the sun had set, but while it was yet somewhat light, we would see the first of the wild animals, a group of deer, approaching through the desert. These were mule deer, of the same species that range over the whole of western Canada, United States, and on down into Mexico. Those of the desert are a separate subspecies known as desert mule deer. They are of a generally smaller size and lighter color than those of their species found in cooler moister climates. Whereas bucks of this species may weigh three hundred pounds or more in some parts of their range, the desert mule bucks average about 150 pounds. This pattern—smaller size and lighter color among the desert-inhabiting races of species that occur both in and out of the desert—is very common for warm-blooded animals.

Arctic species tend to have heavier, more compact bodies than closely related species living in warm climates. With a higher volume-to-surface ratio in the polar animals, there is less surface area from which heat can be lost to the cold air. However, with a higher surface-to-volume ratio— as found among the larger types of desert animals, which are less compact than the arctic animals—there is *more* surface from which body heat can be radiated to the atmosphere. The ears of hares in the north tend to be small; those of the desert jackrabbits are huge and serve as a surface from which heat can be lost from the body. These generalizations apply only to warm-blooded animals. The opposite is true for cold-blooded animals; for example, the largest species of snakes are found in the tropics.

The reason for the lighter coloration among desert mammals is open to some debate. Certainly the lighter colors allow them a greater degree of protective coloration in an environment where the soil is light-colored for the most part, and where much of the vegetation borders on a gray-green color. A tendency toward lighter coloration in desert animals—and this includes not only mammals, but some birds and reptiles also—could thus be a matter of natural selection: lighter, more protectively colored individuals surviving to pass on their lighter colors to offspring, the darker individuals falling prey more often and not living to reproduce. However, some animals which are also lighter in the desert are never abroad in the light of day, when light protective coloration would be important. These include burrowing animals which seldom come above ground and animals active only at night. Adherents of the natural selection theory say that even at night, there is often bright moonlight reflecting off the desert's surface; and so light coloration to more closely match the environment would still be of value. Another explanation for the tendency to lighter colors is the possibility that dry, hot air causes depigmentation and hence lighter colors in desert animals.

The desert mule deer spends hot summer days in shade, as along the edge of a wash where tree growth is heavier. At night it travels to water, such as a waterhole, or is reported sometimes to dig holes in washes to obtain water occasionally trapped by rocks beneath the sandy surface. (Coyotes, too, are known to do this.) During the night the mule deer feeds on the leaves and twigs of trees, many of these spiny. The deer also feed some on cactus fruit, a small nutritious shrub known as jojoba, and grass. This deer is dependent upon drinking water. Not only must it endure the high air temperatures which prevail even in its shady retreats in the desert, but due to its diet it generates a good deal of internal heat. Feeding on plant material containing large amounts of cellulose, the deer is dependent upon internal bacteria to break much of this food down into a form that the deer can utilize. This causes the production of heat, which is an added burden in the desert.

White-tailed deer are also present in parts of the Southwest. The range of this species covers the entire eastern and mid-United States. In the Southwest, the white-tails occupy higher elevations than the mule deer and are smaller than the latter. This race is called the Sonoran white-tailed, and is a small deer: bucks seldom weigh more than one hundred pounds, and here again individuals are paler and thinner in the Southwest than in most other parts of their range.

Another visitor at the museum waterhole is the peccary. In the summer darkness, a herd of from five to fifteen wild peccaries will approach with no pretense of stealth. They come grunting and scraping their hooves on the gravel, and whatever deer are present usually give way and allow the peccaries to take over. Peccaries are pig-like creatures, but belong to a different family than the domestic swine and European wild boars. The two species of peccaries are the only living members of their entire family. One of these, the white-lipped peccary, ranges from southern Mexico into South America. The other species is the collared peccary, which reaches its northern limits in southwestern Texas and in small areas in southern New Mexico and Arizona. From there it extends south to Patagonia in

South America, and in this range, inhabits environments as varied as deserts and rain forests. Collared peccaries are hunted for sport in the saguaro forests and nearby grasslands. In other parts of its range, it is hunted as an important source of food. We once observed a Maya Indian in Yucatan walking home with a peccary he had shot in the forest. He carried it by means of a band about his head, and it rested on a bed of palm leaves to protect the bearer's back.

Peccaries weigh approximately forty to sixty-five pounds. They have a typically pig-like nose, short, thin legs, hoofed feet, a stout body, and almost no tail. The animal is covered by long, coarse, bristly hairs which are black with some white and which give it a salt-and-pepper appearance. A light band of hair extends across the back behind the neck, giving rise to the common name "collared." This peccary has spearlike tusks and is called *javelina*, from the Mexican word for javelin or spear. The tusks are upper canine teeth which grow downward over the lower canines; in boars they may be an inch-and-a-half in length. When alarmed the peccary raises the long bristles about its neck and emits an offensive odor from a musk gland on its back. This potent gland must be removed before the animal is cooked. Evidently the musk acts as a warning signal to other members of the peccary's herd, but it may serve other purposes as well. Peccaries are gregarious animals, each herd is composed of both sexes and various ages. They have a reputation for being fierce and belligerent, which is likely an exaggeration. If frightened, a herd may charge, but probably most often its members (whose eyesight is poor) are simply trying to escape. Their tusks, however, are formidable, sharp weapons.

These animals often use caves or old mines to rest in, and if wandering along washes, will bed down under the heavier vegetation. They are mainly vegetarians and like the pack rats, specialize in cactus, primarily prickly pear. In one study, 53 percent of their feeding activity was centered on this cactus. Glochids evidently pass through their intestinal tract with no ill effect to the animal. Peccaries are also reported to feed on the smaller fish-hook cactus, which takes its name from the shape of its spines; and their excrement has been reported as occasionally so full of these spines that it looks like a pincushion. They also feed on the fruit of other cacti, mesquite beans, and annuals; they use their noses to root for tubers and roots; and they are said to relish the fallen fruit of the saguaros.

The peccaries were so ruthlessly preyed upon by men—some of whom considered them a pest on cattle range in the grassland—that it was finally found necessary to place them on the list of protected animals in Arizona for a number of years. The peccaries are now numerous enough in that state to sustain an annual hunting season. The young are very attractive, almost exact miniatures of their parents. They are usually born in litters of two and can run within a few hours after birth. After the first day, they are ready to travel with their mothers and the rest of the herd. Young peccaries are sometimes raised as pets, but often become unpredictable as they grow older.

The peccary is obviously an adaptable creature, for the desert bears no resemblance to the tropical home of others of his species. The peccary uses the food available in the desert, and its succulence must be of help. The peccary still seeks water, however, especially in the heat. It may be active by day in cooler weather, or switch to a nocturnal schedule when heat prevails. Particularly where its range is concerned has it shown its adaptability in the desert. Historically, in Arizona the peccaries were creatures of the river valley bottoms, living in the dense vegetation along the Gila, Santa Cruz and San Pedro Rivers. The white man took over much of this area; cut back the thickets, dammed, diverted, or otherwise cut down on the water in the rivers; and shot the peccary. These animals ranged farther out and away from the river bottoms and the concentrations of humans. Today they are often found on the upper desert parts of the bajadas and also range into higher zones. The peccary, like many other animals, however, can adapt to man only so far. From that point on, man must adjust at least a little to the peccary and the animal species pushed aside like it, if these animals are to survive in an increasingly humanly-populated world. The deer and the peccary represent only two of the many desert vegetarians. A host of other animals live on an omnivorous (both plant and animal) diet or a strictly carnivorous one (meat only). Some members of these last two groups visit the waterhole occasionally or regularly, some do not find it necessary. Occasional visitors include the gray fox—a widely distributed species noted for its small size and light coloration in the Southwest—and two species of skunks, the hooded and spotted. (Two other skunk species, the hognose and the striped, are also present in parts of the Southwest.)

The skunks enjoy priority at the waterhole. When skunks are already present, deer or peccary approaching the hole often hold back and wait their turn. The skunks are good bluffers and have the equipment to back it up. If they tarry too long however, the deer and peccaries will finally re-assert themselves.

Ringtailed cats are occasional visitors to the waterhole. These are

Striped skunk carrying young (*M. W. Larson*)

small, beautiful creatures, more tail and eyes than anything else, known scientifically as *Bassariscus astutus*, "crafty, cunning little fox." Actually, the ringtailed cat is neither a fox nor a cat, but a member of the same family as the raccoons, coatimundis, and pandas. A long, slim, streamlined animal, its total body length is about thirty inches, half or more of which is a bushy and distinctively black-and-white banded tail. This animal stands only six inches high at the shoulder. The body color is a brownish-gray and the face is cat- or fox-like with prominent rounded ears. A nocturnal forager, the ringtailed cat eats a variety of food: pack rats, other rodents, insects, plant materials, and birds. It makes its home in caves, rock crevices, and if possible will move into a deserted cabin. These animals were once known as miners' cats, and were often kept as wild "pets" around prospectors' shacks where they proved to be both good com-

Bobcat (*M. W. Larson*)

panions and expert rodent-catchers. At our home in the desert, we were honored by one ringtail that visited our windowsill each night to collect the food we had left for it.

Bobcats, or wildcats, live very successfully in the saguaro forests. These are an adaptable species whose range includes all of the United States (except the very center portion) and extends into Mexico. The bobcat is a beautiful animal with yellowish brown hair touched with traces of black. Its stomach is white with black spots. The ears have short tufts of hair at the tips. Longer hair on the lower portions of the face gives the appearance of a short beard or a ruff. It has a stubby tail—certainly not long, yet not completely short either—which bears black bars near the tip. The feet are impressively large. Here again, the desert subspecies tends to be lighter in color. Bobcats weigh twelve to twenty-five pounds, sometimes slightly

Mountain lion (*M. W. Larson*)

Badger (*Peggy Larson*)

more. In the desert they are mainly nocturnal and feed chiefly on rabbits, rodents and similar fare. No doubt they are drawn to the waterhole not so much by the water as by the tasty things that come there to drink.

Other cats occur in the desert, at least occasionally and in certain portions. The magnificent mountain lion occasionally comes down from higher elevations in the mountains and is found in the desert proper. Sometimes one or its signs will be seen in the Tucson Mountains near the Museum, but such sightings are relatively rare and best kept quiet by anyone who admires these long-persecuted animals. The beautiful jaguar, the small ocelots and margay cats, and the jaguarundi are primarily Mexican inhabitants and may occasionally enter some of the most southern parts of Arizona, New Mexico, and Texas.

It was our pleasure and our sorrow to once have a badger as a pet. These animals, too, are sometimes seen at the desert waterhole. Badgers are unusual-looking animals. Flattened so that they are very broad and mounted on exceedingly short legs, they live close to the ground. They also live in the ground, being great excavators of burrows and diggers after rodent-food. Males may weigh up to twenty-four pounds.

The badger's overall color is grizzled, its long hairs showing some brown, some black, and some gray. It has a clean white stripe from the nose back to the shoulders. The face is marked on each side with a black patch between the small eyes and tiny, rounded ears. The tail is short. The front feet toe-in and are equipped with long tough claws with which the badger digs very speedily and effectively. It has a scent gland which produces an odor when the animal is alarmed, but is very mild when compared to that of the skunk, which is one of its closer relatives. The badger feeds on rodents, insects and reptiles, many of which it digs out. Its geographical range is a wide one covering southwestern Canada, western and mid United States, and extending south to central Mexico. The badger has been consciously and effectively reduced by man over much of its range as a "varmint"—whatever that means—and as a digger of holes dangerous to cowboys' horses.

Where people are concerned, the badger is shy and avoiding. It is generally respected by other wildlife, for the badger can use its teeth and claws very effectively. It is very muscular, has a loose skin underlaid with fat and heavily covered with long fur, and is endowed with a great deal of courage—all of which make it a formidable enemy. The badger may hunt early in the morning or in late afternoon, but is often nocturnal.

Coyote (*M. W. Larson*)

Some authorities feel that it has probably become more nocturnal as its contacts with man have increased. Certainly it is a measure of man's ignorance that this animal (and others like it) are often shot by hunters who have no higher motive than to hit a moving target—and in this case, a target that is incapable of anything approaching speed or self-preservation in the face of a gun.

Our badger was a pleasure, for she completely trusted her captors and enjoyed human company. She came out of her burrow when called, she "churred" her happiness when scratched, she wrapped her front legs about the human leg attempting to depart from her when she did not want to have that person go. She was a sorrow when she died, for her death was directly attributable to the fact that she was a wild animal, incapable of directing her own destiny, having been circumstantially dropped into the human world. Such is usually the case with wild pets. Seldom is it better for a person to raise a wild animal baby than leave it in the wild, free and with its own dignity.

Coyotes use the waterhole near the museum, but are seldom seen there —only their tracks betray them when morning arrives. It is evident that they are much too wily to approach the water when humans are close by.

Rock squirrel—good coyote fare (*M. W. Larson*)

This is one of the traits that has helped these animals survive the pressures man has imposed upon them. Once these were primarily animals of the western prairies. Their distribution has spread greatly in historic times, and their geographical range now includes much of Alaska, all of western Canada; western, mid and parts of northeastern United States; and south to Central America. A desert subspecies is Mearn's coyote which—true to form—is light-colored and small, males weighing about twenty-three pounds. Coyotes are omnivorous, this too helping them live in the desert: they feed on rodents, rabbits, insects, plant materials and other items. The coyote is an important predator helping to control desert rodent populations. It has long been—and continues to be—persecuted by man, often for little or no reason. Whole books have been written about this symbol of the West, outstanding of which is J. Frank Dobie's *The Voice of the Coyote*. Indeed, the coyote is particularly noted for his voice. His proper name *Canis latrans* means barking dog. The sound of the coyote, whether barking, howling, yupping, or—as the Mexicans say—singing, in the darkness of the desert night is one of the valued intangibles of the untamed desert. May it so remain.

Over a night's time, into the area about a waterhole are funneled a large number of thirsty animals, and certainly predators must be aware that this is a gathering place. Schmidt-Nielsen suggests that those animals which can drink quickly and fully to replace their water loss have a tremendous advantage over those which cannot and must tarry there longer, or who must leave before obtaining sufficient water supplies. A desert waterhole is basically a very dangerous place for animals. It is not for man, but in a time not really so far removed, it may well have been so for him too.

chapter fifteen

The "Desert People"

O F the animals which use the saguaros, there are many. Of the people who used—and even today continue to use—the saguaros there is one main group, the Papago Indians. Fresh saguaro fruit must have been a delicious treat for the Indians during the harvest, for their name for the time of year which is approximately our month of May was "Painful Moon," or "Hunger-Hurting Moon"—referring to the general lack of food at the time preceding the saguaro harvest. So important was the saguaro fruit harvest to the Papagos that it marked the beginning of their new year; the time was known as "Saguaro-Harvest Moon."

The name of these Indians, Papago, comes from a nickname given them by other Indians, garbled by the Spanish, and basically meaning the "Bean People" or the "Bean-Eating People," referring to their use of the native, drought-resistant, cultivated tepary bean as a food staple. The Papagos, however, call themselves "The Desert People." Basically a calm, controlled people among whom pride or boasting is discouraged, they are nevertheless quietly proud to be a group which has made their very successful living wholly in the desert. They were able to do so by taking advantage of any and all benefits, no matter how slight, that the desert offered them and using these benefits to the fullest extent. They have

233

proved that man, too, can use microclimates and microhabitats to advantage for himself, and for his crops.

When the Spaniards arrived, the Papagos were living in what is today known as southwestern and south central Arizona and northwestern Sonora. Their homeland was thus largely within the geographical range of the saguaros. This plant was one of importance in their economy, which was based on hunting, gathering, and some agriculture.

In June and early July, Papago families camped in the saguaro forests. Using a long pole from a saguaro skeleton, women knocked the ripe, red fruit down from the tops of the saguaros. Often two poles had to be tied together to achieve the needed length. Near the tip, a short crosspiece of saguaro rib was tied to serve as a hook to help dislodge the fruit. The women scraped loose the red, seed-filled inner pulp and carried it back to the camp in baskets. The outer part of the fruit was discarded on the ground, but the Papagos were careful to leave the red inner lining of the husk showing, for this was considered of importance in bringing rain. Some of the pulp was eaten fresh back at the camp, but most of it was thrown into large clay *ollas* over open fires. The tiny black seeds were strained out, and the juice cooked down over a period of hours until it became a syrup. When cool, this was placed in clay jars, and each jar was covered with a piece of pottery that was sealed in place with clay or mud. Thus preserved, the syrup would be used as a sweetening through the coming year, or could be fermented to make wine.

Many of the ceremonies the Papagos carried out were for the purpose of rainmaking. Living in an arid land and dependent upon the limited rainfall to produce vegetation and supply water for themselves and the animals they depended upon, it is not surprising that the people were vitally concerned with doing all they could that—through their beliefs—promoted rain. One of the most important ceremonies of the Papago year, then, was the wine ceremony, held soon after the end of the saguaro fruit harvest. Previous to the wine ceremony, the "Keeper of the Smoke," a religious figure, brought from hiding the village fetishes—objects such as stones kept in a basket. In conjunction with the wine-making ceremony, careful handling of these objects, according to certain traditions, was the means of bringing rain. In making the wine each family donated a set amount of saguaro syrup, and this was taken to the village round house.

Travelling through the Papago country in 1910, Carl Lumholtz observed and described the wine-making process. The Indians poured saguaro syrup into large, watertight baskets with symbolic designs woven into them; and added water. One man carried out the mixing for each basket, according to a set pattern. Dipping his arms into the liquid, he drew his hands across the bottom of the container and out again, rubbing them against each other twice over the liquid before the next plunge. After much of this stirring, the mixture was tasted and then poured into large ollas inside the building.

The fermentation required approximately four days, during which time the ollas were watched and cared for by certain men of the tribe. On each of the four nights, the villagers gathered to dance and sing special songs of the clouds, rain, wind, and crops while medicine men waved eagle feathers. When the wine was ready, traditional speeches were made regarding such Papago virtues as peacefulness. The wine was then served to the participants in a certain order, who drank until most were at least mildly intoxicated. They believed the coming of the summer rains depended upon the success of their saguaro wine ceremony, and certainly these rains were vital to support their crops. In their study of these Indians entitled *The Desert People*, Alice Joseph, Rosamond Spicer, and Jane Chesky found that the wine ceremony was not basically a time of revelry. Rather the wine, producing happiness and song, was a symbol of life's renewal, helping to bring rain and erasing the evils and ill feelings of the previous year.

These Indians spent the winter months near the usually low mountain ranges that dissect their land; for here were the occasional seeps, springs, or waterholes they needed so badly. Even so, water was often several miles distant from their homes, and their women used up a great deal of time in carrying it home. As soon as the first summer thunderstorms arrived, the Papagos moved onto the flat lands below the mountains to plant crops of beans, pumpkins, and maize. They practiced a special type of agriculture, planting in soil that lay at the mouths of washes coming down from the hills. Planting immediately followed this soil's soaking by flash floods or brief stream flows. In some cases, slight provisions were made to channel the water out over a piece of nearby land. In either location the crops had to get by with whatever water had soaked into the ground just previous to planting, though later storms sometimes provided additional moisture. Indeed, a hard run-off after planting could completely ruin the growing plants, just as surely as a complete drought could doom them to failure. Such flash flood farming was a precarious under-

A reconstruction of what early Papago Indian homes used to look like (*Courtesy of Arizona-Sonora Desert Museum*)

taking. The Indian families camping near their fields depended on rainfall caught in *charcos,* large holes scraped in the soil or naturally gouged in the washes.

Because they could not always depend upon their crops, the Papagos had to be ready to survive, if necessary, on the natural products of the desert. Even in years of good crops, approximately three-fourths of their food supply came from wild plants and animals. The women spent much time gathering fruit from the saguaro and organ pipe cactus; cholla buds, fruit, and joints; the fruit and buds of the prickly pear cacti; mesquite beans, seeds of ironwood and palo verde, and the roots and seeds of various plants. They pit baked the crowns or centers of agaves when these were available. The men hunted deer, black-tailed jackrabbits, antelope jackrabbits, cottontail rabbits, antelope, mountain sheep, peccaries, pack rats, and some birds. In season, they feasted on the large caterpillars of the sphinx moth, and animal skins provided their scant clothing.

Papago homes were basically circular grass huts. The framework was formed by mesquite posts. Bundles of a special, long, coarse grass were applied around the basic framework and held in place by hoops of ocotillo stems. The entrance was a low doorway.

Life in this desert environment was never easy for the Papagos, but by industry and hard work a family could usually support itself. Certainly each member of the family must have felt great satisfaction when, working as a group, they were able to store a harvest of wild and cultivated foods to sustain themselves. Out of such cooperation developed an industrious, peaceful group of Indians who were generous and helpful to one another. Gifts were freely given and received; their language has no phrase for "thank you." Generosity was considered a virtue, and was no doubt a kind of insurance against a future time when the giver might have needs of his own. Quarreling was avoided, and children were taught that peaceableness was most important. The opinions of others were of extreme importance, and guided the actions of most members of the society.

The Spanish added many things to the Papago culture including horses, cattle, and wheat. Cattle were used for food, and horses made travelling easier and became a status symbol. Horses also came to the Apache Indians through the Spanish. The Apaches were neighbors of the Papagos to the east, and with the increased mobility that their horses afforded them, they became a serious threat to the Papagos, causing them to gather in larger villages for a time to protect themselves. Wheat could be planted in the fields in the late fall, grown, using the winter rainfall, and harvested before the coming of the summer rains when other crops could be planted. This second annual crop was of great value, filling the void that had previously been known as the "Hunger-Hurting Moon." The Spaniards also brought their religion and created a largely unfulfilled desire for missionaries. Father Eusebino Francisco Kino established the San Xavier del Bac Mission near present day Tucson and worked tirelessly with the Papagos, but after his death, Spanish mission activity among the Papagos declined. From the Mexican people, the Papagos later adopted the wattle-and-daub house, built of saguaro ribs or ocotillo branches plastered with mud or adobe. Mexican influence also provided them with the adobe brick house and the tortilla, and a diet largely based on tortillas and beans is common with many Papagos today.

Fortunately for the Papagos, their land had few of the resources the white man wanted, so they were largely protected from encroachment. However, some mining took place in what are now ghost towns dotting the Papagos' area, and cattle grazed across part of their land. In a few places, miners and ranchers sunk wells that the Indians were quick to take advantage of. Finally in the early 1900's, the United States Government drilled wells in various parts of the Papago country. This allowed the Indians to build permanent villages near their fields, since drinking water (although not water for irrigation) was then available to them and their stock the year around. Their nomadic existence between the springs and the fields was no longer necessary. Today the Papagos are located on three reservations: a very small one near Gila Bend, Arizona; a slightly larger one around San Xavier Mission on the outskirts of Tucson; and a third very large one stretching west along the Mexican border from the Baboquivari Mountains west of Tucson to the Ajo Mountains, not far from Ajo, Arizona. Not until 1917 was this last, main reservation established by the government. The Papagos' total reservation area is approximately 2,855,000 acres.

Today there are approximately 15,000 Papago Indians. The some 7,000 that still live on the reservation are faced by an expanding population that is confined by the reservation's boundaries. Much of their land has deteriorated from attempts to raise too many cattle, and the Desert People have increased desires for certain advantages they see in the surrounding Anglo culture. Large numbers are leaving the reservation, but most are educated for only the lowest paying jobs. Elementary schools are distributed about the reservation, but only a single high school provides classes through the eleventh grade for this entire area. A high school student's one alternative is to go away to an Indian boarding school, but for a people with strong family ties, this is a difficult step to take.

Partly out of necessity and partly out of desire, the Papagos retain many of their old ways. They still gather the saguaro fruit, camping among the giant cacti during the hottest time of year. They still construct traditional *ramadas* or shade-giving roofs of mesquite posts topped with ocotillo stems or saguaro ribs, and the women still set forth in the early morning and late afternoon with saguaro-rib poles to gather the fruit. But now they arrive in pickup trucks, and tin pails have largely replaced the handmade baskets. Not long ago I talked to a Papago woman who had invited me to come to their saguaro-collecting camp at midday. While the temperature pushed past the 100° mark and the rubber soles of my tennis

Papago Indian woman working on saguaro fruit pulp (*M. W. Larson*)

shoes made my feet decidedly uncomfortable on the hot soil, she and her mother sorted the fruit and tended a good sized, aromatic, mesquite wood fire out in the sun, over which boiled a large olla of saguaro pulp. "We pick the saguaro fruit mostly for my mother," the woman told me. "She says we must keep the old ways." She and her husband had not attended high school, but they very much hoped their daughters would do so. Her husband sometimes had jobs off the reservation, but he had none on this hot June day and was camped with the rest of the family. She said they still practiced flash flood farming, and "We must, just must have good rains this summer." Indeed they did. On an appointed day when we were to visit them on the reservation, we were stopped at the grandmother's house, since the dirt road beyond was muddy and impassable. Nevertheless the younger woman and her husband and daughters came by horse and wagon to meet us there instead. An outdoor ramada provided shade and cool breezes, and here most of the cooking and living were carried on. The yard was scrupulously clean and neat. Not far away, a field with rows of corn interspersed with melon plants was green and thriving. The son-in-law was hoeing weeds in it under a clouded and thundering sky that gave promise of even more rain.

The Papago tribe is working hard to improve their range and their stock. They are managing tribal affairs in a businesslike manner. Mineral rights on their land may ultimately be of value, but at present, poverty and lack of education are major obstacles, especially since their resources are limited and since some of the Indians themselves do not wholeheartedly embrace the Anglo culture. This certainly is their right, although one that has been rather steadily denied to all Indians since a certain memorable October day in 1492.

The Papagos are but one of the many Indian tribes who made the Southwestern deserts their home, and it does seem strange that such arid and semi-arid areas would have attracted so many. It seems less unusual, however, when you consider that some of the world's great civilizations and cultures have arisen in arid lands. The Indians of the Southwest never reached the advanced stages of the Egyptians, for example, but many achieved rather high levels of advancement nonetheless. The Pueblo cities of northern Arizona and New Mexico developed a distinctive and sophisticated culture.

At the other extreme, some tribes merely subsisted on a precarious hunting and gathering economy in Lower California, and in the Mohave

Cooking the saguaro fruit pulp into syrup (*M. W. Larson*)

and Great Basin Deserts. The Apaches were latecomers on the scene, but having once received horses and a not entirely unwarranted hatred for Mexicans and Anglos, they became experts on warfare, striking terror throughout northern Mexico and southern Arizona and New Mexico. The Navajo, too, were late comers, but more adaptable. It is hard to imagine what they were like before they adopted their now-familiar habits of raising sheep and horses, and weaving, pottery making, and house building. Other tribes lived along the rivers and unlike the Papagos, depended on the year around water supply. Along the lower delta region of the Colorado River, in what is today Lower California, lived the Cocopa. Higher up the mighty river lived the Yuma, Mohave, and a number of other tribes. The Gila River in Arizona supported various others, the most outstanding of which were the Pimas. The Papagos are considered a division of the Pima group, though the Pimas were the "River People." The Pimas dug canals from the Gila River to irrigate their fields and were very successful farmers. It was they who often provided sorely needed food to the fur trappers and Anglos attempting to reach the California gold fields by way of the Gila River. South of the border (an artificial boundary where the Indians were concerned) lived more Papagos and other tribes like the Gulf-oriented Seri Indians. And before all these and the many other tribes that the Spanish and Anglos found when they arrived, lived still earlier groups of people.

Excavations of Ventana Cave on the Papago Reservation uncovered signs of human occupation there as long ago as 10,000 years. These early people killed and ate animals such as the sloth, tapir, and four-horned antelope, now extinct. With the animal bones were found stone choppers, scrapers, and points. Other even older dates of human occupation have been recorded for sites in the Southwest. Future studies will be required to establish definitely the length of man's occupancy there, but it is obvious that it has been a long one.

A Pima Indian term refers to some of these ancient people as the Hohokam (ho-ho-*kam*), "that which has vanished." Dr. Emil W. Haury of the University of Arizona recently reported on his excavations of Snaketown, an ancient Hohokam site in the present day Pima Reservation along the Gila River. Explorations of the ruins revealed that perhaps even before 300 B.C., the Hohokam were carrying on irrigated agriculture by means of at least three miles of well-designed, hand-dug ditches. Later the Hohokam dug many other irrigation ditches, both at Snaketown and in other locations along the Gila and Salt Rivers. As a community, Snake-town probably died sometime in the period between 1100 and 1200 A.D. Dr. Haury believes that its people continued to live in the valley in smaller settlements, and that their culture was blended with that of newcomers to the area. He feels that the modern Pima Indians are descendants of the Hohokam.

"That which has vanished" did not do so quickly. What appears to have been a period of relative peace and plenty reigned for approximately 1500 years at Snaketown. The society even accrued enough extra re-sources to allow certain members to develop fine pottery, a ball court, elaborate stone tools, and sculptured stone vessels. Dr. Haury's work revealed that these people developed the world's first acid-etching process, hundreds of years before Europeans made the discovery during the Ren-aissance. The Hohokam prepared their etchings on sea shells, which they obtained through trade with tribes nearer the Gulf of California. Beautiful examples of such work were uncovered in the Snaketown excavations. Drawing inspiration from the familiar things about them, the long-dead artists had created representations of horned lizards, snakes, and other desert creatures. The discovery of one uncompleted etching revealed exactly how the process worked. The desired design was first painted on the shell with pitch, then the shell was placed in a mild acid bath that slowly dissolved away the upper layers of the shell surface not protected by pitch. And once again the useful saguaro enters the picture, for Dr. Haury suspects that the acid used for the etching was none other than the fermented juice of the saguaro cactus fruit!

chapter sixteen

Palms, Yuccas, Agaves, and Boojums

THE forests are mostly composed of trees, the grasslands, of grass, but the desert is a lot of things from trees, to shrubs, to grass, to cacti. The diversity of plant life in the North American Desert provides a variety of differing backgrounds or bases around which living communities are built. Insofar as animals are concerned, in this book we have focused primarily on the community that exists in the saguaro forests, since many or most of the animals present there—or species similar to them—are also present in many other parts of the desert. Similarly, one could focus on any number of other distinctive large desert plants and explore the interrelated community of living plants and animals that live in, on, and around them.

Various types of palm trees occur in the deserts of Mexico and Baja California. The distinctive California fan palm, *Washingtonia filifera,* is found in desert oases in southern California, parts of Baja California and in the Kofa Mountains of western Arizona; and is now grown as an ornamental in suitable areas around the world. There is a certain thrill, however, the first time one sees these palms growing wild in a desert oasis. Perhaps this is due to the plethora of movies and stories laid in the desolate Sahara with the palm-studded oasis providing background or constituting the goal of the hero beset by thirst, nomads, or other trials. Perhaps it is exciting to see palms in a natural oasis simply because these large, green plants are so very striking when viewed rising out of the sparse, dry desert surrounding them.

The palms usually shown in movies of the Sahara Desert are date palms, which have an elongate leaf blade. The splits or divisions in the blade reach to the center midrib. The frond of the California fan palm, however, is nearly circular in outline, with the divisions extending about one-half or two-thirds of the length of the blade and arranged palmately. This palm may reach a height of fifty feet. The large dead leaves tend to remain on the tree, hanging downward along the trunk and forming a dense thatch or shag which may eventually cover the entire length of the trunk. Long ago, in a wetter age, these palms were more numerous and widespread, but as the climate became increasingly arid, they became restricted in range. Today they grow only where sufficient permanent water supplies are available, clustered about an occasional hillside seep or in a canyon or rare wash area with springs or subterranean water supplies.

In an oasis, the palms form the dominant plant species, but they are joined by other plants as well. The plant species present depend upon numerous factors including the terrain and the type of soil. Some water plants grow where permanent standing water is available. About the water source grow the palms, and beyond these is a transition zone from the oasis to the desert.

Other plants sometimes found associated with the palms in the oasis are mesquites, cottonwoods, tamarisks, smoke trees, and halophytes or salt tolerant plants. The fan palms are able to tolerate fairly high concentrations of alkali. In some oases, alkali may even produce a crust on moist soils. Such soils, of course, prevent the growth of many species of plants. In a study of twenty-four fan palm oases in California, Richard J. Vogl and Lawrence T. McHargue recorded an average of only eleven species of plants per oasis, and this included the plants of the three zones—water, oasis, and oasis-desert transition. The species of tamarisk trees found in these oases and in other locations in the North American Desert were native to Europe and Asia and introduced into North America where they have prospered. They grow only where water is rather readily available, and they have become dominant along many southwestern streambeds where they have crowded out native vegetation. (Their invasion of oases is also serving to crowd out some of the native vegetation.) So prolific and so wasteful of water are these trees that attempts to eradicate them are sometimes made, in certain areas, but this is often difficult to achieve.

Smoke trees are plants of the washes in southern California, southwestern Arizona, and northern Sonora and Lower California; therefore they often occur in wash-type oases. The smoke trees are restricted to frost-free areas. The seeds of these trees require abrasion before germination can occur, and this action takes place in the wash during floods. This is a small tree, approximately twelve to thirty feet in height. Most of the year it is leafless and consists of many slender spine-tipped branches. The overall color of the leafless tree is a definite grayish-silver. When seen from a distance it resembles a puff of smoke—hence its common name. In the late spring it produces a profusion of bright purple flowers; in or out of bloom it is an attractive, unusual plant.

The fruit of the fan palm was eaten by certain Indians. They sometimes burned the dead thatch from the trees, reportedly to increase fruit production and also in the belief that it harbored evil spirits. Even today, fire may play an important role in the palm oasis. The thatch and fallen leaves of the palms are highly flammable. If a fire starts in an oasis—and such an occurrence is usually due to man or lightning—the thatch, ground debris, and some of the smaller plants growing in the area are burned. The palms are relatively fire-tolerant and usually survive. Actually, such a fire sometimes benefits the oasis. Removal of dead debris leaves clear, moist soil in which new plants may begin growth; it removes small shrubby species of plants which through their shade prevent optimum development of young, small palms. Destruction of the water-using shrubs also enhances the palms' water supply. Vogl and McHargue concluded from their study that these palms may live as long as 200 years, although most probably die before 150 years of age; and that optimum conditions for germination and growth of seedlings need occur only once every hundred years in order for stands to reproduce themselves. They reported that the annual crops of seeds appeared to remain dormant on the moist alkaline soils and hypothesized that prolonged rains may be necessary to leach inhibiting materials from the seeds or the soil before germination can occur.

An oasis may support one or two palm trees or several hundred. When present in some numbers, they provide a distinctively humid microhabitat for a number of animals. Birds such as orioles, towhees, sparrows, finches, quail, and doves take advantage of the oasis. Small mammals make it their home, and certain snakes in turn come to prey upon them. Bats swoop over the oasis at dusk or after nightfall to obtain water and insect food, and large mammals such as mule deer and coyotes come to partake of the water supply. Just as the saguaro hosts insects that tunnel into its tissues to spend their larval stage, so does the palm support a special beetle, whose larvae eat and tunnel their way through its trunk. Coyotes eat the fallen palm fruit, and since palm seeds are found in large numbers in their droppings, they are considered to be important disseminators of these seeds.

One interesting and rare animal that visits oases for water is the desert bighorn sheep. This heavy-bodied sheep is approximately three feet tall at the shoulder, occasionally up to five in length, and weighs approximately 120 pounds. (Individuals of 200 pounds have been recorded.) The coat is a pale tan, with a white rump patch around the short black tail. Both males and females have horns which they never shed and which continue to grow both in length and circumference throughout their lifetime. Those of the females usually do not exceed a half-circle, but those of the rams are magnificent, gradually curling backward and then forward to make a complete spiral. The horns on a mature ram may attain truly gigantic proportions and the weight of such a headdress is impressive. One sheep from the Pinacate Mountains has been recorded with a horn basal circumference of fifteen-and-a-half inches and a horn length of thirty-seven-and-a-quarter inches. J. Ross Browne, reporting on his tour of the Arizona frontier in the 1800's, described the desert bighorn: "These animals have prodigious horns, upon which they alight when they tumble down the cliffs. How they get up again is difficult to conjecture. My own impression is that they are born there, and are pushed over by other sheep." Obviously Browne never let facts get in the way of his reporting.

When the first Anglo settlers reached the Colorado River Basin, large numbers of desert bighorn sheep occupied the mountain ranges of the area, but their number was greatly reduced by 1900. Man hunted the sheep, first for food and later for trophies. Drying up of many previously permanent streams (partly due to overgrazing of the watershed) reduced the water supplies upon which the sheep depended. Domestic stock ate up much of the sheep's forage and introduced diseases to which the desert bighorn also were susceptible. Burros that escaped from their owners or were turned loose on the desert fouled the water sources, devoured foliage for considerable distances around, and reproduced prodigiously. So fast did the bighorns decline in numbers that the killing of them was unlawful in Arizona even before that area became a state.

Today the desert bighorn is present only in limited numbers in some of the most isolated of the dry, rugged mountain ranges dotting the North American Desert. Various pieces of land have now been set aside as desert bighorn reserves. One, the Cabeza Prieta Game Range near the Mexican border in southwestern Arizona, is an arid, lonely, desolate region through which passed a portion of the infamous Camino del Diablo highway. Another is the Kofa Game Range in the Kofa Mountains— which is also the site of Arizona's only natural palm oasis. Arizona law now allows limited and tightly controlled hunting of old rams.

The desert bighorn consists of several subspecies of *Ovis canadensis* which are found today in localized areas of southeastern California, southern Utah, Nevada, Arizona, New Mexico, western Texas, northern Mexico, and Lower California. The rugged, precipitous terrain of the desert ranges provides these sheep with some protection from coyotes, bobcats, and man. The sheep subsist on the sparse vegetation and make visits to rare desert waterholes, particularly during hot, dry periods.

In low mountainous country not far from the Kofa Mountains lies a special desert bighorn sheep watering site which we visit occasionally. Where a certain desert wash drops from an upper level, water is held in a series of deep rocky basins. Vegetation is sparse, mostly creosote bushes with a good deal of bare ground surface between them. Along the washes grow small desert trees. A long dirt road leads to the general vicinity; a four-wheel drive vehicle is necessary for making the last part of the trip into the area of the rock "tanks." Here on the cliffs you can see the sheep's beds, although one is seldom fortunate enough to see the wary sheep themselves. Long ago this was a popular Indian gathering place, as is evident by the broken pottery, manos, and metates. Black volcanic rocks abound in the area, upon which the Indian artists chipped their petroglyphs. One such petroglyph represents a desert bighorn sheep. The figure, not more than about two feet in height and composed of only a few chipped lines, nonetheless stands clear, beautiful, and expressive on the hill above the wash. To obtain food, the "savage" Indians killed and ate the desert bighorn sheep and also honored it through their artistry. Strange then that "civilized" man, who no longer needs the desert bighorn even for food, often prefers to honor the species by hanging its stuffed, disembodied, and glass-eyed head upon the wall of his "civilized" home.

Yucca with "candles" (*M. W. Larson*)

Another species of yucca, this one with a slight trunk (*M. W. Larson*)

There are many species of distinctive plants known as yuccas in various portions of the North American Desert, all members of the genus *Yucca* and placed within the lily family. These, depending upon the species, are trees, shrubs, or heavy-based plants which develop from a caudex or stem base, are sometimes branched, and have thick clusters of very long, stiff, sharp-pointed leaves. On some yuccas, these leaves, when dead, form a dense shag on the trunk of the plant. In this respect—and also in the general appearance of some species—the plant slightly resembles a palm tree. A large panicle of flowers, white, slightly greenish, or with tinges of purple, are produced, usually upon a tall, quick-growing stalk. The sharp-tipped leaves are the source of one common name for the plant, "Spanish Bayonet." The strikingly beautiful plumes of flowers provide another, "Candles of the Lord." And the fact that a "soap" which was used by Indians, exudes from severed roots and stems provides yet another name, "soapweed."

Yuccas were useful plants to many of the southwestern Indians. Besides soap, they provided a source of fibers for basketry, ropes, nets, and other necessary items, and food in the form of the young shoots, flowers, and seeds. The yucca is the state flower of New Mexico, and yuccas are one of the few plants which colonize the white dunes composed of gypsum in New Mexico's White Sands National Monument. Here as the white sand drifts about a yucca, the plant's roots continue to extend in an attempt—sometimes successful, sometimes not—to keep the plant's head above the sand, and its roots help to bind the otherwise shifting sand about them.

For its pollination, the yucca is not indebted to the proverbial birds and bees, but rather to moths of the genus *Pronuba,* known as yucca moths. The dependency of a plant upon an insect for cross pollination is, of course, a very familiar story. The insect is lured to the flower by color or odor, and is rewarded for its visit with edible pollen or nectar. In its activities in the flower, bits of pollen become dusted upon the insect's body and are carried on to the next flower visited. Incidentally, some of this loose pollen thus comes into contact with the female portions of the various flowers visited, and pollination is achieved. This relationship between plant and insect is a case wherein both participants benefit. Such relationships are commonplace, but nonetheless extraordinary when one stops to consider the long evolutionary history that was involved; first in the flowers—in the development of colored petals, attractive odors, rewarding nectar and production of sufficient pollen for both pollination of other members of the species and feeding of the visiting insects—and secondly in the adaptations of certain insects and some other animals to best take advantage of the plants' offerings. *Pronuba* and *Yucca,* however, carry the plant-insect relationship beyond the usual level.

The small, white female pronuba moth visits the newly opened yucca flowers by night. As she moves from one flower to another, her specially modified mouth parts gather pollen which is gradually formed into a large ball and tucked under her head. Moving on to yet another flower, the moth climbs part way up the pistil, the female portion of the plant, and inserts her ovipositor, or egg-laying organ, into the plant's ovary, where she lays her eggs. She then climbs to the top of the pistil and with her head rubs into the stigma some of the pollen grains she carries, thus fertilizing the flower and insuring seed production. The larvae which will develop from her eggs are thus assured of the only food on which they will feed, the developing seeds. Repeated many times over by many moths, most of the yucca flowers are fertilized and produce seeds within their seed pods. The moth larvae eat only a portion of the seeds within the pods, eventually bore their way through the wall of the capsule, and enter the ground. They remain there until the following year, enter the pupal stage, are transformed into the adult moth, and finally emerge to initiate once again the complicated ritual vitally necessary for continuation of both the yucca and the moth species.

In the more traditional insect-flower relationship, the insect reaps an immediate gustatory reward for its visit and the benefit to the flower is simply an accident on the part of the insect. Not so with *Pronuba* and *Yucca.* Here the pronuba moth—although her action is instinctual—appears to be able to reason, for she carries out the activity of gathering pollen (which she does not eat) and through a complicated maneuver places it on the flower so as to achieve fertilization and seed production. This in turn will ultimately benefit the moth species, but in no way directly benefit the *individual* moth. Add to this remarkable behavior the fact that as different species of yuccas have evolved, so have different species of pronuba moths; particular species of moths being associated with particular species of yuccas!

We can say the action the moth carries out is based on instinct, and we can name the process by which this relationship developed as "mutually-adaptive evolution on the part of both moth and yucca." In both cases, science has better labels than explanations.

Outstanding among the yuccas is *Yucca brevifolia,* the Joshua tree. This is the most distinctive plant and the popular symbol of the Mohave

Joshua trees (*M. W. Larson*)

Desert. This yucca normally has a single trunk which forks a few feet above the ground. The branches in turn fork and refork with additional growth of the plant. The branches usually lack leaves near their base, above which is a thatch of dead, reflexed leaves. The end of each terminal branch is covered by encircling dense, green, stiff, tooth-edged, and spine-tipped leaves. A flower cluster is eventually produced at the end of each branch, after which the branch forks; and this procedure of flowering and forking continues. Thus a mature plant assumes a tree form with a generally rounded crown. These trees may occasionally reach forty feet in height, though thirty is a more common large size.

The Joshua trees' range is limited almost completely to the Mohave Desert, although scattered plants do occur in the Sonoran Desert's extreme northern part in Arizona, where they may mingle briefly with the saguars. But in portions of the Mohave, the Joshua trees form impressive, distinctive forests where they are the dominant plant. Joshua Tree National Monument in southeastern California preserves extensive forests of these wierd but wonderful plants.

The Joshua trees' name was bestowed upon them by Mormon pioneers who apparently drew some symbolic analogy between the Biblical Joshua and these craggy, desert dwelling plants. Whatever their reasoning may have been, the name stuck. In the middle 1800's, Lieutenant J. C. Frémont described the "yucca tree" as "stiff and ungraceful . . . the most repulsive tree in the vegetable kingdom." Some forty years later, an English company attempted to use these plants as a source of pulp to manufacture paper stock for the *London Daily Telegraph!* A mill was reportedly constructed on the Colorado River for this purpose, and a few editions of the *Telegraph* actually appeared on Joshua tree paper. Fortunately, however, the pulp tended to heat and spoil on the ocean voyage, and the costs became prohibitive.

In an intensive study of the animals in the Joshua Tree National Monument, Alden H. Miller and Robert C. Stebbins reported twenty-nine species of reptiles and amphibians, fifty species of birds, and twenty-eight species of mammals present in the yucca plant belt. (Two other plant belts are represented in the Monument: the creosote belt at a lower, and the piñon belt at a higher elevation than the yucca belt.) Among the yucca belt's twenty-eight mammals were such creatures as desert bighorn sheep, bobcats, badgers, gray foxes, kit foxes, coyotes, pack rats, a variety of small mice such as grasshopper, deer, cactus, and pocket mice, kangaroo rats, gophers, ground squirrels, black-tailed jack rabbits, cottontails, and bats. The birds included turkey vultures, hawks, golden eagles, quail, mourning doves, roadrunners, owls, poor-wills, red-shafted flickers, verdins, and cactus wrens. The reptiles ranged from desert tortoises, geckos, collared and leopard lizards, to chuckwallas, desert spiny lizards, side-blotched lizards, desert horned lizards, red racers, king snakes, Mohave rattlesnakes, speckled rattlesnakes, and sidewinders.

One seldom seen reptile that is actually numerous and closely associated with the Joshua trees is the yucca night lizard, *Xantusia vigilis*. This small, secretive lizard is approximately one-and-a-half inches in body length, with a slightly longer tail. It lives almost exclusively under dead Joshua tree limbs or among the dead leaves on living plants. It is also sometimes found in the dead thatch of other yucca species and occasionally in other locations. The yucca's extensive debris provides this night lizard with a favorable microclimate, a degree of protection from predators, and a profitable hunting ground for termites, ants, and beetles.

Another of the desert's more distinctive plant groups are the agaves, sometimes known as century plants. The short subterranean stem sends up a basal rosette of leaves: long, narrow, and succulent, they are spine-tipped and often adorned with spines along their edges. Most agaves live from about seven to twenty years before producing a tall, quick growing flower stalk with a panicle of light colored flowers. Following its single flowering, the plant dies. One small species, *Agave lechuguilla,* is often considered a symbol of the Chihuahuan Desert. The species and common name for the plant, *lechuguilla,* is the diminutive form of the Mexican word for lettuce. These are small agaves with approximately ten to thirty leaves, each about eight to sixteen inches in length. The flower stalk may reach twelve feet.

Larger species of agaves are raised commercially in extensive fields in tropical America. Nearby are large processing areas with racks on which agave fibers are dried, before being made into ropes, sacking, cords, hammocks, and other items. The famous alcoholic drinks mescal, tequila, and pulque are made from the central stem and leaf bases of some agaves; in fact, *mescal* is one of the common names for certain species of agaves. The crowns or center portions of agaves were often pit-baked by numerous Indian tribes, providing a sweet, nourishing food. Such agaves formed a primary food item for some of the Indians of the central desert portion of Lower California, where especially during dry periods, the agave crowns were one of the few harvests they were able to obtain.

The taking of the agave crown killed the plant. After the establishment of the Spanish missions in Lower California, the agaves often became scarce in the vicinity of the missions, for the Spanish priests brought numbers of the Indians together in one location. Food to feed the group sufficiently oftentimes could not be raised, and the meager resources of the land in the immediate vicinity were soon exhausted. The land could support small groups using the resources of large areas, but could not support large groups restricted to small areas.

The early explorers and missionaries commented on and deplored two of the food customs of some of these central Baja California Indians. During what was believed to be a ceremonial activity, the Indians tied a cord of agave fiber or human hairs around a piece of meat. A participant in the affair chewed the meat somewhat and swallowed it, but retained his hold on the cord, which he then used to pull the tidbit back out of his stomach. The masticated meat, plus string, was passed on to the next individual in line, and so on *ad nauseam.* Another noted custom

The incomparable boojum (*M. W. Larson*)

was known as "the second harvest." When available, quantities of fruit of a large cactus known as *pitahaya dulce* were eaten by the natives. During that harvest period, the Indians all defecated in one chosen location. Several weeks later, they collected their dried feces, ground them up, and winnowed out the undigested seeds. These were toasted, ground and eaten, providing additional nourishment at a time when food was not abundant.

The Spanish attempted to ameliorate these natives' harsh desert environment by introducing agriculture, grazing, and mission life. The most successfully introduced aspects of "civilized" life, however, proved to be syphilis, typhoid, and similar diseases which largely annihilated the Indians; the missions collapsed. Even today, with the advantages of modern technology, portions of Lower California support only a small fraction of the number that lived there successfully before the arrival of the Spaniards. Regardless of some of the methods they used for survival, the original inhabitants had reached—before the advent of the missions toppled it—a rather delicate equilibrium in relationship to their environment. And although modern man lives far more comfortably, this equilibrium with the environment is more than he can rightfully claim.

Of all the bizarre plants of the North American Desert, probably the strangest is the boojum tree. Forests of these plants are so incredible that even standing among them, you feel rather obliged to disbelieve what you are seeing. As we noted earlier, the boojum looks like a huge, somewhat wizened, inverted carrot. The tree may reach sixty feet in height; the circumference at the base may be as much as thirty inches, from which the grayish trunk tapers up gradually to the tip. Along the trunk grow a few very short, small, twiglike branches, arranged at regularly spaced intervals on great spirals about it. The top of the plant usually produces slightly longer branches, but even these appear so insignificant that the boojum gives the impression of being all trunk. Boojums belong to the same family as the ocotillos, and indeed, the boojum trunk bears a slight resemblance to a single ocotillo branch. Like the ocotillos, the boojum produces small leaves during favorable periods, and the leaf stems remain on the plant as spines after the leaf blade has been shed. Some boojums develop a trunk that forks near the apex, or occasionally, one gradually grows with the tip bending downward, and forming a great arc, finally reaches the ground surface.

The boojum trees are confined to the central section of Lower California, with but a single exception—they are also found in one location on

Boojum tree forming an arch (*M. W. Larson*)

the Mexican mainland, directly across the Gulf of California from their peninsula homeland. In Lower California the boojum is the distinctive plant of the Vizcaíno Region of the Sonoran Desert. In certain portions of this region the boojum forms great forests where the spires of the many plants rise far above all the other vegetation and stand naked and startling against the sky. Other plants in this impressive region include species of yuccas and agaves, a certain species of ocotillo, the cardon cactus, and the elephant tree. The latter is a small tree, usually about ten to fifteen feet tall. The trunk and limbs are exceedingly heavy and thick, and the limbs are often grotesquely branched. The bark of the tree is white, and the outer layers are shed as thin sheets.

The land of the boojums is difficult to reach and consequently is not visited by large numbers of people. Only one road traverses the length

A roadway in boojum country, Baja California (*M. W. Larson*)

of the Lower California peninsula, and it is barely a road, certainly no highway. In Sonora you can reach the mainland stand of boojums by leaving the main highway and driving approximately eight hours over dirt roads. To visit the boojum forests is an exhilarating experience—strange and unusual plants abound, the scenery is lonely and magnificent, and the wilderness complete.

Cirio (candle) the Mexican people call the boojum. *Idria columnaris* the scientists promote. But boojum, a good many Anglos say, deriving this strange name from a most unusual source. In *Hunting of the Snark* Lewis Carroll wrote a mythical account of an explorer and of a legendary "thing" called a boojum, said to dwell upon distant, unfrequented, desert shores. In 1922 Mr. Godfrey Sykes of the Desert Botanical Laboratory in Tucson organized an expedition to study strange plants that had recently been discovered by his son Gilbert. Upon first seeing the plants, the elder Mr. Sykes is reported as having said, "Ho, ho, a boojum, definitely a boojum." And boojum—a distinctive name for a distinctive plant—it is.

A fallen boojum; only the skeleton remains (*M. W. Larson*)

chapter seventeen

Life on the Dunes

S AND is a difficult environment in or on which to live. It represents
one of the restricted, special types of habitats within the desert. Some
animals, however, are particularly adapted for life on this friable founda-
tion. Notable among these are certain reptiles, and notable among the
reptiles is a small lizard known as the fringe-toed or sand lizard, of the
genus *Uma*. This reptile has several body modifications which contribute
to its success in the loose sand; in fact, it is restricted to this habitat, only
being found in dunes, hummocks, and sand flats.

These are medium-sized lizards, up to four-and-a-half inches in body
length plus tail. They are attractive with light-colored bodies, usually
matching the ground color of their area. On this background color are
black markings which tend to outline circular areas, with dots of color
within the eye-like circles. The back feet of these lizards are equipped
with lateral fringes of long, pointed scales—hence the common name
fringe-toed. These fringes are an aid for running over sand, increasing
the surface of the foot: a little like man's snowshoes but much less cum-
bersome. When disturbed, a sand lizard runs at great speed over the sand.
Occasionally one moving very fast does not even use its front legs in running, but holds them above the ground surface and propels himself with
the back feet only. The lizard may dash down a rodent burrow or bury

Pinacate beetle (*M. W. Larson*)

Fringe-toed sand lizard (*M. W. Larson*)

Hind foot of a fringe-toed sand lizard (*M. W. Larson*)

itself in the sand. In the latter case, the lizard, after this burst of speed, literally dives into the loose sand, swims under the surface far enough to completely cover itself, and then remains still and hidden. This is a most effective defense maneuver. Its speed puts a good distance between the lizard and its enemy; its entrance into the sand is so rapid that it is often difficult for the predator—including man—to see exactly where it disappeared; and it makes such a neat getaway that it leaves very little trace in the sandy surface to betray its presence. To achieve this sand "swimming," the lizard holds its front legs back against its body. Its head moves from side to side, and its hind legs kick alternately to produce the push. Finally the end of its tail is rapidly vibrated, bringing this also under the sand.

The "fringe" on the toes is also of value in helping this lizard kick his way under the sand. Its body is flattened and its surface very smooth, almost velvety—both of which help it glide easily through the sand. But even more impressive are certain modifications that keep sand grains from entering or irritating parts of its body. This lizard has valvular ear flaps to keep sand from entering the ears; overlapping eyelids help keep it out

A close-up of a fringe-toed sand lizard; note the underslung jaw (*M. W. Larson*)

of the eyes. If sand does accumulate in the eyes this lizard—and some other lizards also—has a nictitating membrane, a semitransparent tissue which sweeps across the eye, helping to clean it. The head is wedge-shaped, in keeping with the way it is used. The lower jaw is countersunk into the upper. These lizards have sand-trap nasal passages and nasal valves which prevent sand from reaching the lungs; thus they are able to breathe under the sand.

The *Uma* are found in portions of southeastern California, extreme southwestern Arizona, south into Sonora, and in northeastern Lower California. They are reported as often hibernating underground from about November to February. Their diet consists chiefly of insects, and for these they are dependent upon vegetation. Therefore, although they do often inhabit sand dunes, they do not live in completely barren areas, but rather in those which have at least some vegetation.

Sand cricket (*M. W. Larson*)

A study of *Uma notata* was carried out by Wilbur W. Mayhew on the
Sonoran Desert's Algodones Dunes just west of Yuma, Arizona. These
impressive dunes cover about 160 square miles of southern California
and extend into Lower California. In the area studied, temperatures as
high as 122°F occur, and temperatures of 109°F and above have been
reported for many consecutive days. The annual rainfall averages about
two-and-a-half inches, enough to support some widely spaced perennials,
primarily in the hollows between dune crests. Annuals bloom in the early
spring, following the winter rains, and the sand lizards there feed on
insects that are dependent upon this ephemeral vegetation. When annuals
and insects are both available, the sand lizards reproduce in the early
spring, but when the moisture has not been sufficient to promote the
growth of annuals, the sand lizards must depend upon insects from the
larger perennial vegetation. They are more difficult for these lizards to
obtain, and breeding is delayed until sufficient insect food has been
obtained to prepare the lizards' bodies for this activity. Mayhew states
that during dry years he has observed these lizards climbing as much as
two feet into the perennial vegetation—evidently in search of food—but
they have not been seen there in more favorable years when food could
be obtained on the low annuals. For these lizards then, low rainfall at

least delays the advent of breeding. With some animals in other desert areas (particularly quail) reproduction may be almost completely absent in years of low rainfall. In years of plentiful moisture—and therefore plentiful vegetation usually resulting in many insects and a good crop of seeds—the number of young produced may be extremely large. In the quail and similar cases, just what triggers excessive reproduction or inhibits it is physiological, but not completely understood; vitamins are probably one of the factors.

One particular species of horned lizard, *Phrynosoma m'calli*, is restricted to sandy areas and occurs only near the head of the Gulf of California, its range similar but not identical to that of the sand lizards. It feeds largely on ants, but takes other insects also. It, like the *Uma*, uses the sand for concealment and may dive into it headfirst or often buries its flat self by rapid sidewise movements of its body which quickly cover it. Although they live in an exceedingly hot environment much of the year, this horned lizard and the *Uma* are not capable of withstanding extreme temperatures, and both retire underground when the surface becomes well heated. The horned lizard is reported to retreat under the sand when the surface temperature reaches 106°F.

Of the lizards which inhabit sandy areas, the desert crested lizard, *Dipsosaurus dorsalis,* is best able to endure high temperatures. This lizard holds the record for the highest voluntarily tolerated temperature for any reptile; one individual having had a temperature of 115.5°F when that temperature was taken in the field. The desert crested lizard also has a range centering about the head of the gulf in California and Arizona but reaches as far north as southern Nevada and extreme southwestern Utah. It extends to the tip of Lower California, and through Sonora to Sinaloa. It is found in a variety of habitats from subtropical scrub, to sandy soils, to areas of windblown sand which is held in place by creosote bushes. It also occurs in the Algodones Dunes, already mentioned as one of the areas inhabited by the sand lizards.

The desert crested lizard is one creature that truly appreciates the creosote bush. In the spring when these bushes are in bloom, this lizard eats quantities of its blossoms, climbing up into the bushes to feed on them. During other parts of the year it feeds on other plants and scavenges. Being principally herbivorous, it stands in contrast to most other lizards. The creosote bush is also an important source of shade for this lizard, and under and among its roots these lizards often prepare their underground burrows or use those made by small mammals. Within its shallow burrow in the soil the lizard may—particularly at night—plug the entrance with sand. This probably serves to exclude predators; during the day, however, these lizards may remain in unplugged burrows. Dr. Kenneth Norris studied the ecology of the desert crested lizard and found that temperatures within the unplugged burrows ranged from approximately 95°F to 100°F. The burrows are used as retreats from the heat, as nocturnal resting places, and as the location for winter hibernation.

Norris found that of the North American desert reptiles, the desert crested lizard is able to remain active in hotter environments than any other genus. On a summer morning, it is the last of the lizards to appear aboveground. In fact, the sand lizards are just about to start their siesta when the desert crested lizards crawl out of their burrow beds and come aboveground. The activity periods of the two overlap only briefly. Once the desert crested lizard is warmed sufficiently after emergence, it begins foraging. The body temperature of such a foraging lizard ranges between 104°F and 107°F. As air and ground temperatures increase, the lizards often climb high in the creosote bushes or other plants to reach cooler layers of air. In this location they rest and also eat—if the creosote bushes are in bloom. As temperatures continue to rise, these lizards usually descend and rest in shade. Continued heat increase finally sends them down into burrows.

The desert crested lizard displays some interesting behavior in regard to the hot sand surface of its environment. If the lizard stops on hot sand, it may press its body into the surface and rapidly move its body and tail from side to side. In so doing, it breaks through the top layer of hot sand and reaches the slightly cooler levels below. At the same time, it may also use its front feet to dig in the sand, and move its body forward into the depression just formed. Unlike the sand lizards, the desert crested lizard is not burying itself, but simply reaching a slightly cooler layer on which to rest. If you have ever tried running barefoot on very hot pavement, you can empathize with the desert crested lizard trying to move across the hot sand. Moving or standing, it may flex its toes, hold its tail high above the hot surface, and elevate its abdomen.

An animal's tendency to have a color similar to that of the background becomes particularly apparent in a sand habitat. Here the sand background is rather uniform in color, and for protective coloration an animal primarily needs to approximate only that one color—it is unlike a more

Zebra-tailed lizard (*M. W. Larson*)

complicated habitat where numerous colors are present. A reptile whose color closely matches that of its background, such as sand, is in a more favorable position to avoid being seen by predators. Thus, protective coloration can develop in a species under predator pressure, through survival of the best-matched individuals. Kenneth Norris and Charles Lowe studied this color matching in certain reptiles and found that the reptile's colors often match very closely the colors of the surface on which it lives. The horned toads, *P. m'calli,* which occur on the reddish Algodones Dunes are themselves of that color; the same species living on whitish dunes, matches them. Specimens of the sand lizard *Uma notata* living on white beach dunes in northwest Mexico were found to be whitish. Only a short distance inland where there are reddish dunes—derived from a different source than those along the coast—the same species of lizard was reddish. In his study of the desert crested lizard Norris found that it, too, shows adaptation of its dorsal coloration to the soil, as in the Algodones Dunes.

Protective coloration can become an exceedingly complicated matter. Since an animal predator may see colors very differently than man does, the value of a certain animal's colors and patterns may not be immediately obvious to the human observer. For example, *Uma notata,* the sand lizard is distinctly marked, as we noted earlier, with dark eye-like spots over its whitish-to-rusty background color. Norris and Lowe state that a man can see this pattern from several yards away, but beyond this distance, the lizard, pattern and all, blends into the sand. At close range to a smaller predator the color and design on this lizard may tend to produce a disruptive pattern that helps conceal it. Horned lizards have developed great dependence on protective color and pattern which together closely approximate the background. Rather than running as a means of escape, they tend more often to press their well camouflaged bodies against the soil and depend upon this defense. It is highly effective where the human eye is concerned and must be the same for predators' eyes, for horned lizards are a successful group.

The desert crested lizard and the sand lizard are both diurnal and live in areas subjected to a great deal of solar radiation. It is of interest to note that they, like some other lizards, have a black coloration on at least portions of their interior anatomy. The locations of this internal coloration vary among the species. The desert crested lizard has a black tint on portions of the peritoneum, on the gall bladder, the blood vessels of the liver, and a portion of the brain. It is theorized that this dark pigment may shield certain vital areas of the body from ultraviolet radiation.

Among the snakes too, we find some species that burrow efficiently in sand. One, the western shovel-nosed snake, ranges northward from the head of the Gulf of California to southern Nevada. It is most common in sandy areas, but does range into other types of desert. It is reported as inhabiting some of the most barren sections of the desert, but does not extend into areas where vegetation is lacking. It feeds on spiders, insects, scorpions, and centipedes. The western shovel-nosed is small and nocturnal, about ten to sixteen inches in length. It readily crawls under the sand with the help of its shovel-like snout, countersunk lower jaw, smooth scales, nasal valves, and lateral ridges along the abdomen that give better traction and reduce slippage. The streamlined shape of a snake is of course a natural one for this activity; it has no troublesome projections like legs to get in the way. Another snake highly and similarly specialized for burrowing in sand is the banded sand snake. This burrower's favorite habitat is loose sand with bush-held hummocks. It is reported to be inclined to "cruise" just below the surface of the sand.

The sidewinder is a rattlesnake whose sidewinding motion is a valuable means of locomotion on loose surfaces such as sand, and helps this snake to exploit a special habitat. Sidewinders are not restricted to sand, sometimes being found on firm soil, but in these localities they are usually not far from a sandy area. This snake lives around the head of the gulf and northward, through southeastern California into southern Nevada and

Sidewinder rattlesnake (*M. W. Larson*)

extreme southwestern Utah. It reaches east to south central Arizona and extends southward into Sonora and Lower California. It is a fairly small rattler one-and-a-half to two-and-a-half feet long. Its head is large and broad and sports two hornlike projections over the eyes, giving rise to another of its common names, "horned rattlesnake." Over a ground color that matches its general habitat appears a slight blotched pattern; the tail is marked with light and dark bands. Sidewinder food consists of rodents such as kangaroo rats and lizards like the sand lizards. The snake is usually nocturnal; during the day it will enter burrows of small mammals or partially bury itself in the sand, usually in the shade of a bush. In doing so, it coils its body, and with slight outward movements of the loops, sinks into the sand until its back is approximately flush with the surface. In this position, with the sand lightly drifted over it, the snake's protective coloration is very effective.

Sidewinding is a complicated maneuver by which a snake progresses at an angle toward its goal. Throwing its body forward diagonally in a series of loops, the snake appears to be crawling sideways in a flowing S curve. By so doing, the force exerted is vertical, rather than horizontal, which represents the best way of pushing against a loose surface. The track left by the sidewinder is a series of short, unconnected straight lines at about a 30° angle with the direction of progression. Each track has a J-shaped mark at one end made by the head and neck, and the hooks of the J's show the direction of travel.

Movement by sidewinding may sometimes be carried out by other species of snakes if they find themselves on a very smooth surface where their usual means of moving is ineffectual. These are often awkward attempts and are not commonly used by such species. With the horned rattlesnake, however, sidewinding is the normal means of locomotion. Some Old World snakes also use sidewinding as their normal means of movement—these include the horned viper and the sand viper of the Sahara Desert and the South African horned viper of the Kalahari Desert. These sidewinding snakes are examples of convergent evolution, whereby genetically distinct organisms that share a common type of environment come to mimic one another. (Or in other words, similar adaptations to similar environmental conditions often produce animals which bear superficial resemblances to one another.) The common environment in this case is sand. By adaptation to the environment, each of these species has independently hit upon the same general formula for success in their particular environment—sidewinding locomotion.

Convergent evolution is particularly apparent among desert organisms, for in this environment conditions are extreme and clear cut, and adaptations to them must often be equally extreme. Cacti, for example, are a product of adaptation to the desert environment in the Western Hemisphere. In Africa there are succulent, spiny, large plants which to all appearances are large cacti. Actually these are members of a separate family—Euphorbiaceae—far removed from the cactus family, Cactaceae. The cactus-like euphorbias have simply hit upon the same basic plan for survival under conditions of heat and aridity. There is an Australian lizard, *Moloch horridus,* which occurs in arid regions, looks superficially much like our horned lizards, and even tends to feed on ants! The chuckwalla is a large, blackish North American lizard which lives among piles of large rocks in which it can obtain protection. It is a vegetarian. In the Old World are spiny-tailed lizards, *Uromastix,* which live among rocks, eat vegetation and look like the chuckwalla. Even the solution to food storage needs in an arid environment by development of repletes, or honeypots, has developed in separate subfamilies of ants.

Among the mammals, two foxes of separate genera have each evolved many of the same behavioral and physical adaptations to their desert environment. The fennec fox, a very small long-haired, light-colored creature with exceedingly large ears, lives in the desert regions of North Africa and on the Sinai and Arabian peninsulas. The head and body length are about fifteen inches, the tail about six to ten inches, the ears approximately six. It lives in burrows which it digs in the sand, is nocturnal, and eats plant materials and animals such as rodents, lizards, and insects—some of which it digs out of the ground. These foxes can evidently subsist without free water for considerable periods.

The fennec's North American counterpart is the kit fox, again a small animal about twenty-four to thirty-one inches in length, plus a nine to twelve-inch tail. It stands only nine to twelve inches at the shoulder and weighs a mere three to six pounds. Like the fennec, it is pale in color, grayish to buff-yellow, and has a bushy tail and very large ears. It digs its den in soft soil or in sandy areas among roots and is shy and nocturnal, only seldom seen in the wild. This delicate looking, dainty, and extremely attractive fox may dig out its food or run it down with a short fast dash. It eats lizards, insects, and rabbits, but especially rodents; it evidently has a distinct liking for kangaroo rats.

It is thought that perhaps the development of large ears in the kit foxes and the fennecs aids them in detecting the movements of their prey from a distance during their nocturnal hunting. (The development of large ears is a rather common feature among some other desert animals as well. The large ears of the antelope jackrabbits, also appear to have at least one slightly different purpose—that of radiating heat—although no doubt they do afford the rabbit an excellent sense of hearing.) The kit fox is adapted for its life in the sand by heavy stiff fur just inside the ears, thought to help exclude sand, and by the possession of hair pads on the feet to help the fox move more effectively on sand. The kit fox has a rather wide geographical range in western and southwestern United States, extending in one area from Canada into Mexico.

Some of the arid and semi-arid areas of the Old World are populated by small hopping rodents known as jerboas. They live in burrows in the ground and plug up the entrances during the hot day. They are active nocturnally, feed on seeds and plant materials, and can survive on metabolic water alone. They have long tails and back legs four times as long as the very short front ones. Their primary means of getting about is by jumping on the two hind legs. In other words, their adaptations are almost unbelievably like those of our North American kangaroo rats. These two types of animals, however, have evolved from two different families and are further examples of convergent evolution. In addition, there are other animals in the world, such as gerbils, which exhibit much the same adaptations to desert conditions as the jerboas and kangaroo rats.

We discussed the kangaroo rats as examples of animals beautifully adapted—physiologically and behaviorally—to living without free water supplies, metabolic water in conjunction with certain living habits proving sufficient for their needs. Mechanistically, we can say that these animals are very important links in the desert food chain producing moisture-filled meat from dry seeds for a wide variety of predators like kit foxes, coyotes, badgers, bobcats, snakes, and others. With more feeling we may note that these are some of the most attractive, interesting, and downright miraculous of the desert animals.

The kangaroo rats stand only about two inches high, but vary in length, depending upon species, from about eight to fifteen inches—more of this length is tail than body. Their dorsal portions are yellow to brown, the underparts white. The eyes are large, the end of the tail tufted. The legs and feet are the strangest part of its anatomy. The front legs and feet are very short and used approximately like hands; they may rest on the ground, but often do not. The rat uses them to pack seeds into its cheek pouches and to empty them out again by shoving forward with the front feet against the outside of the pouches. The back legs and feet are modified for jumping; the kangaroo rat rests and progresses on long appendages that look like miniatures of the back legs of kangaroos. This animal's general appearance is a little kangarooish, and certainly its mode of locomotion is.

The kangaroo rat may move about on all four feet, but when really

Kangaroo rat (*M. W. Larson*)

going somewhere he moves forward by great springing leaps, using only his hind legs to propel himself. These animals can cover about twenty feet a second and leap two feet per hop. The tail acts as a balancer and as a rudder, helping the animal zigzag and turn in mid-hop. (It is also used as a prop when the rat is standing.) This tremendous leaping activity is the kangaroo rat's chief means of defense, allowing it speedy and unpredictable flight from its predators. If caught in close quarters with an enemy, the kangaroo rat kicks sand in the enemy's face with its large back feet.

The kangaroo rats live singly in their burrows, which often have a mound over them with several entrances. Emerging only at night—and even then often not on bright moonlit nights—they collect seeds and plant materials. They carry these home in their cheek pouches, or may cache them along the way, returning for them another time—occasionally they forget some, the seeds germinate, and the kangaroo rats thereby act as plant disseminators.

There are many species of kangaroo rats. As a group they are located west of the Missouri River, from southwestern Canada into Lower California and south-central Mexico. They inhabit arid and semi-arid areas and prefer open ground which is better for leaping and better for seeing who's in the neighborhood. And just as the kit fox has big ears to hear the stirrings of creatures like kangaroo rats, so does the kangaroo rat have special aids to help him to hear the kit fox and similar predators. It possesses what are known as large *tympanic bullae,* or enlarged hearing chambers within the skull that serve to amplify sounds. Not surprisingly, certain jerboas also have large tympanic bullae.

Besides the kangaroo rat, other animals in our North American Deserts can live solely on dry food. These include at least two species of pocket mice of the genus *Perognathus* and the kangaroo mouse, *Microdipodops pallidus.* Pocket mice, harvest mice, deer mice, pack rats, ground squirrels, and similar small creatures—regardless of the means they use for making a living in the desert and whether independent of all except metabolic water or in need of water in succulent food—provide a very plentiful and very basic food supply for many other creatures of the desert. And as though one of the mice finally decided this matter of always being the prey had gone absolutely far enough, he and his progeny have become predators.

Surely there was never a more un-mouselike beast than the grasshopper mouse, for this animal (weighing in at a full two ounces) is a killer. One species inhabits much of the western United States; another lives in southwestern sagebrush, grass, and creosote bush areas. These mice are nocturnal, short-legged, and stout, and their diet is about 90 percent animal matter. They stalk their prey, and rush in and seize it; then they lay back their ears, close their eyes, and kill it by biting. The victims may be anything from grasshoppers (which along with other insects, make up about a fifth of their diet) to rodents or other grasshopper mice, to scorpions which are eaten in large numbers. As if to round out their image, these mice are reported to stand on their hind legs, point their nose to the sky, open their mouth, and produce a miniature wolf howl audible for fifty feet! Webster's says to be mousy is to be lacking in boldness or definition, colorless, timid, quiet, making no noise. Certainly Webster never met the two-ounce wonder of the mouse world. And if anyone ever compares you to a mouse, you can at least choose your species.

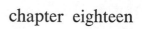

chapter eighteen

Grasslands and Mountain Country

IF you travel across the desert, ultimately of course, you reach its limits. These are not always immediately obvious: often you will only suddenly realize that you have left the desert behind. Reminders of it in the form of certain plants often continue for some distance, yet other new plants are appearing. The desert and its neighbor blend their boundaries for a distance until finally the new replaces the old. You may reach the desert's limits by travelling to its outer borders, or you may reach its limits by travelling up one of the tall mountain ranges that here and there rear above the desert surface. The North American Desert is bordered at its outer edges by a variety of types of vegetation depending upon the location—oak woodland and chaparral, piñon-juniper woodland, short grass plains, thorn forest, and desert grassland. If you ascend a tall mountain from the desert floor, you may leave the desert at the lower elevations and, depending upon the height of the mountain, pass through one or more different vegetational communities.

The desert grassland acts as a bridge between the Sonoran Desert and the Chihuahuan Desert, and is often the transition between desert and chaparral or evergreen woodlands as one ascends to higher elevations on the desert mountains of south-central and southeastern Arizona. These grasslands vary somewhat depending upon the soil, the topography, and

279

Desert grassland (plus a few yucca) in southern Arizona (*M. W. Larson*)

their history of use. Some support a good cover of grasses. Others have grass in combination with such larger plants as prickly pears, chollas, agaves, yuccas, ocotillos, and mesquites. Much of this desert grassland has undergone drastic changes within the last eighty years, with some of the more typically desert vegetation becoming much more prominent. This has proved very disturbing to cattlemen as well as a good many others, and investigations show how exceedingly interrelated are the many factors that determine what grows where.

Mesquite is usually classed as the number one villain in this story. More than one white man has swung at the end of a rope tied to a mesquite limb and J. Ross Browne, writing of his travels through the Southwest in the latter part of the 1800's, described an Apache Indian killed by white men, then hung from a "mesquit-tree" as a lesson to other

Mesquite bean pods, which demonstrate the tree's relation to the pea family (*M. W. Larson*)

Indians. The Indian was still hanging there two years later when Browne happened by. Dried, shrunken, and parchment-like, the body was adorned with arrows added by hostile Indians, and on the face was a "horrible grin" as the body swung in the slight breeze. Yet the mesquite has long been a blessing to the animals of the desert and was equally valuable to the Indians and early settlers. In many parts of the Southwest up to a hundred years ago, mesquites of the genus *Prosopis* were primarily trees of the bottomlands and washes, where they often grew to considerable heights and girths to form heavy, thick mesquite *bosques* or forests. Today, the bosques are gone—cleared to make way for agriculture and cut for firewood. Their replacements, if any, have had to make do with the reduced amounts of water available along the streams.

These trees belong to the pea and bean family and produce hard seeds enclosed in a pod which does not split open. The pods are eaten in quantities by many of the desert animals, and were formerly consumed by various Indian tribes. The Yuma Indians were described as having large mesquite harvesting celebrations. They gathered the pods, saturated them with water, and buried the sticky masses in the ground. In a day or two these were unearthed, shrunken and solid, ready to be stored and later ground into flour. White settlers, too, sometimes learned to use mesquite flour. The wood provided fence posts and lumber for the first settlers and continues to be used as an excellent, aromatic firewood. Mexican woodcutters travel into remote parts of their country (in trucks that only those of great faith would use to venture forth) to cut mesquites, ironwoods, and other trees, which they sell for firewood. The mesquite often helps stabilize sand dunes, for if parts of the tree are drifted over, it puts out more shoots which finally emerge triumphant above the sand. This process, if repeated often enough, may result in a tree with more trunk underground than above, and woodcutters sometimes dig out the subterranean portions too. If the upper part of tree has been cut down, the mesquite roots can also send up new shoots.

In order to germinate, mesquite seeds need to have their seed coats worn, eroded, or scarred. This service is admirably performed by the deer, cattle, and other animals who eat the seed pods. The seeds themselves pass undigested through the animals' digestive tract, but the seed coat is changed sufficiently to allow germination to take place. Cattle are therefore efficient disseminators of the mesquites: after carrying the seeds to new locations, they leave them with a deposit of fertilizer.

The 1880's saw the intensive overgrazing of these grasslands by cattle, which in turn was followed by the disastrous drought of the early 1890's. In *The Changing Mile,* Hastings notes that the major streams of southern Arizona were strikingly changed in the brief span of one summer. They tended to dig deep trenches. Waterflows were greatly decreased, greater erosion occurred along washes, and farmland was washed away. Marshes disappeared, and with them went the mosquitos and beavers. The grasslands, already overtaxed by grazing, now suffered from lack of moisture, and their grass cover was further reduced. Into the gap stepped the adaptable mesquite, which was followed by some "undesirables"—prickly pears, chollas, and burro weed—which often drastically lowered perennial grass production. Since then, these species have continued their takeover and have expanded in many areas. In one study, H. G. Reynolds and J. W. Bohning found that perennial grass production was cut 25 percent by burro weed, 10 percent by cactus, and 100 percent by mesquite. Over a seventeen-year period, George E. Glendening studied the changes in vegetation on one area of desert grassland. In his study area, mesquites

A fruiting prickly pear cactus (*M. W. Larson*)

more than doubled in number, while the density of perennial grass decreased more than 95 percent! Mesquites in such grasslands do not become the big shady trees they did in the bosque bottomlands, but still, a 30 percent crown canopy cover of smaller and shrubier mesquite will for the most part prevent the growth of perennial grasses. Cacti rapidly join the mesquites, for as soon as some of the grass cover is gone, they can make use of upper soil moisture previously used by grass roots. Without a good ground cover, erosion and run-off are added to the area's woes. Interesting studies of such changes have been made using "before" and "after" photographs—old photographs of grasslands have been located and compared with new ones taken at the same sites. Some of the differences are nothing short of phenomenal.

Certainly the extreme drought of the last century is far behind, and

Jackrabbit (*M. W. Larson*)

cattle have since been reduced to more sensible numbers. But if so, why are mesquites and cacti still multiplying so quickly in grasslands? No one is about to answer that question with any degree of certainty. There are some who still blame cattle for overgrazing, disseminating mesquite seeds, and compacting the earth. Rodents and rabbits come in for their share of the blame also. Where cholla and prickly pear abound, so does the pack rat who finds the remodeled grassland a fine homeland and helps to distribute cholla joints which can grow into new plants. Conversely, the pack rat has been found to eat very little grass, but to live primarily upon mesquite and cholla, the enemies of the grassland. Rats also exert a favorable influence upon the soil by collecting vegetative litter which eventually reduces to humus. There are two types of rabbits common to the southwestern desert: the cottontails and the jackrabbits. The desert cottontail, as an example of the first type, is present in many of the western states and Mexico. So, too, is the black-tailed jackrabbit. (A near relative of the latter, the antelope jackrabbit, is found along portions of the northwest coast of Mexico and enters only a part of southern Arizona.) Actually, the cottontails are rabbits, and the jackrabbits—so-called—are hares. The young of the rabbits are born naked, helpless, and blind. The young of the hares are born haired, with eyes open, and are able to run about a few minutes after birth.

In the desert the cottontails inhabit underground burrows, live on succulent vegetation, and are mainly nocturnal—which combination allows them to survive the aridity. They inhabit areas of brush as are found along washes, sufficient to afford some protection from predators. If pursued, they make a zigzag dash for a burrow or into brush to hide. They fail often enough—and also reproduce often enough—to feed an impressive number of desert reptiles, birds, and mammals.

It is the jackrabbits, rather than the cottontails, however, which are blamed for range deterioration when "rabbits" are being condemned. The jackrabbits are able to do without free water, surviving on the moisture in their succulent food. These animals are known to live in areas where the distance to water would be prohibitive. The jackrabbits stick it out on top of the ground, not retiring to burrows. This, combined with their rather common disregard for water supplies, proves their fine adaptation for desert living. These impressive-looking members of the rabbit clan are large, long, and lean, and appear to be predominantly ears, legs, and muscles. The black-tailed jackrabbit averages five-and-a-half pounds. Its total length is about twenty inches, plus three-and-a-half inches of tail. Its body is grayish; the top of the tail is black and its undersurface white. The antelope jackrabbit is even larger, with an average weight of eight pounds. Some females weigh up to ten pounds. The antelope jackrabbit has a slightly larger body than the black-tailed, and ears that may be eight-and-a-quarter inches long! This hare has whitish sides and underparts with a slightly darker back. It derives its name from white hair on its rump, similar to that sported by the pronghorn antelopes. Its long ears are not black-tipped, as are the black-tailed jackrabbit's.

If disturbed, both species run hard and fast, bounding over obstacles in their path. Theirs is not the zigzag course of the cottontail but a first-class show of speed, up to thirty and thirty-five miles per hour. The antelope jackrabbit is particularly noted for its leaps, which may cover ten to fifteen feet. The hare may jump to get a better view of the area around and in back of him. If hard pressed, his leaps become ground-hugging bounds that carry him along at a record speed, usually leaving his predator far behind. When the animal is undisturbed, darker hair largely covers the white fur on its rump, but when bounding away, the long white hair is erected and the very light patch is in evidence. The rabbit runs diagonally away for a distance, while the white rump patch flashes on the hip closest to his pursuer. Soon the rabbit changes course diagonally in the opposite direction, and the white patch shifts to the opposite hip. To achieve this showy maneuver, muscles pull the skin of the hind quarters over the back and up on one side, while also everting the hairs on that side. When the direction of travel is changed, the muscles of the one side are relaxed, and those of the opposite side cause the flash to occur there. The purpose of this flashy display is not known; it may be a means of startling and confusing predators.

Between their two species, the jackrabbits blanket the desert from grassland to creosote bush desert, with the antelope jackrabbit showing preference for grassland. The jackrabbits have as their resting place a form, the simplest of which may consist only of a favorite place where the rabbit lies in the shade and partial protection of a plant. The forms are often a little more elaborate; a slight depression having been scratched out in the soil. These average about three to six inches in width and from about a foot to a foot and-a-half in length. They may be dug below the ground surface to a depth of 3 or 3½ inches. The forms are often located beneath the branches of mesquite or catsclaw, or under cholla where they are among the fallen cactus joints. Relaxed in the form, the jackrabbit may lie with its forelegs under the front part of the body, the backs of them down and the palms up, or may stretch its front legs out in front of it. Its ears lie lowered and relaxed along its back. An alarm usually causes its ears to snap to attention and its body to come erect. At this point it may choose to run, or conceal itself in the form by crouching low, with the long ears held tightly against its back. Jackrabbits evidently use numerous forms in their territory which may be several miles in diameter. This is not to say that the jackrabbits live singly, for Charles Vorhies and Walter P. Taylor report that small groups of two to six individuals— especially antelope jackrabbits—are often seen together at all times of the year.

Jackrabbits have a good sense of smell. Their large eyes are evidently more proficient at discerning movement than they are at distinguishing still objects. Thanks to their enormous ears, they have a good sense of hearing. These ears, however, also probably serve as heat radiators, as we have already suggested. Schmidt-Nielsen states that the jackrabbit is too small to use water for successful heat regulation, but that it does not "avoid" heat by going underground. These hares have no sweat glands, but do lose some moisture through insensible perspiration in addition to respiratory losses. Evidently the jackrabbit survives in the desert by making the greatest possible use of microclimates. Schmidt-Nielsen suggests that when they are resting in the shade of vegetation during the hot day, both the ground on which they lie and the surrounding air have a temperature lower than that prevailing in the open desert. In the depressions of their forms, the rabbits are largely protected from indirect radiation from adjacent hot ground surfaces. In this position, their large ears, only lightly-haired and well supplied with blood vessels, are valuable tools with which to radiate heat from the body to the surrounding atmosphere.

The hares make a good living in the grassland. Following the winter rains they eat grass and in dry May and June they switch to mesquite and cactus. After summer rains they return to the grass until it dries up once again. They also chew on catsclaw, palo verdes, crucifixion thorn, and other plants. Prickly pear cactus is a favorite nibbling item, as are some of the smaller cacti and even the saguaros. If a rabbit can make a start among the spines of a barrel cactus, it will often consume the plant almost completely. Vorhies and Taylor, who carried out a study of these animals, report that the jackrabbit carefully pushes its nose between the clumps of spines until its teeth can get a hold on the flesh of the cactus and pull it loose, thus making an opening in the plant. These rabbits are not immune to the spines, however, for they reportedly get stuck frequently and have trouble removing spines from their paws.

This study found that 56 percent of the antelope jackrabbit's diet brings it into competition with cattle; the black-tailed jackrabbit has a 41 percent score. It would take 74 antelope jackrabbits or 148 black-tailed jackrabbits to consume as much as one cow.

Cattle, unfortunately, are often the measure of almost everything, and comparisons like these were enough to exterminate millions of prairie dogs. The jackrabbits increase on overgrazed areas and are often given the blame for the condition, when in actuality the overgrazing is more

Prairie dog (*M. W. Larson*)

the cause of the rabbits. When there is fresh grass, it is usually sufficient for both the cattle and the rabbits of the area. But when this is gone, the rabbits can still feed well for the remainder of the year on mesquite and cacti, whereas the cattle cannot. The rabbits are thus usually well provided for the year round, even on overgrazed land. Much the same is true of the pack rats, which are sometimes partially blamed for the condition of the range. They can simply thrive on the vegetation that cattle cannot, and overgrazing provides this vegetation.

Some specialists feel that a distinct climatic change has taken place over at least parts of the Southwest since the 1890's, and that this hotter, drier trend is the main cause of some of these dramatic vegetational changes. Most are inclined to say there are a good many interrelated factors. The range has often been overgrazed, and cattle today are a part of the total picture, interacting with the environment. Damaged grass cover allows the entrance of shrubs, weeds, and cacti; and cattle help distribute mesquite seeds. Of course, erosion on damaged range plays a part in its future. Records do show that in at least a part of this area there have been generally higher temperatures and lower rainfall since the turn of the century. Some wildlife has evidently increased due to some of these causes, and they in turn may now be affecting the total picture. Man has shot, poisoned, and otherwise attempted to "control" predators who feed upon the rodents and rabbits of the grassland. Something once started is difficult or impossible to stop. Momentum often is gained along the way, strange side-effects are spawned, and the whole spirals to a situation that man can neither wholly predict nor wholly dissect to explain.

It is easy to leave the desert, at least in some of its parts (particularly south-central and southeastern Arizona) by ascending a mountain, many of which rise rather abruptly from either the desert or from the intervening desert grassland. A person travelling up a high mountain can pass through several different vegetational zones, each with its characteristic animal inhabitants.

Leaving the saguaro forests around Tucson, you can ascend within an hour to the top of the nearby Catalina Mountains, where there is winter skiing among the pines. In southeastern Arizona lie the beautiful Chiricahua Mountains, in and around whose lower levels lived Cochise, the famous leader of the Apaches. In south-central Arizona, the smaller but equally interesting Huachuca Mountains rest atop the Mexican border. Numerous other ranges, many not as large as these, dominate the landscape of much of the southwestern deserts. These mountains tend to rise abruptly and completely, with little of the "foothill" prelude that one finds with some of the extensive mountain ranges in other parts of the country.

The view of the desert mountains is an ever-changing and rewarding one. Deep purple in the waning light; stark and gray in midday, contrastingly light and dark when clouds shade parts; dark, ominous, and powerful when the storm clouds build over their tops; gray and silver with the pattern of falling rain upon their sides illuminated by an unclouded sun— all these moods make the mountains a dramatic backdrop for the lower deserts about them. The mountains are the great procurers of moisture. Their height captures the rain and snow that bypass the lower deserts, and in turn some of this water flows down to the needy lowlands.

The vegetational zones on a mountain are termed "life zones," under

Ladybird beetles in the autumn, massing for hibernation; they often spend the winter on desert mountains (*M. W. Larson*)

a system set up by C. Hart Merriam, who worked in the San Francisco Mountains of Arizona just before the turn of the century. Life zones are a convenient way of classifying an area, and are primarily applicable to western North America. For example, the Sonoran Desert lies in the Lower Sonoran Zone. The Great Basin and grasslands lie in the next higher zone, the Upper Sonoran. Next, at about 7000 to 8000 feet above sea level in the southwest, is the Transition Zone, supporting oaks and pines. This is followed by the Canadian Zone at about 8000 to 9500 feet, with a cover of Douglas fir and aspen. The Hudsonian Zone extends from 9500 to 11,500 feet and supports white fir and spruce. The final area above timberline is the Arctic-Alpine Zone. As you can see, ascending a mountain in Western North America is similar to travelling north in the same area. The Lower Sonoran Zone is found at sea level in Mexico. Going north, you would pass through the intervening zones until finally reaching the Arctic-Alpine Zone at sea level near the pole.

Each of these zones on a mountain supports special vegetation and special animals, some of which range through more than one zone, others of which are rather restricted. Many of the animals are confined by the surrounding country to the mountain range on which they find themselves as surely as if they were on an island surrounded by water. The birds, if they so desire, can come and go, as can some of the largest mammals, but the smaller creatures are there to stay. Evidently this was not always so in a cooler time when many of the northern-type plants and animals reached these mountains. Their ancestors arrived long ago, and with the climatic changes that have occurred since that time, these animals have now been isolated on their high islands.

The Huachuca Mountains lie along the Mexican border between Nogales and Douglas, Arizona. At their foot lies Fort Huachuca, established as protection against the Apaches, and still active today as a military camp. A small town named Fry once existed there, and no doubt in the early days the soldiers and their families living there did just that in the summer. Today it is a city, and so has been given the more prosaic name of Sierra Vista. The Huachucas consist of a single range approximately twenty-five miles long and four miles wide, covering only about 100 square miles. Its highest peak barely reaches the 9500 foot level.

Streambeds, sometimes dry, sometimes flowing, follow the canyons down to the bajadas that skirt the base of the range. By taking a narrow dirt road with a good many switchback turns, one can climb very nearly

Mountains and grassland in the Huachucas of southern Arizona (*M. W. Larson*)

to the top of the range in a matter of thirty minutes. The views along the way are impressive. You stand in the pines with the mountainside dropping very nearly straight down, and below at the mountains' base, the grassland and desert stretch to the far horizon, and you can see to the next mountain range and on to another and another.

There are four life zones represented in this area (as delimited by Donald Hoffmeister and Woodrow Goodpaster who studied the mammals of the Huachucas)—the Lower Sonoran, briefly represented; Upper Sonoran; Transition; and Canadian. (The two highest life zones do not occur in these mountains.) Several different plant belts occur within these zones, and the various species of plants present at any one location is dependent upon many factors including elevation, slope, exposure, moisture, and insolation. There is thus an interesting and fruitful blending of plants providing extremely varied habitats. Ascending the mountain there are, in general, zones of grassland, then oak woodland, pine-fir forest, and aspen.

Animal life is richly represented in this mountain range. Habitats are varied; northern species of animals are well represented, having reached this far south at some past time, and some of them making it no farther. Southern species of animals are plentiful. For some of these, the Huachucas represent their actual or approximate northern limits; they lie along the border, and some species, like the wolf are thus here allowed easier access across the border than would be possible in many other locations. Place all these factors in an area of approximately 100 square miles and you have a rich field for observation and study. For that reason the Huachucas have long been popular with scientists who here find concentrated large numbers of species of plants and animals in interesting and complex interrelationships with each other and the environment.

In this mountain range, Hoffmeister and Goodpaster listed seventy-eight different kinds of mammals (this is 40 percent more than in the listed seventy-eight kind of mammals (this is 40 percent more than in the entire state of Illinois!) and 536 different plants. They reported eleven kinds of hummingbirds alone. Of all the birds that breed in North America, about one-quarter of these species are represented in the Huachucas. This survey, including the bajada area about the base of the Huachucas, revealed ten species of bats, plus six more species which are rare or known only from museum specimens for this area, four kinds of skunks, ring-tailed cats, badgers, gray foxes, coyotes, bobcats, various squirrels, many species of small mice, three species of kangaroo rats, two species of pack rats, porcupines, raccoons, two species of cottontails, black-tailed jack-rabbits, peccaries, mule and white-tailed deer, and brown bears. Prong-horn antelope, black-tailed prairie dogs, and kit foxes were exterminated from the area long ago. Jaguars have been sighted here in the past. Occasional wolves come into the area from northern Mexico, where their extermination fortunately has been less thorough than in the United States. Mountain lions are permanent residents in spite of the fact that they are hunted for a sixty-five-dollar bounty. These are beautiful, tawny cats who mainly inhabit the rimrock in the Huachucas. They may be up to eight feet in length, including the long tail, some weighing as much as 200 pounds (although most are smaller). They are excellent predators

Coatimundi (*M. W. Larson*)

and concentrate primarily on deer. The mountain lion, the wolf, and coyote are efficient biological controls, weeding out sick and weak animals; and man's harsh treatment of these three has not often been in his own best interests.

One strange immigrant into the area is the coatimundi or "chula." This is a medium-sized brownish mammal with a body approximately two feet long, terminating in a tail of about the same length which the coatimundi usually carries in a vertical position. The animal has the face mask of the raccoon, but an elongated, pointed nose. Coatis are gregarious, roaming in groups, rooting with their strange noses in loam or leaf litter for insects and roots. They will eat small mammals and birds if they are able to find them, and also feed on berries and other plant foods. They climb trees readily. Within the last fifty years, the chulas have been extending their range northward into the higher elevations of Arizona and New Mexico. There are three species, only one of which reaches the United States. This particular species also ranges down into South America.

We once gave a ride to a Mexican who was travelling along a dirt road in the thorn forest of southern Sonora. He loaded into our car a burlap sack containing deer hides and a tin bucket in which reposed a very dead chula. In my less than fluent Spanish I inquired what he planned to do with the chula. Even I could understand his happy answer, "Tacos, Señora, tacos!"

chapter nineteen

The Desert and the Sea

WHERE the desert meets the sea, man comprehends something of the enormity and power of natural forces in the world. Here the very-wet meets the very-dry, and each stretches magnificently unbroken and unsubdued, to its respective horizons. Going to the sea is yet another way in some areas to reach the desert's limits, and the contrast between the watery medium which supports life abundantly and the desert land which succors it less amply is striking.

In the Sonoran Desert there is a large amount of desert shore line, arid country encircling much of the Gulf of California. In these many hundreds of coastal miles, the desert assumes various appearances, but is almost everywhere still wild and relatively unchanged by man. Such a piece of wilderness near the ocean lies between the Mexican-American border and the Gulf of California in the area southwest of Ajo, Arizona.

Access to the area is not easy, however. A Mexican highway completed only in 1956 now traverses its northern edge along the boundary. By turning south from this and travelling over dirt trails established by woodcutters' trucks, one moves slowly through sparse desert to a 600 square mile wonderland of ancient volcanic activity known as the Sierra Pinacate. Dominating the area are two main black, striking peaks, the tallest slightly over 4000 feet in height. Surrounding the main peaks and extend-

297

The Pinacate Region (*M. W. Larson*)

Cloverleaf crater (*M. W. Larson*)

Caldera, seen from the rim (*M. W. Larson*)

ing for many miles beyond are lava beds, irregularly punctuated with cinder cones.

The area's outstanding geological features are a number of "craters" specifically known as *calderas*. Seen from the air, they appear as gigantic pockmarks in the terrain, but from the ground the craters appear as low, flat-topped hills. Climbing such a hill, however, one is suddenly astonished to top the rise and see spread out below a magnificent crater sunk in the earth. Such a caldera is MacDougal, which measures approximately 5000 to 5700 feet in diameter and 430 feet in depth. The walls of the depression fall steeply to the almost flat floor, where here and there grow the giant saguaros, dwarfed by their distance below the rim. MacDougal is but one of several calderas of various sizes.

Each is considered to have been formed by a process whereby ejected volcanic material was built into a cone at the site. The magma underground lost great amounts of gas, and some of the magma itself was lost, hence the magma reservoir under the cone shrank. The center part of the cone and parts of the vent wall collapsed into this underground void.

Edge of a lava flow, with brittlebush in the foreground (*M. W. Larson*)

The result is known as a collapse caldera, and the Pinacate region has an outstanding representation of this volcanic formation.

The black lava surface of the Pinacates is in some areas stark and bare, but much of this country supports sparse desert growth of cacti, ocotillo, brittlebush, crosote bush, and along the washes, paloverde, ironwood, and other plants. The black rocks and dark sand and soil meet on their southern, western, and—to some extent—eastern borders, with light-colored sand dunes, derived from the gulf. To the south these dunes stretch approximately twenty miles to the gulf waters; to the west, they flow inland from the coast and ultimately end at the point where the Colorado River meets the gulf. This forbidding sandy expanse to the west of the Pinacates is often called El Gran Desierto. Photographs of the area taken from space show strikingly the expanse of lighter sand, abutting and flowing from the dark Pinacates toward the River and the sea.

Sandy desert in the Pinacate Region (the tree is covered with mistletoe) (*M. W. Larson*)

An ancient trail once led from northern Mexico across what is now northwestern Sonora and southwestern Arizona, whose ultimate destination was California and Lower California. This trail skirted around the Pinacates, stayed generally north of the dunes of El Gran Desierto and followed an irregular route through extreme desert from one slight water source to another. Indians first developed the route; later they led the Spanish along it. Father Kino travelled this path, and it is thought that he and his party climbed Pinacate Peak in 1706 to view the country and Gulf to the west in their attempt to determine if California was an island. This difficult trail was known as El Camino Real, but ultimately came to be called *El Camino del Diablo*—the Devil's Highway, and the trip along it called *Jornada del Muerto*—Journey of Death. Used by unknown numbers of people who, lured by gold, land, or simply fate, attempted to reach California from the United States and Mexico, the "highway" reaped a

Natural "water tanks" (*M. W. Larson*)

The same tanks filling with water (*M. W. Larson*)

grim human toll. Graves along it were common. Lack of water, strength, and foresight killed many; robbers and plunderers—Indians, Anglos, and Mexicans—added to the travellers' woe. Travel on this trail was possible only due to certain "tanks" to be found along it—that is, holes naturally gouged in the rock of washes which caught water during occasional storms and consequent brief streamflow, and which were deep enough to retain this water for some time.

Such tanks also exist in the Pinacate region, and because of their presence in this dry land, small numbers of Indians were able to live in the

Indian metate in the Pinacate Region, used to grind seeds (*M. W. Larson*)

Pinacates and in the barren desert around this lava area. These people generally were known as Sand Papagos or Areneños. The particular group that dwelt in the Pinacates has been termed Areneño Pinacateño. If the river-dwelling Pima Indians considered the desert-dwelling Papagos their "poor relations," then certainly the Areneños must have been the "poor relations" of the Papagos in general.

The Pinacateños were a small group dependent upon the water stored in the *tinajas* or tanks of their area. They practiced no agriculture, but lived off the wild products of their environment.

Although they spoke a Papago dialect, they were generally hostile to other Papagos and appear to have been on good terms with only the Yumas, who lived along the Colorado River to the west. They traded with them and obtained pottery; the Pinacateños did not manufacture any pot-

Indian shell mound. An earth-colored pottery shard is visible in the center (*M. W. Larson*)

tery of their own. Near the tinajas today, one finds their manos and metates, an occasional obsidian arrow point, many sea shells, camp clearings, gyratory cone crusher bases, and broken pottery. It is easy to imagine the woe of the Pinacateño women over the ages who dropped and shattered the precious bowls or jars that produced these fragments. Occasionally complete pieces of pottery, from large water jars to smaller bowls, are discovered in the Pinacates; long ago the Indians carefully secreted these in rocky crevices for safekeeping. Pinacateño life involved considerable travelling from one tinaja to another, and valuable possessions such as pottery were no doubt cached from time to time until the owners could return. To the archaeologist, the discovery of such an artifact is extremely exciting and provocative. Who hid it and why? How many hundreds of years has it remained here? Surely its owner did not

San Esteban chuckwalla (*M. W. Larson*)

simply forget. Did catastrophe strike before he or she could return to the hiding place? These questions go largely unanswered.

In this large, lonely land bathed by sun and today stirred only by the wind, one can imagine the people camped near the tinajas. Long ago the women collected plant products and ground seeds in their metates or in deep holes worn into the rocks near tinajas where they must have gathered to work and gossip. The men hunted desert bighorn sheep, once more plentiful in the rough terrain provided by the Sierra Pinacate peaks and craters. (Today they are only occasionally seen in the area.) The flat lands provided grazing for the pronghorn antelope, which they hunted, but which is rare in this region today.

Among the dark volcanic rocks lived the big, fat chuckwalla lizards, and it is possible that these were eaten. Chuckwallas are heavy-bodied lizards up to eight inches in length, plus a blunt-tipped tail. Black, dark

306

Indian shell mounds in the Sonoran Desert (*M. W. Larson*)

gray, or brown with blotches of lighter colors, they live among jumbles
of rocks, and the piles of volcanic debris in the Pinacates are ideal for
them. When threatened, they retreat among the rocks, puff themselves up
with air, and thus lodge themselves in, making it difficult or impossible
for a man or animal to remove them. The chuckwallas, strangely, are
vegetarians, living largely on creosote bush and the bright yellow flowers
of a plant especially common in the Pinacates known as brittlebush. Other
Indian tribes were reported to stab chuckwallas as they were wedged in
the rocks, deflating them, after which they cooked and ate them. The
Pinacateños may well have done so too, since chuckwallas are still plentiful in parts of the Pinacates. Rabbits, too, were present and were a staple
food. It is said that the Areneños were capable of running rabbits to death
on the sand dunes. The importance to these people of the sea—to which
they must have journeyed frequently—is apparent by the great numbers

of sea shells, bleached and white, lying on the dark rocks and soil of the Pinacates. They were dropped by the Indians who ate the meat from them and then discarded them or used them as implements for a time.

The Pinacate region is criss-crossed by trails—smoothly-worn paths in the gravel surface. These connect one water hole to another, and they probably stand out today almost as clearly as they did when they were regularly trod by Indian feet. Along them, an occasional sea shell or pottery shard gives evidence of an ancient pedestrian. The ground surface of this country is only slightly covered by vegetation. Desert pavement, rocks, gravel, isolation, and only meager precipitation combine to produce a surface that has changed very little over hundreds of years. For this reason, any signs left by man are readily apparent. Sleeping circles built of rocks, paths worn in the gravel, clearings for camps, large figures outlined with rocks on the desert pavement, tools, pottery shards, shrines —all remain much as the Indians left them long ago. Thus apparent, they are unfortunately vulnerable to the tampering of modern man, who also leaves his marks on the Pinacates—not only by his regrettable habit of leaving tin can artifacts on the desert (where they almost never deteriorate due to the dryness) but by simply driving off the roads onto the desert surface, where tire marks disturb the desert pavement and remain apparent for years.

The Papago Indians from farther north regularly made pilgrimages near and through this area to the Gulf shore where, with much ceremony and tradition, they obtained quantities of salt. They utilized tinajas and rare springs on their journey; out in the dunes near the shore where they gathered the salt, they knew locations where brackish water for drinking could be obtained by digging. In later years some of these Papagos described the Pinacateños as "bad people." In 1851 evidently, the Pinacateños, who were never present in large numbers, very nearly died out from the "black vomit"—perhaps yellow fever. The few survivors went to live with the Areneños, who then eventually made some use of the Pinacate area.

Today the Indians are gone from the Pinacates. A few Mexican cattle roam the northern area around Papago Tanks, which unlike many of the smaller tanks, usually retain some water year round. Occasional Mexican cowboys work in the area, and a few Anglos come to hike, camp, and explore. Otherwise, the Pinacates are still one of the isolated, quiet, little-changed natural desert areas of North America. To the north, El Camino

Automobile tracks in the Pinacate Region (*M. W. Larson*)

del Diablo has been largely obliterated by the Mexican highway and the international boundary fence. The trail's western portions that are located on what today is American land largely fall within an area used by the United States Government, and this is closed to unauthorized persons most of the time. West of the Pinacates, El Gran Desierto is cut by a set of Mexican railroad tracks, but otherwise probably remains much the same as J. Ross Browne described it in the 1860's when he and his party traversed it by horseback, travelling from the Pinacates along the shore to the mouth of the Colorado River, "this miserable shore . . . these interminable sand-hills—having no grass for our animals, and nothing but the brackish water obtained by digging wells in the sand along the seashore."

As with almost every region difficult to reach or little known, there are tales of treasure. One old story relates that somewhere in the sand dunes east of the Colorado River, there lie the remains of an old mission. Its crumbling walls are near a spring, and an ancient smelter suggests hidden riches. Another bit of folklore relates a story of treasure hidden in the Pinacates. Travellers along El Camino del Diablo had no choice but to use the only waterholes available. There, like thirsty desert animals, they were easy prey for predators—in this case, bandidos of any of several races. Robberies and murders were common. Supposedly, the Indians had developed the nicotine habit and by the mid 1800's robbed travellers either coming to or going from the California gold fields of tobacco and gold. According to the story, the Indians smoked the tobacco, but hid the gold in the Pinacates.

These make good, unbelievable yarns, but probably the region's best tales are ones we can only surmise. On a dusty flat near Papago Tanks we once found a pendant. Triangular in shape, with a small hole drilled in one point and with the edges carefully ground smooth, it was a piece of china, suspiciously resembling the old-fashioned blue willow ware. Where it came from, how it was obtained, who proudly wore it, and what ultimately brought it here to lie in the dust no one will ever know. In the same area, exposed in a small wash, we found the front half of a large, rusty padlock. A dent suggested the lock was opened by a blow or a shot. The raised letters revealed its ownership: *"U.S. Mail."*

Many stories have been written with a "desert" island background. Adorned with coconut palms and exotic plants in most cases, these were anything but desert islands. The real thing, however, exists in the Gulf of California. Approximately 225 miles south of the Pinacates on the Mexican mainland coast lies Kino Bay, and west from Kino Bay to the shore of Baja California stretches the narrowest portion of the Gulf of California. Spread like steppingstones across the approximately sixty miles of watery gulf are approximately fifty islands. This region comprising the two opposing desert coasts and the desert islands lying between them is known as the Midriff.

The gulf itself is a long narrow arm of the Pacific, surrounded on three sides by the Mexican mainland and the peninsula of Baja California. It is only at the gulf's narrow southern end that its waters connect with those of the Pacific. At its northern end lies the mouth of the Colorado River. The gulf dead-ends in extreme desert country such as El Gran Desierto, and much of the coast that borders the gulf, both on the mainland and the peninsula, has been only slightly developed. Therefore the gulf has never become of great significance for waterway transportation and has remained relatively little-used, except by Mexican fishermen and in late years, by tourist fishermen from the United States. Long ago the Spanish explorers utilized it to some extent; and another name for this body of water, given it by those Spaniards, is *El Mar de Cortez*, or the Sea of Cortez, after the conqueror of Mexico.

In about 1540, Hernando de Alarcon commanded three ships sent with supplies to aid the army of Coronado in its search of the Southwest for the fabled seven cities of gold. Alarcon sailed up the gulf, and with a great deal of difficulty, ascended the Colorado River for some distance by ship. Unfortunately the overland party and the supply party arriving by sea never made contact with each other. Eventually Alarcon sailed back down the gulf, and when a scouting party from the main expedition finally reached the Colorado River all they found was a message from Alarcon carved on a tree and letters buried beneath it. (This was only one of the many disasters of the expedition; the seven cities of gold also failed to materialize.) In the 1800's, some ship travel, particularly of United States Army personnel and materials, took place up the gulf and the Colorado River, but the river travel was exceedingly difficult at best. In that same century, Guaymas on the Mexican coast near Kino Bay was a port used by southwestern mining interests in their attempts, beset by difficulties, to carry on mining activity. At the same time there were a good many individuals in the United States who urged Congress to buy enough Mexican territory to give the United States a port on the gulf. Their pleas went unheeded, and today it is interesting to speculate what changes an American port might have wrought on the gulf itself. All in all, however, the Sea of Cortez remains today a relatively isolated, little exploited body of water.

The waters of the gulf are among the world's richest in animal life. Air-breathing man is forced to remain on top of the water's surface or is burdened by equipment and awkwardness when he attempts to probe beneath it, but from the gulf he receives many obvious signals of abundant animal life. Commercial Mexican fishermen have long made their living from the fish, shrimp, and turtles of these waters. Sports fishermen report the fishing in the gulf as some of the very finest in the world; they drive to Mexican mainland ports or fly in increasing numbers into Baja, from whence they take boats into the gulf.

A trip by ship across the Midriff gives much evidence of the teeming

Dolphins (*M. W. Larson*)

underwater life in the gulf. One or more schools of dolphins, often containing hundreds of individuals, is almost certain to be encountered. They can be seen from afar as they swiftly approach the ship, leaping from the water, swimming gracefully and with remarkable speed. They move—seemingly almost effortlessly—in the wake of the ship, at its sides, and beside the bow, leading it through the blue-green waters. If any animals in the world can be said to display curiosity or joy, and to approach what egotistical man might term a "human" level of awareness, certainly they must be these sleek, beautiful animals which abound in the gulf. Stranger, less well-known animals such as the manta rays, leaping forth momentarily from the water, are also seen in the waters of the Midriff. Divers who enter the waters surrounding the islands encounter multitudes of fish. Green sea turtles are numerous. So, too, are sharks; and one of the

Finback whale in the Gulf of California; note the light spray of water droplets from the blowhole (*M. W. Larson*)

large islands of the Midriff is called *Isla Tiburón,* Spanish for "Shark Island."

Most awe-inspiring of the gulf's inhabitants are the whales, often in evidence in the waters of the Midriff. An individual whale may be seen in the far distance as a faint, dark curve on the water's surface, and periodically above the curve rises the spout from the animal's blowhole. This is not liquid water being shot into the air, but is water vapor from the lungs condensing as it hits the open air. Whales are magnificent creatures, unbelievable even when in sight. Like the dolphins, they, too, sometimes appear to be moved by curiosity and to approach ships.

Anchored in an island bay in the Midriff, we were one day startled to hear a whale spout as it surfaced within twenty-five feet of the ship; it then submerged and swam on. On another memorable day of whales,

Osprey nesting in cardon cactus (*M. W. Larson*)

aboard an 85-foot boat in the Midriff we watched these gigantic creatures, and saw as many as fifteen spouting at a single time. Cutting the boat's motors we drifted, alone except for the blue sea and sky and the whales. Two were interested in the boat, and kept coming ever closer over a period of an hour. One finally lost its reserve and surfaced numerous times beside the ship—it was almost as long as the ship itself. Climbing to the top of the ship's cabin, we gazed down upon this mammal so different from ourselves. As its great length rolled up from the depths, we saw barnacles growing upon its fins and could look down into its blowhole. Its body continued to roll up, then downward out of sight. Finally, instead of surfacing parallel to the ship, the whale surfaced as it travelled head-on towards us. At the last minute it dove, skimming under us, and again surfaced on the ship's opposite side. It repeated this maneuver several times and then, its curiosity satisfied—or tiring of the game—it left us. The Mexican crewmen laughingly shouted "¡Cuidado! ¡Cuidado!" (Careful!) as it approached, and we shouted in excitement, yet I don't think any of us seriously feared the intentions of the mammoth animal—nor, I think, did the animal fear ours.

The islands that rise out of the waters of the gulf in the Midriff section consist of extreme desert country. Most (although not all), are without any source of fresh water. Plant life is generally sparse, but one large type of cactus triumphs over the environmental conditions and thrives in large numbers on many of these islands. This is the cardon, which in many ways resembles the saguaro cactus. Like the saguaro, it is composed of a fluted trunk and branches, but the cardon is more massive than the saguaro. It branches nearer to the ground, is more compactly branched, and may have as many as thirty branches. It may reach thirty to forty feet in height.

The desert island of San Pedro Martir is one of the many in the Midriff, and it well illustrates the abundant resources provided by the ocean waters in comparison to the scarce ones provided by the desert environment. Almost all of the animal life—and they are present in exceedingly large numbers—consists of species which although based on the land, derive their livelihood from the sea.

Most of this particular island consists of tall, steep desert hills that drop off to the ocean in sheer cliffs; in these are rocky caverns. We once visited this island in late May and found along the entire shore line thousands of sea lions. Large males, smaller females, and young rested on the rocks or swam in the water. Day and night their constant chorus, against the noise of the swirling water, echoed and reechoed by the caverns and cliffs, punctuated with the deep coughing sounds of the bulls, variously resembled the talk of sheep and goats. On a low beach were more sea lions, including females with newly-born, big-eyed, soft-haired young. About the rocks of the beach were large crabs of a beautiful orangish-red adorned with turquoise and other colors. Small lizards ranged along the beach—desert creatures evidently adapted to scavenging and eating material derived from the sea. Circling the beach from the cliff in back of it and the area above it were gulls, two kinds of boobies, and pelicans. In one section of the cliff, on the ground under a jumble of huge rocks, were nesting striking tropic birds, white with black markings, a red bill, and extremely long white tail feathers. The numbers of birds were phenomenal, as was the noise they produced. At sunset, particularly, looking up-

Sea lions (*M. W. Larson*)

Sea lion and young; the fatty roll around the neck is one of the few places the mother can get a good grip (*M. W. Larson*)

Blue-footed booby (*M. W. Larson*)

Brown pelicans (*M. W. Larson*)

Cardon cactus on a guano-whitened desert island (*M. W. Larson*)

Young pelicans (*M. W. Larson*)

ward one could see "layers" of many, many birds wheeling and circling over the cliffs.

Leaving the beach one day, we climbed to the top of the island. Over much of the area, little grew except for small amounts of low brush and cardons. The latter were widely spaced and exceedingly numerous. Except for the very highest portions, the land was completely white-washed with bird guano. In the meager shade of the cardon trunks or out in the sun were the dirt-hollow nests of the blue-footed boobies, or the slightly fancier stick nests of the brown pelicans. Often nests were only a few feet apart; and the occupants ranged from fluffy teddy-bearish white young boobies to baby pelicans which, featherless or quilled, purplish and awkward, must be among the least handsome members of the bird society. On this desert island base there were literally thousands of animals which

A somewhat older young pelican (*M. W. Larson*)

Terns (*M. W. Larson*)

Gull stealing eggs from a nesting tern colony (*M. W. Larson*)

Herrmann gull chicks; note the camouflaged baby plumage (*M. W. Larson*)

Petrel nesting in rock slide (*M. W. Larson*)

Young duck hawk on a rockslide (*M. W. Larson*)

Chuckwalla on San Lorenzo Island (*M. W. Larson*)

found room, but which depended upon the sea for their board. In striking contrast, on our hike to the top of the island we found only a few truly "land" animals—a raven, a few small birds, several small lizards, and one rattlesnake.

The animal species present on these islands vary, often markedly, from one island to another, although the distance between them is small. Thus on another—Raza—there were no sea lions at the time of our visit, but there were vast quantities of nesting sea birds, in this case terns and gulls. Another island only a few miles away supports large populations of two kinds of petrels under and in the rock slides along its coast. These small, all-black birds betray their dependency upon the Gulf by their webbed feet. Also living in these rocky niches are numbers of fishing bats. During the day these large, brownish bats remain under the rocks, or (in some

Rattleless rattlesnake on San Lorenzo (*M. W. Larson*)

cases) under old, overturned turtle shells or in caves. At night they leave
to obtain their food from the ocean. It is not definitely known exactly how
they accomplish this, but it is thought that their long feet and claws
aid them in capturing sea life. In the slides inhabited by these animals
overturning rocks during the day often discloses resting petrels (in the
spring one finds them with all-white eggs). Or a bat may be seen scurrying away through the crevices, sometimes with her young attached to her
and being carried along. By day, hiding, rather than flying, is the defense
taken by both the petrels and the bats, probably because the danger from
predators in the air, such as duck hawks, is great during daylight hours.

Of the strictly desert-type rather than ocean-related animals, the species
represented on some (but not necessarily on all) Midriff islands include
various species of lizards, spotted night snake, king snake, rattlesnakes,

pack rats, and mice. On Tiburón, a very large island, coyotes and deer are native, and the Mexican Government is planning to introduce other large animals. Some fresh water is available on this island, and it was formerly the home of one of North America's interesting Indian tribes, the Seri. These people now live on the mainland not far from Kino Bay.

Islands are strange places. What animals are present; how the species originally arrived there—by storm, swimming, or by the hand of man; and what has happened to them in terms of evolution since the arrival— all are interesting, involved questions. The desert islands of the Midriff have been relatively little studied by the ecologist; they offer a fascinating field of inquiry. For example, on one island south of the Midriff, Isla Catalina, lives a species of rattle-less rattlesnake! And on another of the Midriff islands, San Lorenzo, lives a species of rattlesnake which in this island population is in the process of losing the rattles: snakes both with and without rattles are found there. Why are the rattles being lost? No one definitely knows. Their loss seems rather astounding, but when you stop to consider the matter, it is no more astounding than the *presence* of rattles on a snake's tail in the first place.

Tern in flight (*M. W. Larson*)

chapter twenty

How Shall the Desert Blossom?

"AND the Lord God formed man of the dust of the ground." Later that same man was to learn "... and unto dust shalt thou return." From basic elements and eventually back to basic elements is the path followed by all living things, and man is no exception. He is a part of the total earth community, and he cannot divorce himself from the basic laws which govern it, although he often tries. Whether one views man as a Divine creation, as a product of Divinely guided evolution, or as simply a result of undirected evolution, man with his superior intelligence is now placed in the position of the world's caretaker. Thus far he has been a miserable flop in that role. Mankind in general operates on the philosophy that all things were created for man to use as he sees fit. Used them he has; conserved, reserved, or deeply considered them he often has not. The showdown is fast approaching between the single species of

327

Homo sapiens, and the rest of the earth's total biosphere. By really intelligent action, man may avoid that confrontation; if he cannot, he may ultimately prove to have been an exceedingly brief and unsuccessful experiment when viewed in terms of the earth's history.

Much of the earth's surface lies ravished. Filthy water, dirty air, eroded soil, ugly sprawling cities, extinct and declining animal species, decimated forests, pesticide and radioactive contamination, and crowded populations all point to man's lack of concern for his identity as an integral part of the earth community and to his carelessness in fulfilling his role as the earth's keeper. The deserts are among the least damaged portions of the earth. We cannot stop, nor reverse time to recover the grass of the Great Plains nor the great forests of the eastern United States, but we can still preserve much of the desert before it too is ravaged by the pressures of an exploding world population.

It was not until the middle of the sixteenth century that the world's human population reached the half billion mark. By 1950, the world population was estimated at about 2.4 billion; by 1960 approximately 2.8 billion. In 1958 the United Nations estimated that by the year 2000, there will be a world population of more than 6 billion! In his book *Standing Room Only* Karl Sax estimated that if the present rate of population growth were to continue, in less than 200 years it would reach 100 billion, and in less than 500 years, 3000 billion. In 1700 years, the weight of the human population would exceed the weight of the earth itself! In *The Next Hundred Years,* H. Brown, J. Bonner, and J. Weir state that more than half the world's people today are hungry, but that each day approximately a hundred thousand babies are born to join the human herd.

Pressure for space in which to live and produce food for this expanding population is building, and increasingly, mankind looks with covetous eyes upon the desert. Only one factor really blocks the complete "development" of the desert, and that is lack of water. Much desert soil produces crops abundantly if water is supplied, and with a long or year-round growing season, several crops a year may be grown. Sufficient water supplies could support industry and its consequent grown in population. Given or provided sufficient water supplies, the desert, like a good deal of the rest of the earth, could become carpeted with people from horizon to horizon.

In many ways, the desert is already being exploited as though water were no problem. As an example, the state of Arizona is currently using approximately 7.6 million acre-feet of water annually. Of this amount, 5 million acre-feet is pumped from groundwater supplies, and about 3 million acre-feet of that pumpage is groundwater that is not being replenished! The city of Tucson pumps its city water supply from wells, and it is estimated that the water obtained is approximately 4000 years of age. The decline in the water table it comes from is approximately three feet per year.

In search of additional water supplies the city considered the nearby Avra Valley as a location for additional wells. In 1963, the Southern Arizona Branch of the American Society of Civil Engineers stated in a report that water levels in the Avra Valley were declining at a much faster rate than in the Tucson basin. In the Avra Valley, where extensive pumping for agriculture is taking place, the decline of the water level averages more than ten feet a year. The report stated that additional pumping from the Avra Valley reservoir would only hasten the water level's present decline. Today, however, Tucson is proceeding with its plan to drill wells in the Avra Valley and pump the water into the city. Landowners in the Valley fear the loss of the groundwater on a personal basis, but all the citizens of Arizona may well deplore the loss of groundwater throughout the state. Around Eloy, Arizona, ground water levels declined sixty feet in a recent five-year period; in certain parts of this area, the decline of water levels has led to land-surface subsidence of as much as three-and-a-half feet. Near Stanfield, Arizona, under intensive pumping, water levels declined a maximum of one hundred feet in five years.

More intelligent use of existing water supplies, better management to prevent evaporation and recover run-off, increased reuse of water, and similar changes in water usage can make the desert's water more efficient, but they cannot produce miracles. The only possible foreseeable "miracle" is the desalinization of sea water at a cost that will make it feasible for use in the deserts. A great deal of study and research is being done in this area today, but it appears that costs will continue to be prohibitive for some time to come.

If water could be supplied so that our North American Desert could be completely utilized for agriculture and cities, it would no longer be the desert, but a man-made oasis. Is this what we want? Many people would answer affirmatively. They see a changed desert in terms of jobs, food, homes, dollars, and prosperity for increased numbers of people. They assume the only "human" course of action is to feed and house the masses of humanity to be expected on this planet within the next few hundred years. Would it not be more humane to deaccelerate our breeding immediately? Is mankind's purpose on this planet the sheer production of numbers? Or can he, by use of his intelligence, serve higher purposes and in so doing provide a better life for fewer, rather than an increasingly poorer life for increasingly greater, numbers? Population growth cannot continue unchecked for long. Either man must control the number of births or find an efficient predator—probably man himself—to control his numbers by death. If he is to breed like the proverbial rabbits, then a portion of his numbers must be slaughtered through diseases, war, or other methods, just as the rabbit population is efficiently reduced by the coyotes, the foxes, the bobcats, and the snakes.

As man in the desert today is mining his water supplies while the water levels drop beneath his feet, so by his fantastic reproduction is he reducing the environmental base on which he stands. With a rapidly increasing human population, the deserts no doubt will be—as will almost all of the earth's surface—irrevocably changed to serve man's immediate physical needs. Man has more than physical needs, however, and the desert and other wilderness areas have a more important purpose to serve. In these areas man can literally escape from mankind at least briefly, see laid plainly before him the power and complexity of natural forces, and thereby begin to see himself in perspective to the rest of the universe. If, howver, he is doomed by an exploding population to be crowded permanently among other men and the works of men, is he not likely to believe that man is all-powerful and all-important? It seems significant that primitive man saw his gods in the powerful forces of nature—in the sun, in thunder, in lightning, in animals—while modern man visualizes his God and himself in similar images.

Eventually we may be forced to develop water supplies such as desalinated ocean water, to scrape the desert's surface clean and flat, and build it into cities, plant it with crops, and reap a harvest to feed a few billion people—who will in turn soon double their numbers (and who knows where they are to be fed and housed). Ultimately, however, the population issue must be met. We can only fervently hope that it is met and solved before all the earth's land surface, including the magnificent, lonely, and inspiring desert, is subdued. There are a good many people who hope that the desert will never "blossom as the rose," but that for posterity it will continue to blossom as the desert, *just* as the desert.

Index

Agaves (century plants), 18–19, 25, 71, 236, 256, 259
Agria, 97
Alarcon, Hernando de, 311
Alcorn, Stanley M., 125, 127, 128, 129
All-thorn (shrub), 18
American Society of Civil Engineers, Southern Arizona Branch of the, 329
Andrews, Roy Chapman, 6
Antelope jackrabbits, 285–88
Ants, 203–14
Ants of North Dakota, The (Wheeler), 211
Apache Indians, 237, 242, 289
Arabian Desert, 6, 41
Arctic tundra, 7–8
Areneño Pinacateño Indians, 304–8
Areoles, 93
Arizona crested-flycatcher, 139
Arizona-Sonora Desert Museum, 50, 107, 143, 161, 173, 219
Arizona State Game and Fish Department, 107, 184
Arizona Upland, 23–25

Arroyos (dry washes), 30
Ash-throated flycatcher, 139
Atacama Desert, 7, 11
Austin, Mary, 29
Australian Desert, 7
Avra Valley, 329
Axelrod, Daniel I., 29

Badgers, 229–30
Bajada, 30
Ball-moss, 81
Banded sand snake, 271
Barrel (cactus), 95
Bartholomew, George A., Jr., 153
Bats, 141
    See also Fishing bat; Long-nosed bat; Vampire bat
Beadle, N. C. W., 80
Beaver-tail (cactus), 95
Bighorn sheep, 248–49, 306
Birds of Arizona, The, 151
Black-tailed jackrabbits, 285–88
Blue paloverde, 78, 220
Bobcats, 227–29
Bohning, J. W., 282